Teaching the Art of Poetry

 *The Moves*

Teaching the Art of Poetry

∿ *The Moves* ∿

Baron Wormser
Poet

David Cappella
Wabash College

LEA
LAWRENCE ERLBAUM ASSOCIATES, PUBLISHERS
2000   Mahwah, New Jersey   London

Lawrence Erlbaum Associates, Inc., Publishers
10 Industrial Avenue
Mahwah, NJ 07430

Front cover design by David Cappella and Jonathan Sturm

Library of Congress Cataloging-in-Publication Data
Wormser, Baron.
Teaching the art of poetry : the moves / Baron Wormser,
   David Cappella.
      p.   cm.
   Includes bibliographical references and index.
ISBN 0-8058-3337-4 (pbk : alk. Paper)
1. Poetry—Study and teaching. 2. Poetry—Authorship—Study
   and teaching. I. Cappella, David. II. Title.
   PN1101.W67   2000
   808.1'07—dc21
                                          99-049027
                                             CIP

Books published by Lawrence Erlbaum Associates are
printed on acid-free paper, and their bindings are chosen
for strength and durability.

Printed in the United States of America
10 9 8 7 6 5 4 3 2

For Kate Barnes and Marion Stocking
—B. W.

≈ ≈ ≈

For Gale Goodwin Gomez and Janet Wormser
—A. D. C.

Contents

Preface

This book is written with classroom teachers in mind. It is the teacher who is the institutional gatekeeper of poetry in our society. There is no poetry (particularly contemporary poetry) in most students' homes; they do not see poetry on the television or in the newspaper. What they hear on the radio is determined largely by the exigencies of commerce. For millions of young people their like or dislike of poetry depends on their teachers. The task is a serious one and many teachers discharge their responsibilities admirably with great feeling and insight. Over the course of decades of talking with teachers, we have come to realize that many teachers would like to make poetry a classroom staple rather than an occasional unit. We have written this book with those teachers in mind.

Teaching the Art of Poetry is, as its name indicates, a guide to the art of poetry and a focused approach to how to teach poetry. To teach poetry, a teacher needs a knowledge base and a methodology. The art of poetry represents a crucial knowledge base for every teacher; imparting that knowledge by means of experiential learning represents a methodology. The over 160 exercises and 19 weeklong lesson plans in this book speak to the importance we place on the actual classroom. For too long the teaching of poetry has been lumped together with other aspects of literature under the rubric of teaching for meaning. First and foremost, poems are instances of art.

There are 19 chapters in this book devoted to various aspects of the art of poetry and a 20th chapter devoted to pedagogy. The chapters are organized so that the book begins by focusing on the physical basis of poetry (without which there is no poetry), then moves to structural issues such as syntax and grammar, then to aspects of language use such as word choice, details, metaphor, and image. Chapters 10 and 11 examine the stanzas and forms that distinguish poetry. The remaining chapters treat some of poetry's special techniques and concerns. The pedagogy chapter provides a rationale for how to teach poetry and includes a hierarchy of methods that enables the teacher to build skills sequentially.

Having said all we have said about teaching and teachers, we feel that this book is for anyone who is interested in learning more about the art of poetry. Although it contains dozens of poems in their entirety, the book is not an anthology; it is a guide, a series of signposts, vistas, predilections, observations. We have cited much contemporary poetry because its richness is scanted in classrooms and in our society generally, but we have also quoted the likes of Shakespeare (many times), Keats, Wordsworth, Milton, and many other worthies.

What we cite in passing are merely indications of how much exists. As with any good guide, we hope this book will allow you, our reader, to get some ground under your feet and go your own way. To have poetry be a force in one's life, day-in, day-out, is a great blessing.

We wish to thank the following people who have helped make this book possible: George Drew, Donald Hall, Jo Josephson, Naomi Silverman, Cathy Stutz, Deborah Butler, and Marc Hudson.

How To Use This Book

Each chapter contains four sections: an essay, a set of classroom exercises, a weeklong lesson plan, and a bibliography. For the classroom teacher, each essay provides a foundation for discussing an aspect of poetry. The classroom exercises originate from salient points in each essay and are numbered accordingly. Each exercise offers an opportunity for the student to experience a particular aspect of poetry. These experiences involve reading, writing, listening, and speaking. The Five-Day Lesson Plan is designed to give the teacher a hands-on, integrated, weeklong set of classroom activities. Each week has an additional activity to reinforce the chapter beyond the confines of a week. The chapter bibliography lists the books in which the poems cited can be found. Also, in some cases, it lists further readings related to the essay topic.

We envision this book as a complete, low-budget guide to the teaching of poetry. By "low-budget" we mean that the teacher can integrate this book with available literature texts and library resources. Books, of course, go out of print so English teachers who use this book may well want to consult with their librarians regularly to help them locate poems and to generally keep up with the literature.

Additionally, teachers who use this book do not need to stand around the photocopier. We advocate reading poems aloud to students at every opportunity and having them write those poems down in their own notebooks (either paper or electronic). There is no more fundamental way to get students to directly experience the language of the poem. Hearing and writing down poems anchors the student in the physicality of language. It represents mental and kinetic engagement. This book's epilogue, "Getting Started," speaks to this issue.

We feel strongly that this book can aid teachers in their struggles with the hydra of curriculum. If the basis of the English classroom is the responsible and expressive articulation of the English language, then poetry, as the art of language, deserves pride of place in the classroom. To cite one of the most basic aspects of poetry, students should know what every word in a poem means. Any word a student does not know should be defined by the student in his or her notebook. Vocabulary is generated within a meaningful context, since the act of reading a poem is a natural and exciting way for a student to make sense of some very carefully chosen words. Thanks to poems, people have been learning new words long before *Hot SAT Words* came along.

Other typical aspects of the English classroom such as grammar can be taught in terms of reading poetry. Poems provide natural contexts for learning; they are not unrelated exercises or drills but purposeful syntheses. Since poets continually rethink basic issues such as punctuation, poems are great places to observe the choices and decisions that confront any user of the English language.

Poems, of course, are of worth in and of themselves. The art of language has many lessons to offer, but poetry can never be reduced to a set of rules. This book can be used in its entirety (for instance, as the basis of an elective class devoted to poetry) or chapter by chapter or exercise by exercise. The teacher, student, and general reader should feel free to use this book as imagination dictates. Imagination is, after all, the heart of poetry.

— *David Cappella*
—*Baron Wormser*

Introduction

Poetry frightens. Over the years when it has come up in conversation that we write poems, dozens of people from all walks of life have paused and then diffidently or straightforwardly confided that poetry means nothing to them. We have heard in those various voices puzzlement, anger, longing, contempt, and very often a note of betrayal, of having been denied a right that goes with speaking, reading, and writing a language. They have shaken their heads, as if to forswear the very notion of poetry.

In truth, poetry—to a degree—should frighten. Poems cannot be condensed, systematized, or quantified. Poetry concisely registers on the nerves the whole skein of human emotions. It harrows, enthralls, awes, dazzles, confides. As the African-American poet Walter Dancy has written, "A poet is a mind sailor soul dweller and teller of heartbeats." Poetry in the words of Langston Hughes is "the human soul entire, squeezed like a lemon or lime, drop by drop, into atomic words." According to Nobel prize winner Joseph Brodsky, "Poetry is essentially the soul's search for its release in language."

These are heady definitions but not unfocused ones. Although all three poets use the word "soul," there is nothing fuzzy about that word. The soul is the depth of our being and poetry is one means of sounding that depth. To be sure, not every poem seeks that intensity but as the lives and works of many poets show, poetry emphatically embraces that quest. It isn't fainthearted. It isn't an aspirin or a tonic. It isn't entertainment. A poem doesn't wile away time; it engages our fleetingness and makes it articulate. It seizes time and shapes it.

This is not to make an idol of poetry. As the literary historian David Bromwich has noted, "We have to think of the poet as nothing more special than a representative of a community of speech, who sometimes recovers a knowledge others repress in order to live. They forget and he [sic] sometimes remembers with a shock, how far we are at once servants and masters of language." There is no idol here and the complaints about poetry are very understandable in the light of the "shock" Bromwich mentions. Poetry has been held to be arcane, immoral, impractical, at once coy and overbearing. What does the poem mean? Why doesn't the poet just say it and get it over with? Why all the breathy mincing and feinting? As a department head once remarked to a then 1st-year teacher of our acquaintance, "Isn't it a bit early in the year to be getting to poetry? It's only November." Thank goodness for prose and grammar exercises.

"Servants and masters of language," "atomic words," "release in language": these are different takes on the same theme. Poetry is the art of language and that is the glorious difficulty of it. To belittle our fears about poetry either by making it cozier and more plainspoken or by elevating it to an unattainable height is no answer. Even at its most expansive Whitmanesque moments, poetry remains an art of essences and essences are unnerving. Poetry is respectably referential—it talks about the Boston Red Sox and Route 128—but it also exists unto itself and it cares only for its own perfection—the consort of sounds, rhythm, words, form, pauses. Poetry is a very demanding art as the poet is dealing at once with words that exist meaningfully in dictionaries and conversations and newspaper articles and ads and with words as pure, dumb, vocal sounds. Pigment is pigment, musical notes are musical notes, but the words in poems are two-faced, looking both toward the everyday world and that which is art and exists on its own terms.

It is here that teaching typically has failed poetry. The mention of "art" brings to mind, on the one hand, a welter of rules about stanzas and pentameters and, on the other hand, the bogey of subjectivity. The teacher who is bound by rules may lose the spirit of the enterprise; the teacher who goes in fear of subjectivity may scant the texture of art for mind reading ("Who knows what the poet meant?") or retreat to multiple-choice test objectivity ("What sort of sonnet is this?"). The teacher who revels in poetry's subjectivity may have nothing solid to teach. This is emphatically not to blame teachers. Uncertainties and dogmas are passed on from generation to generation and there is much that is left unsaid and unapproached. That our society prides itself on airing out all manner of once-closeted misapprehensions and avoidances is not a bad thing. Poetry, for one, deserves to be studied as an art.

The critic I. A. Richards put it very clearly when he wrote that "What a poem is is essentially what it does." A poem must be considered an animate body. Its constituent actions are its being. An analogy from the world of sports seems germane. To score a basket in basketball a player must make a series of moves that allow him or her to get a good shot at the hoop. The basket doesn't happen simply because the player wants to score. There are resistances of all sorts—hands in one's face, one's own less than perfect skills, referees partial to the home team. When the player makes the right moves and executes the shot properly, the player scores. A poem is similar in that a writer is using a series of moves—metaphor here, image there, succinct rhythm at one moment, looser rhythm at another. The resistances are things like dull syntax, cliché, unwanted overtones of words. As with the sport, everything depends on the inspiration and ability of the individual. One can't will oneself to be a Richard Wilbur or Adrienne Rich any more than one can will oneself to be Michael Jordan. One can, however, learn the various moves and the variations on the moves and the variations on the variations: hence our subtitle. The degree of structure varies from poem to poem (and from shot to shot) but the repertoire is as large as the poet's (or athlete's) aspirations.

To study the moves is not to lessen the mystery of the endeavor. It is to switch the focus from the final sum of two points to how one gets to that basket. For poetry the basket has been something called "meaning." "What does the poem mean here, class?" Twenty-five young people tense up simultaneously, start to sweat, look straight ahead or stare desperately into their textbooks wondering what the teacher wants from them, what the right answer is. Ah the joys of poetry! No wonder so many adults dismiss poetry as an ordeal that mercifully lies in the past.

The intent of this book is to delineate the moves. You will not find any talk about what the poem means herein. We have nothing against meaning *per se*; we simply feel as poets and teachers that the cart tends to be put before the horse. If the reader or auditor has no sense of how poems are put together, meaning can never be more than an abstraction somehow extracted from the mortified poem. For the reader or auditor who has a sense of the moves, meanings take care of themselves. As thoughtful intuitions they are, after all, personal—as they should be. Poems make us feel and there is only so much to be gained in explicating feelings. To be able, however, to articulate how one comes to a feeling; what delights, challenges, and perplexes is no little thing. Informed analysis is appreciation. And every reader can try her or his hand as a writer and experience first-hand what it is to try to make a poem. Michael Jordan's genius as a player hasn't stopped anyone from playing basketball. On the contrary, he inspires.

Although one reads and writes a poem for the sake of doing it, poems exist in a social context and have social tasks. Poems are sharers. As they praise, lament, ridicule, narrate, anguish, catalog, commemorate, plead, discourse, wish, regret, take leave, commiserate, confess, charm, protest, teach, and grieve, poems acknowledge bonds that link us as human beings who face life's perennials—grief, joy, evanescence, to cite three mainstays of poetry—and face at the same time the particulars that denote a time and a place. The hubbub about meaning (to say nothing about meaning's more sophisticated cousin, theory) may distract us from the position that poems may hold in our day-to-day lives as they offer solace, make us laugh out loud or start crying, instruct or beguile us.

A poem is a gift (as Lewis Hyde has noted in his book about the economies of poetry entitled *The Gift*) and we need in a society that attaches commercial values to every situation to acknowledge how crucial poetry is as a gift upon which no market price can be set. When we share poems of our own devising or others'—be it in a classroom or at the kitchen table or by e-mail—we honor the social bonds of poetry. We steadily need light and food and water and air, but at all manner of moments we need the nurture of poems. It is sad how few of us are able to avail ourselves.

A corollary of poetry's social nature is that as an art existing in time, poetry changes. This may seem to go without saying but many people do not hesitate to define poetry by some unyielding rule of thumb such as "Poetry must rhyme" or "Poetry must be in meter." These notions are imbibed in classrooms and it is quite possible over a lifetime to never further encounter poetry and thus preserve old saws. In fact, the beauty of poetry in twentieth-century America has been the degree to which it has refreshed every aspect of the art as it has addressed every aspect of life. It has embraced without compunctions the diversity of human experience.

Indeed if we look at history, it is plain that the agony of World War I shattered the genteel murmur of what once was called "poesy." It seems a tenable generalization to say that the work of American twentieth-century poetry has been to honor the fragments of the century's damnable wars, its race hatreds and genocides, its belittlement of the value of the individual life. As poetry has been constructed of fragments (initially and most famously in *The Waste Land* by T. S. Eliot), poets have been careful to distance themselves from sheer eloquence. The poem of rhetorical exhortation of which the nineteenth century was so fond died in the mud and thunder and poison gas of World War I, to say nothing of Auschwitz and Hiroshima. There is great pith in the fragments of human experience and poetry has kept faith with them. What is especially exciting is how many previously marginalized voices have taken hold of poetry and emphatically made it their own. American poetry is all the richer for the multiplicity of our voices.

Canons without living cultures are worthless and students whose educations are limited to brisk tours of canonical texts may wonder what it all has to do with their own worlds. How does one appraise art without canonical road signs? Do students have access to cultures beyond commercial ones in their own lives? Is the classroom providing them with that access? How democratic is art in a democracy?

Every teacher cares about standards and the above questions posit the testing of standards. Works of art are made of discrete elements; they are at once the sum of those elements and more than they are. The work of evaluation is never to be discarded on the grounds that it is subjective. The joy of being articulate about an art lies in part in being able to discuss why one likes a poem according to how it works as a poem. Or dislikes it because it doesn't work. Intelligent disagreement about the standards of practice is a source of genuine culture and the soul of the humane classroom that recognizes the validity of individual responses. If the ways of artistry are infinite, the aspects of an art are modestly finite. To return to the basketball court, one can dribble all sorts of ways but the ball still has to bounce up and down, up and down. Standards are not confining rules; they are models of the attainable. They are practical ideals.

Cultures are literally media that promote growth. Cultures are soil and that is the physical note on which we wish to end this introduction. For poetry is above all a physical experience. It is the stuff of sound and rhythm and speech, of muscle and voice box and vision and breath and pulse. It affects us physically when we speak it and listen to it. Without that physical basis there is no poetry. As we move through the many aspects of the art of poetry, let us not forget our bodies. All the moves are physical motions.

1

Rhythm

Summary

Rhythm is the key physical basis of poetry. It is what gets a poem
into us; it is visceral. Since English is an accentual-syllabic language, the play of those accents among the words that make up a
poem's lines is a main determiner of rhythm. In traditional English-language poetry, accents are patterned so as to form meters
in which each line has a definite number of accented units. In
the free-verse poetry of the nineteenth and twentieth centuries,
accent is looser and embodies the provisional, moment-
by-moment quality of daily living and speaking. Free verse is less
arch and dramatic than meter; it is more conversational and
open-ended. Whereas meter keeps a beat, the rhythms of free
verse insinuate themselves.

There is no more subtly powerful compeller than rhythm. Rhythm
literally defines life for us as human beings: Blood circulates within
us, we breathe in and out, we lie down and get up, we chew our food
and walk down the street and make love, and for decades of their lives
half of the human race menstruates each month. Rhythm is all around
us and woven into us in the seasons, day and night, tides, lives and
deaths. Living in Maine, we feel the winter solstice as a rhythmic
depth, a near stillness, whereas the summer solstice is the elongated
height of light. The equinoxes are poises, fulcrums, balances. (1)
  Rhythms are surging, lilting, insistent, and we humans convey all
manner of rhythm as we chat, dance, strut, orate, sing, clap hands,
whistle, drum, run, chant. Rhythm expresses emotions that range

from a parent's intimate, calming pat on an infant's back to the chilling, mass display of goose-stepping Nazis. Rhythm is the motive feeling of the life force, the "green fuse" as Dylan Thomas (a very great rhythmer) put it. In poems rhythm is capable of producing trance-like states of mind. Rhythm puts us so deeply into ourselves that we may feel we are outside of ourselves. (2) In the section of N. Scott Momaday's poem "New World" printed below, the reader is made to experience the primal pulse of life-energy in lines that are as rhythmically stark as is possible—typically one accent for each of the two syllables that make up each line:

> At noon
> turtles
> enter
> slowly
> into
> the warm
> dark loam.
> Bees hold
> the swarm.
> Meadows
> recede
> through planes
> of heat
> and pure
> distance.

The stillness of the scene absorbs and mesmerizes us; we hear a beat that is, at once, insistent and minimal. It is as if Momaday captured on the page the very rhythm of time. There is no racing through the poem, each line—though it is little more than a second—will have its say. (3)

As an oral and mnemonic art poetry always has honored the force of rhythm. Poems are meant to be spoken aloud and the rhythmic force communicated in a poem insists on the passion in the human voice. Every poem is the movement of words in time and that movement as it embodies the particular soundscape of a particular language conveys some shade of rhythm, from the tight structure of meter to the amble of collo-quial cadence. A monotone seems inhuman and the adjective is a term of opprobrium because a monotone rejects the rhythmic pulse of being. The vocal rises and falls that distinguish human utterances, the stuff of pitch, energy, and loudness, are part of the body's instinctive rhythmic feeling. Every articulation from an elaborate oration that piles orotund clause upon orotund clause to a simple exclamation ("Yikes!") be-speaks rhythm. (4)

English is an accentual-syllabic language and it is no exaggeration to say that it is a language with a built-in pulse. All multi-syllabic Eng-lish words have an accent; long ones have a primary and a secondary accent. As for monosyllables, one cannot go through three of them without accenting at least one of them to some degree (unless, of course, one speaks in a lifeless monotone). English abhors a rhythmic vacuum. To say "for the sake of our dogs" is to voice a readily discern-ible accentual texture, as "sake" and "dogs" seem relatively strong in relation to their companion words. The syllables we speak are rising and falling, falling and rising, always surging and lolling on the throb-bing tide of rhythm. To the force of dictionary-defined accent, there is always being added the pressure of human meaning. (5)

The simplest and strongest rhythm is that of alternation: Tides rise and ebb, valves open and shut, feet (and hooves) go up and down. Duple rhythm (as it is called) is the rhythm of alternation and it has been the workhorse of English-language poetry. One syllable is rela-tively stronger than the other syllable, thus an accented syllable fol-lows an unaccented syllable, an accented syllable follows an unaccented syllable. This relative strength may be patterned (weak/strong, weak/strong, weak/strong) to create a momentum that is, at once, brisk and lulling, that creates a trance of sorts. This is the rhythm of the majority of metrical poems in English and any reader of poetry will have her or his favorite that comes immediately to mind. We have always especially liked Shakespeare's "Sonnet 30," which begins:

> When to the sessions of sweet silent thought
> I summon up remembrance of things past,
> I sigh the lack of many a thing I sought,
> And with old woes new wail my dear times' waste ...

The terms (such as iamb and foot) that are used to describe this rhythmic occurrence are derived from classical prosody via the Elizabethans and though they have the merit of time-honored usage are not particularly helpful in apprehending rhythm. Indeed, they are probably more of a hindrance as they promote the dissection of lines into units that make accent seem compartmentalized, one-dimensional, and altogether neater than it is. A prosodic concept based initially on the syllabic rules of Greek poetry, the so-called *foot* has in all likelihood confused more people than it has helped. Talk about "trochaic substitutions" (replacing weak/strong with strong/weak), for instance, has an artificial, pedantic quality to it as if poems were the sums of numerous organized effects and the poet a clever engineer. We do well to remember that the root of the word "rhythm" means "flow" and its physical source is a word for stream. The foot-unit is a notional convenience of sorts while the physical truth remains the salient fact: The art of pulsation is rooted in the rhythm of alternation. Thus when *Mad* magazine changed Irving Berlin's "A Pretty Girl is Like a Melody" into "Louella Schwartz Describes Her Malady" and Berlin sued for copyright infringement, Berlin lost the case. The judge reputedly scolded Berlin for not being willing to share worldwide rights to the iambic (weak/strong) rhythm. Certainly, it is much more important to listen than to fret about terms and procedures. The play of accent among the syllables is sturdily audible. (6)

The prominent artistic issue of duple rhythm is how forcefully the poet wishes to assert it. To maintain a strict accounting of duple rhythm is to write in meter, the patterning of syllabic accents so many to a line: weak/strong, weak/strong, weak/strong, weak/strong, weak/strong = Shakespeare's "With éyes sevére and béard of fórmal cút" (The accent mark over each stressed syllable is known as an "ictus"). The virtues of meter in the hands of a competent poet are numerous: Its pace is even, yet unless the author is repeating identical phrases, every pair of alternations differs from the proceeding and following pair; it is engaging without being overbearing, persuasive yet measured, comforting without being boring. A metrical pattern is artificial in the sense that we do not routinely talk in meters but it isn't perniciously artificial. As poetry is a heightening of language (we do not go around speaking poetry), so meter is a heightening of rhythm. (7) The numerous monosyllables and rising rhythm of English-language speech make meter's orderly heightening of accents perfectly plausible. The five-beat, accentual-syllabic line that has been the rhythmic hallmark of English-language poetry from Chaucer to Robert Frost has no affectation about it. It is flexible, commodious, capable of great suppleness yet possessing an unflinching backbone. The time from "O mighty Caesar, thou dost lie so low?" to "One could do worse than be a swinger of birches" is centuries; the tones are vastly different yet the integrity of the meter, its compelling aptness, is unassailable. The contexts of poetry change greatly because the ways people live change greatly. However, as Paul Fussell has noted, "essential changes in the structure of the English language cannot be willed." The accents endure and the rhythm of alternation endures. (8)

It has always taken a firm hand to adapt meter to the poet's concerns. As a pattern it is a sort of engine and easily can get the uppermost of an inexperienced poet. The poet must, at once, relish its possibilities and subdue it to his or her expressive ends. There are rich cadences such as Christopher Marlowe's

> Now eyes enjoy your latest benefit,
> And when my soul hath virtue of your sight,
> Pierce through the coffin and the sheet of gold,
> And glut your longing with a heaven of joy.

> *Tamburlane the Great, Part II*

and unassuming ones such as William Wordsworth's

> A freshness also found I at this time
> In human life, the daily life of those
> Whose occupations really I loved ...

> *The Prelude, Book IV*

There are balanced deliberations such as Alexander Pope's

> Some beauties yet no Precepts can declare,
> For there's a happiness as well as care.
> Music resembling Poetry, in each
> Are nameless graces which no methods teach,
> And which a master hand alone can reach.

> "Essay on Criticism I"

and expressionist clamors such as Hart Crane's

> O, I have known metallic paradises
> Where cuckoos clucked to finches
> Above the deft catastrophes of drums.

> "For the Marriage of Faustus and Helen, II"

These quotations are from different eras and they remind us that meter exists in a social context, that it is historical and as an artistic medium changeable so that although we can say that Shakespeare and Frost both wrote in meter, the language each poet was deploying was hardly identical. Pronunciations, usages, meanings, poetic customs (such as elision and word order) all change, to say nothing of human outlooks. It was precisely the degree over centuries to which meter in all its varied usages—songs, nursery rhymes, ballads, nonsense verse—became synonymous with poetry that spelled a lessening of the vitality of meter. To assume something must be a certain way in an art form is a sure way to weaken the medium, for art thrives on practicable surprises. There is no point in doing what already has been done. Poets, as Robert Frost put it, don't imitate, they emulate, and, indeed, for his own part Robert Frost matched the cadence of New England speech to meter—something new in the annals of rhythm. Allen Ginsberg, to cite another instance, took Walt Whitman's long lines and made them even longer, giving them a breathless, out-of-control quality—again, something new. Eternal as rhythm is, its manifestations change. **(9)**

Whether artists at any given time and the public at large want to acknowledge the issue of change is another story. Many poets in the latter part of the nineteenth century felt that rhythm should not change. Well-regarded poets such as A. C. Swinburne felt that submitting to a metrical imperative was an affirmation of the eternal value of poetry. Poetry was above history; its rhythms were timeless:

> In a coign of the cliff between lowland and highland,
>   At the sea-down's edge between windward and lee,
> Walled round with rocks as an inland island,
>   The ghost of a garden fronts the sea.

> "A Forsaken Garden"

Lovely stuff that is technically known as logaoedic verse—lines combining duple rhythm (weak/strong as in "with rocks") and triple rhythm (weak/weak/strong as in "In a coign"). The swing is the thing here; the context is simply the excuse for rhythm to vaunt its thrilling, hypnotic wings. Swinburne wants to captivate and captivate he does. Meter exists unto itself in Swinburne's hands; it literally is calling the tune.

Swinburne's lines are a sort of performance and that is what is troubling about them. In the hands of a poet such as Swinburne, meter seems like an ultimatum, a last resort, a self-conscious reveling in the magical powers of poetry in a world devoted increasingly to commerce, steel, and speed. It was an understandable enough impulse but in many ways a heedless one. Donald Justice, one of the most acute craftspersons of the second half of the twentieth century, has noted that in meter "a subjective event gets made over into something more like an object." This facility is precisely what Swinburne indulged in, yet a talent may be too facile for its own good. In the course of the nineteenth century, poetry became more and more (in Cynthia Ozick's stern but just words) "a useless bellows that had run out of breath." Swinburne was hardly breathless but scads of published poems in the latter nineteenth century and well into the twentieth seem rote exercises in meter. Meter as a dumb, dependable pulse could dignify staple sentiments, *ad infinitum*, and did:

If this be but a house, whose stone we place

> Better the prayer unbreathed, the music mute
>
> Ere it be stifled in the rifted lute;

Better had been withheld those hands of grace ...

This is by Robert Underwood Johnson, a founder of the American Academy of Arts and Letters, and bears along with its burden of poeticism (i.e., artificial language) and stilted syntax a thoughtless reliance on meter as a *sine qua non* of a poem. The lines were written in 1921. Meter thus came to seem not so much an instrument of rhythmic artistry, as the accomplice of a wearisome afflatus. The lively pulse had become a trivial clog. (**10**) A syllogism of sorts was at work: meter bequeathed stature; poetry was written in meter; therefore poetry had stature. The free verse of Ezra Pound and T. S. Eliot typically was decried as "unmetrical," hence not really poetry.

Poets of the twentieth century (and some in the nineteenth) thoroughly skewered the metrical syllogism. Particularly in America this revolution resulted in an important rhythmic change, from meter to free verse. The rhythmic medium was decidedly not above the hubbub of history; it was implicated in the tide of human events. Although there is still a certain degree of shouting on both sides of the divide (metrists complaining that free verse is artless and free-versers complaining that meter is restrictive), most readers and writers are happy to acknowledge the successes free verse has wrought and also how it has made meter rethink and thus reinvigorate itself. Free verse opened up new artistic territory and for that act alone it deserves respect.

To be appreciated properly the freedom of free verse must be viewed in the positive light of its freedom to pursue new rhythmic courses as opposed to the negative supposition that free verse means nothing more than jettisoning meter. What free verse says is that meter is not everything, although for centuries meter has appeared to be everything. This is similar (to personify a bit more) to what abstract art said at the beginning of the twentieth century, namely that representational art was not everything although for centuries it too had appeared to be everything. There were other modes of apprehension and they were not inferior but different. (**11**)

The artistic successes of free verse are inarguable. It has broadened the spectrum of poetic rhythm and opened up new areas of expressiveness. What is twentieth century poetry in English without the gravely sinuous poems about animals by D. H. Lawrence; the indelible sensuousities of William Carlos Williams; the sheer, sad tumult of Allen Ginsberg's "Kaddish"; the delicate yet sinewy legerities of Denise Levertov? Between the poles of strict meter and the abandonment of the rhythmic line-unit in the so-called prose poem (see Chapter 19) lies an enormous range of rhythmic shadings. The accentual pulse, after all, never goes away. Again, the great issue is what the poet chooses to do with that pulse. Rarely is it an issue of all or nothing. Indeed, much of the greatest poetry of the century lies in the realm that at once acknowledges the pleasures and strengths of meter and the subtleties of looser rhythms. One need look no further than T. S. Eliot who over the course of his career culminating in "The Four Quartets" demonstrated how the conclusiveness of meter could consort with ephemeral tags of conversation, random observations, names, and disconnected exclamations to create a whole that was profoundly life-like and profoundly artful.

What exactly does free verse offer? More things than are simply categorizable. It offers the amplitude of declamation, the sheer volume of incidents and feelings and geographies that Walt Whitman in the nineteenth century deployed in his long meter-dwarfing lines:

> Afoot and light-hearted I take to the open road
> Healthy, free, the world before me,
> The long brown path before me leading wherever I choose.
> Henceforth I ask not good-fortune, I myself am good fortune,
> Henceforth I whimper no more, postpone no more, need
>   nothing,
> Done with indoor complaints, libraries, querulous criticisms,
> Strong and content I travel the open road.
>
> "Song of the Open Road"

The breath and breadth of the United States could not be held in mere parcels, and one feels that free verse retains for Americans an aspect of national feeling, of almost ungovernable diversity and plenitude. However one judges the products of Whitman's epigones, of poets such as Carl Sandburg and Allen Ginsberg, the rhythmic truth of Whitman's poetry seems undeniable: it is an impulse that has no use for meting out anything, that must speak vastly and variously as if to embody the great, vast spaces of America and the remarkable, hectic, appalling, inspiring energies of democracy. Whitman's free verse is the energy of the untrammeled voice; it holds patterns in contempt. To mark accents (known as "scanning") in Whitman's verse is to miss the forest for the trees; his rhythms are supple and flowing, casual and peremptory. His declaiming voice dictates the rhythm; he always is addressing his fellow Americans as he calls attention to the prospects of democracy.

Equally as compelling as the sweep of the declamatory voice (and Whitman, like many nineteenth century Americans, loved oratory) is the free verse of particulars, of the unyielding yet gentle attention that William Carlos Williams personified in his short lines about plums and cats and trees. Whitman exploded the metrical line in the surge of his feelings; Williams, on the other hand, pared the line down in many of his poems until each word, accent, and syllable seemed to take on a grace of its own. The linkage of accents that meter took for granted is broken down in the crucible of Williams' particularism until what emerges is a tenuous gravity that exists conditionally from moment to moment:

> The elm is scattering
> its little loaves
> of sweet smells
> from a white sky!

"Love Song"

Williams did not assume duration; he created duration as he evoked the physical world. For Williams things and people and animals and moments exist in their own right and the rhythmic weight of this presence is much too glancing and firm to be subsumed by meter's organizational energies. Meter assumes fulfillment—so many units to the line; in Williams the rhythm is the pace of the unfolding of the poem. The poem at once treads and hovers as the reader finds his or her way through the poem. However neatly apportioned a Williams poem may look on the page, it is stubbornly unmechanical in its preference for the hazards of attentiveness. Things do not have to be the way they are and Williams enjoys that mesh of uncertainty and certainty. It is the freshness of being alive.

Meter, as it organizes words, favors summary, argument, certainty, disquisition, and completeness. It is literally measure, a consistent pulse. The mind's great fondness for the art of weighing and judging and relating found a great ally in meter. Yet, however adroit meter may be, it is not the sum of all things and experiences. What of inconsistency, moodiness, hesitation, the sheer exhilarating nervousness of living in the present moment?

Free verse (as many modern poets have stressed) is foremost the poetry of the present moment, of the unknown, of palpable, moment-by-moment energy. Where the next accent falls depends on all sorts of factors (subject matter, tone, line length); it cannot be predicted ahead of time. Free verse can thus leap, sprawl, squat, race, plod, jitter, and gyrate. Much of the best free verse is alive on the page with a taut, almost animal energy. The artistry of a poet such as Denise Levertov seems boundless in this regard:

> Let's go—much as that dog goes,
> intently haphazard. The
> Mexican light on a day that
> 'smells like autumn in Connecticut'
> makes iris ripples on his
> black gleaming fur ...
>
> "Overland to the Islands"

In a metrical poem there is no such thing as a line ending with a "The" that begins a new sentence. The end of the metrical line demands an accent (if the last syllable is unstressed it is because it is a two-syllable word whose accent falls on the first syllable of the word, e.g., "harbor"). What sort of accent is on "The?" Certainly it is no metrical accent; it is rather a sort of metaphysical accent, a part of the quickness of the tone that considers all moments to be accented because they are part of the whole experience that the poem itself defines. Levertov's "The" is at once a mockery of convention and an affirmation of the flow of energy. For Levertov, rhythm is close to dance in the sense that the accents are almost literally on their toes; accent is movement and not, as in meter, placement. The wanderings of the sniffing dog are emblematic of the organic, free-verse poem. Nothing is predetermined; the poem is exploratory; anything can and should happen. Whereas the poet writing in meter is a deployer of sorts as she or he utilizes meter, the free-verse poet is someone who (in Levertov's italicized words) "*is brought to speech.*" Rhythm depends on that impulse. (12)

If (to adopt a baseball metaphor) the left field of free verse may be pictured as Whitmanesque volubility and the right field as the moment-by-moment luminosities, dolors, and actualities of poets such as Williams and Levertov, the great center field of free verse is that of the conversational voice. Meter as it patterns speech, heightens language: "Talk'st thou to me of ifs? Thou art a traitor." This is a richly emotional moment (as are many of the archly manipulative Richard the Third's moments) and the accents are like blows. Such intensity stands in contradistinction to the voice of free verse, dwelling as that voice does in the largely good-natured talkiness of American mass democracy that trusts the unremarkable pace of daily conversation. Such free verse dwells in the dignity of talk, of one person talking to another person rather than one person talking at another person. Here are some representative lines by contemporary American poets writing conversational free verse:

> Beyond the meadow
> on Route 2, the semis
> go right on by,
> hauling their long
> echoes into the trees.

> Wesley McNair, "Seeing Mercer, Maine"

The child propped between two adults
   on a low stool
makes a bell with her brown dress
   spread around her
a bell from which the clapper
   has been severed.

      Jeanne Marie Beaumont, "Childhood of the Invisible Woman"

The moon cuts through
night trees like a circular saw
white hot. In the guardshack
I lean on the sandbags,
taking aim at whatever.

      Yusef Komunyakaa, "Somewhere Near Phu Bai"

Sluggish by 9 PM, the hands
would slide along suddenly sharp paper,
and gather slits thinner than the crevices
of the skin, hidden.

      Martín Espada, "Who Burns for the Perfection of Paper"

In these passages the accents do not call deliberate attention to themselves. The rhythmic presence is casual; the modulation of accents feels quite natural. Whereas meter would seem to have the power to turn anything into a poem by bestowing a pattern of accents upon a string of words, free verse invites any—and everything—into the accommodating precincts of the talking voice. The poetry lies in the remarkability of the seemingly unremarkable. The regulated intensity of meter with its dramatizing instincts gives way to the declarative turnings and joinings of syntax as sentences make their way from one not-strictly-patterned line to another. Free verse, as it is contingent upon the slightly irregular pulse of human feeling, instinctively affirms the stature of everyday life, the moment-by-momentness of life—be it in one's backyard or in the Vietnam War. The rhythm of the contemporary, free-verse poem is the variable pace of speech, the significance of one person addressing another person through the medium of the poem. A well-written free-verse poem is just as memorable as a well-written metrical poem but the quality of the memorability is somewhat different: The conversational free-verse poem has an almost halting quality that the metrical poem does not have because the metrical poem is governed by a steady pattern and the free verse poem is governed by the feel of an emotional situation as that translates into the play of accents and syllables. The free-verse poet is listening as intently as the metrical poet, at times even more so, because the moment-by-moment quality of free-verse is so critical. Proceeding as it does without the backbone of meter, free verse runs the risk of seeming spineless, limp, torpid, rhythmically uninspired. Chopping prose sentences into lines and calling it poetry has never been what free verse is about. Free verse speaks to the rhythms of contingency.

The nature of contingency varies hugely and that is a glory of free verse. It can be utterly off-the-cuff as in the poetry of James Schuyler:

> Now I'm back
> in New York on West Twenty-third Street with the buses farting
>   past. And the one
> dog that barks its head off at two or three in the morning.

"A Few Days"

The art of Schuyler's long poem (from which these lines are taken) is to present the whole, sprawling, nervous energy of a human life in a calm, almost rambling voice. Schuyler considers (among other things) the contents of his medicine cabinet, his friends and family, movies, classical music, books he's reading, what's happening on the sidewalk outside his apartment window: There is no hurry because as far as the poem is concerned there is all the time in the world. At the same time, the poem's preoccupation with death makes it clear that there definitely is not all the time in the world: Life is contingent upon a galaxy of factors, very few of which are under our direct control.

Compare Schuyler's lines to a passage by Robert Lowell:

Now the midwinter grind
is on me. New York
drills through my nerves
as I walk
the chewed-up streets.

"Middle Age"

The setting of the poem is the same as Schuyler's but Lowell's lines carry much unambiguous weight. The hellish, physical, full-force of "New York" stands out as Lowell leaves the words by themselves at the end of a line. New York for Schuyler is where he lives, a part of his meditative pace, whereas the feeling Lowell conveys about the city is taut and pressurized. The short lines keep truncating any chance of a broader rhythm. Although the lines move from one to another without punctuation there is a natural, ever-so-slight pause at the end of each line as the reading eye makes its way to the next line. Lowell refuses the rest of an end-stopped line. His free verse is intentionally edgy and exemplifies the rule of thumb about successful free verse: It must be fully alive to its emotional situation—whatever the situation may be. Free verse is not cloth cut so many feet to the bolt and doled out impartially. As it feels its way through a situation, free verse honors the feeling of the content. Lowell's tightness and Schuyler's leisure are two distinctive voices that have chosen the freedom of free verse to express very particular attitudes.

In summing up, we want to stress that none of this discussion is proscriptive. Poets write perfectly metrical lines and passages within free-verse poems. Poets play with meter, tightening and loosening the accents, stretching the pattern and returning to it, as they keep the imperative intent of meter recognizable but not simplistic. As we stressed earlier in this chapter, what matters above all is to listen. Meter proposes the variety of certainty; free verse is the certainty of variety, of natural variation. Meter marshals time as it makes accents orderly; free verse feels its way through time. Many a good free-verse poem has a tactile feeling to it as if each accent and syllable communicated the uneven tread of time—for we do not perceive time as equivalent, metronome-like moments but multivalent ones.

Though free verse prizes the direct, speaking voice, there is no point in trying to convict meter of insincerity. Far from it. The accents of meter are inextinguishable because they are profoundly pleasing to the ear, as in this stanza from a poem about the great cornet player Bix Beiderbecke:

> He lit a cigarette and closed his eyes.
> The best years of his life! The Boring Twenties.
> He watched the morning break across the snow.
> Would heaven be as white as Iowa?
>
> "Bix Beiderbecke (1903–1931)"

Dana Gioia's lines about the jazz musician strike that note (two accents, for instance, on the slim yet three-syllable "Iowa") that is so distinctively meter's—the gravity of measured statement, the tread that demands our attention because it enacts rhythmically the tenor of conviction. Gioia, a contemporary American poet, lays out Beiderbecke's life without literally missing a beat—just as the musician never missed a beat. In meter and free verse the provocative and unassailable accents of the English language endure: "Quick, said the bird, find them, find them." That urgent, haunting line from "Burnt Norton" by T. S. Eliot epitomizes as well as any line of poetry how much rhythm can convey in so little time.

RHYTHM
In the Classroom

1. Rhythm is natural to all of us. Consider these questions about how your life is affected by rhythm: What is the strongest rhythm in your life? Is it physical, like getting up at the same time every morning and going to bed the same time every night? Is it emotional, like relaxing and listening to music? Is it intellectual, like keeping a book near your bed and reading some of it before you go to sleep? How does this rhythm affect you? How aware of it are you? What happens when the rhythm is broken?

2. There are many mechanical rhythms we encounter in daily life as we use or are around different machines. What are the differences between mechanical rhythms and natural ones? Are there rhythms that you dislike? Why? Do different cultures have different rhythms? Give some examples.

3. The slow pace of Momaday's poem summons the world of chants. The anthology, *America, A Prophecy* edited by George Quasha and Jerome Rothenberg (Random House, 1973) contains many sorts of chants. Read, listen to, and speak aloud some chants found in this anthology. What qualities define these chants? Are there chants you encounter in everyday life? Are there chants you encounter at special occasions? Traditional chants often rhythmically celebrate rites. Compose a chant for a rite in your life or a ritual rhythm.

4. Inflection—a change in loudness and pitch—influences rhythm. Take an interesting passage from any text—be it a poem, a history book, a novel—and then read it aloud in different ways, stressing different words or phrases. The listeners can then discuss how each rendition of the passage represents a different intonation. The listeners should try to define how such intonation may change meaning.
   Listen to different recordings of the same poem. Are there differences in inflection? Do you prefer one reading to another? Why?

5. Accent tells the human voice that one syllable is more important than another. Look up and list ten words each of two syllables, three syllables, four syllables, and five syllables. Underline the accented syllables. Are there patterns of accent for each syl-

lable grouping? Are there patterns of accent for different parts of speech?

6. The nonsense verse of poets such as Lewis Carroll and Edward Lear uses meter to give language a rhythmic order. Although the words are nonsense, the meter helps to create a sense of meaning. After reading some nonsense poems, write your own nonsense poem using as many words listed from Exercise #5 as possible. Poems by Carroll and Lear can provide rhythmic guidelines.

7. Meter, the great organizer, deliberately structures meaning. Some poets have written out poems in prose and then put them into meter. Take a passage from a speech such Martin Luther King's "I Have a Dream" speech or Lincoln's "Gettysburg Address." Is there a rhythmic basis to the prose? How would you describe it? Can there be meter in prose? "Cadence" is defined as a "balanced, rhythmic flow." What is the difference in cadence between an oratorical height such as King's or Lincoln's and a stirring poem such as William Butler Yeats's "Easter 1916?"

8. The rhythm of our language inheres in our speech, and a familiarity with inflection and accent can help connect rhythm to speech. First, record an actual dialogue between two people. Second, scan the dialogue for the stressed and unstressed syllables for all the words. Third, shape the dialogue into weak/strong meter. Consult Robert Frost's "The Death of the Hired Man" for an excellent example of metered dialogue. Scan a stanza of its dialogue. How do speech and meter interact in the lines? Finally, write a poem of your own (however brief) with metered dialogue.

9. Slang words often have a strong rhythmic feel to them. Look up slang words of other generations in a book such as *Listening to America* by Stuart Berg Flexner (Simon & Schuster, 1982) and compare them with your own slang words. What differences do you note? List ten slang words from the past that appeal to you. Ask your parents for slang words that they used when they were teenagers. Again, what differences do you note? Do the slang words of different eras have different rhythms, as, for instance, the slang of the 1920s Jazz Age?

10. Rhythm can be plodding and awkward and just plain bad. Wrenched rhythm, for instance, is when the poet misplaces a

word's accent so it will conform to the poem's meter. Consult an anthology of bad verse such as *The Stuffed Owl: An Anthology of Bad Poetry* (edited by D. B. W. Lewis, Capricorn Books, 1962) and locate some specific examples of wrenched rhythm.

11. Meter isn't the whole of poetry's rhythms. Free-verse poets use rhythm to explore the world around them and are particularly sensitive to the rhythm of experience: climbing a mountain, crawling in a tunnel, driving a new car. Write a free-verse poem that describes the moment-by-moment unfolding of a physical experience, whether it is slinging a hamburger or getting ready to go to a party. Use the present tense in writing the poem. In that way, you can use moment-by-moment, line-to-line cadence to make the experience read as if it were being actually lived in the open-ended, present moment.

12. Through language, poets elevate existence. That language, however, does not have to be special, fancy language. Our everyday language is the stuff of poetry. Write some free-verse poems about daily experience, routines, and perceptions. The language in such poems should be of a conversational, everyday nature. Consult poems reprinted in this book and the chapter bibliography for examples.

RHYTHM
Five-Day Lesson Plan

Day 1   This day is devoted to learning about patterns through listening. Students learn the weak/strong rhythm of English verse.
  • The teacher reads Robert Frost's "Fire and Ice" aloud to the class.
  • The teacher then reads the poem a second time having students write down the poem line by line.
  • Students then identify each weak/strong unit line by line.

To further help students become comfortable and secure with the material, the teacher can run the exercise a second time.
  • The teacher reads Robert Frost's "The Most of It."
  • The teacher reads the poem a second time, and the students write down the poem line by line.
  • The students identify each weak/strong unit line by line in their poetry notebooks.

Day 2   Students examine a Shakespearean speech, for example, *Julius Caesar*, Act III, ii, Marc Anthony's funeral oration, in terms of the weak/strong rhythm, line by line by line.
  • Here is an opportunity to assess students' understanding by beginning the activity in class and having them take the work home to complete.
  • The teacher can distribute poems from different periods, and students can identify how noticeable the weak/strong pattern is.

Day 3   Free verse is democratic in a distinctly American vein. The weak/strong rhythm is a pattern, but free verse is rooted in speech rather than pattern. The teacher reads aloud the first page of Walt Whitman's "There was a child went forth everyday" (1855 edition).
  • Students write down the first ten lines in their poetry notebook. These lines do not have a repeated, line by line pattern. What makes these lines rhythmically compelling?

- The teacher reads aloud Emily Dickinson's poem, #861, "Split the Lark ... "
- Students write the poem in their poetry notebook. What makes Dickinson's lines rhythmically compelling? Does she use weak/strong rhythm?

Day 4   In the 20th century, we see the flowering of American free verse. Devote this day to the paragons of 20th century free verse, such as Ezra Pound, William Carlos Williams, H.D., D. H. Lawrence, and Denise Levertov. Bring in a sampling of these poets. Have students read them. Ask students,
- How does free verse differ from poet to poet?
- Is there a weak/strong pattern in any of the poems?
- If not, what holds the poems together rhythmically?
- Do you see any connections between these poets and Dickinson or Whitman?

Day 5   Contemporary free verse is rooted in speech. The teacher brings in a sampling of poetry journals (e.g., the *American Poetry Review, Poetry*, and the *Hudson Review*). Ask students to read various poems from them and then ask the students to determine what elements of rhythm are present in the poems. How do the poems differ rhythmically from one another?

Beyond the Week

Students choose at least one poem by a contemporary American poet that they like in terms of rhythm. They then copy the poem into their poetry notebook and explain their choice.

RHYTHM
Bibliography

Poems

"New World" by N. Scott Momaday from *The Gourd Dancer*, Harper & Row, 1976; "For the Marriage of Faustus and Helen, II" by Hart Crane from *The Complete Poems and Selected Letters and Prose of Hart Crane*, Liveright Publishing, 1996; "Love Song" by William Carlos Williams from *The Selected Poems*, New Directions, 1969; "Overland to the Islands" by Denise Levertov from *Overland to the Islands*, New Directions, 1958; "Seeing Mercer, Maine" by Wesley McNair from *My Brother Running*, David R. Godine, 1993; "Childhood of the Invisible Woman" by Jeanne Marie Beaumont from *Placebo Effects*, W. W. Norton, 1997; "Somewhere Near Phu Bai" by Yusef Komunyakaa from *Neon Vernacular*, Wesleyan University Press, 1993; "Who Burns for the Perfection of Paper" by Martín Espada from *City of Coughing and Dead Radiators*, W. W. Norton, 1993; "A Few Days" by James Schuyler from *Selected Poems*, Farrar Straus Giroux, 1988; "Middle Age" by Robert Lowell from *Selected Poems*, Farrar Straus Giroux, 1977; "Bix Beiderbecke (1903–1931)" by Dana Gioia from *Daily Horoscope*, Graywolf Press, 1986.

Prose

Recent books on prosody and rhythm include *The Sounds of Poetry* by Robert Pinsky, Farrar Straus Giroux, 1998; *The Poem's Heartbeat* by Alfred Corn, Story Line Press, 1997; and *Rules for the Dance* by Mary Oliver, Houghton Mifflin, 1998. Paul Fussell's *Poetic Meter and Poetic Form*, McGraw Hill, 1979, remains well worth reading. A recent collection that takes a fresh look at meter is *Meter in English: A Critical Engagement*, edited by David Baker, University of Arkansas Press, 1996. Shakespeare's prosody is ably accounted for in *Shakespeare's Metrical Art* by George T. Wright, University of California Press, 1988. Louis Zukofsky's *A Test of Poetry*, Jargon/Corinth Books, 1964, is a classic that speaks sensitively and acutely to the often confused notion of the "music" of poetry. The discussion of meter in Donald Justice's essay "Meters and Memory" in *Oblivion: On Writers & Writing*, Story Line Press,

1998, stands out for its being so clearheaded. Cynthia Ozick's remarks are from *Fame and Folly*, Alfred A. Knopf, 1996.

Among numerous books on free verse are *American Free Verse* by
Walter Sutton, New Directions, 1973, and *Free Verse: An Essay on
Prosody* by Charles O. Hartman, Princeton University Press, 1980.
The Poetics of the New American Poetry, edited by Donald Allen and
Warren Tallman, Grove Press, 1973, offers important discussions by
many leading practitioners of free verse including William Carlos
Williams, Robert Creeley, and Denise Levertov.

2

Sound

Summary

The pleasure we get from hearing poems read aloud has much to do with the sounds of the poem's words. Each word has a meaning but the vowels and consonants exist in their own right as particular sounds. The best known sonic aspect of poems is probably full end-rhyme where the same vowel-consonant combination (the "ing," for instance, of "bring," "string," "ring") chimes at the ends of successive or neighboring lines. Poems do make use of numerous other sound devices including alliteration, assonance, consonance, onomatopoeia, and partial end-rhyme (typically known as slant rhyme or half rhyme). The sonic aspect of words sparks poets' imaginations. Not only are poets seeking certain words in terms of meaning; they are also seeking certain sounds at the same time.

Like musicians, poets are always saying that so-and-so has a good ear. What do they mean exactly? Certainly no two sets of human ears are the same but poets are referring to a feeling for the myriad textures of sound. Here is the beginning of "Meditation on Song and Structure" by Charles Wright, a poet with a fine ear:

> I love to wake to the *coo coo* of the mourning dove
> At dawn—
>   like one drug masking another's ill effects,
> It tells me that everything's all right when I know that
>   everything's wrong.

It lays out the landscape's hash marks,

> the structures of everyday.

It makes what's darkened unworkable

For that moment, and that, as someone once said, is grace.

But this bird's a different story.

It is common for English language speakers to identify poetry as something that rhymes. End-rhyme is, indeed, a prominent device in many poems but it is very far from representing the totality of sonic effects that are available to poets. Every syllable in every word is a facet of sound, whether it be a vowel by itself or a vowel accompanied by one or more consonants. How the poet orchestrates these sound-facets constitutes a poet's ear. There is no jouncing, emphatic end-rhyme in Wright's lines but there is a wealth of delectable sound, particularly of what the critic Northrop Frye has termed "the varying sonority of vowels," the poetic music of the various pitches and sounds of vowels. (1)

Wright does at times rhyme—"love / dove" in the very first line is as basic a rhyme as there is in English—but the poet is more interested in the sameness and variety of vowels. The repetition of similar or identical vowel sounds is called assonance. Look, for instance, at how Wright repeats the long *a* sound in the middle of the passage we have quoted—"lays," "scapes," "day," "makes," and the somewhat distant but still echoing "grace." Wright doesn't call undue attention to the sound but he does repeat it and we hear it. Just as this subtle repetition is a pleasure so is the sheer variety of vowel sounds. Sometimes Wright uses a string of short vowels—"one drug masking another's ill effects"—or the passage's last line where another string of short vowels is brought up short (pun intended) by a long vowel—"But this bird's a different story." That long *e* is decisive and rousing, a spark after a clump of subdued sounds. Typically Wright varies the long and the short of his vowels: "It tells me that everything's all right when I know that / everything's wrong."

Consonants are present too, of course, and they, along with other factors such as rhythm and line, play a part in the pleasure of sound. A wry, unmistakable finality is achieved by Wright in "everything's wrong," as the *ng* sound ends two successive words. Wright is using consonance when he does this: He is repeating identical (or merely similar) consonants in neighboring words whose vowel sounds are not the same—as the *i* in "thing" is different from the *o* in "wrong." Or as the *i* in "ill" is different from the *e* in "tells," while the *l* consonant is repeated.

Wright steers clear of outright alliteration, the repetition of initial consonant sounds in neighboring words. He inserts "once" between "someone" and "said," as he bridges the initial *s* sound between the two words with the intermediate *s* in "once." Alliteration is a quickener, a stimulant, as successive words are launched with the same consonant. "Woman wailing ... " and "mazy motion" Coleridge writes in "Kubla Khan;" "Leaping light for your delight discovers," W. H. Auden writes in one line from "On This Island;" Louise Bogan alliterates but syntactically splits the words, "Mariners! Make way ... " in "Putting to Sea." In all cases alliteration speeds the poem's pulse and thus typically is used sparingly since overuse wears out alliteration's effectiveness. (2)

As always there are exceptions to the rule. Sometimes poets want extended alliteration for the sheer rowdiness of it. W. H. Auden does this at the end of "Domesday Song":

> Once we could have made the docks,
> Now it is too late to fly;
> Once too often you and I
> Did what we should not have done;
> Round the rampant rugged rocks
> Rude and ragged rascals run.

Clearly Auden wants a forceful contrast within the stanza and a forceful ending to the poem and alliteration does it for him superbly. At other times, the poet may want to evoke the Old English origins of alliteration. In Old English, alliteration organizes the line as each line is divided by a caesura into two half-lines of two strong stresses. Usually both of the two stressed syllables in the first half of the line alliterate with the first stressed syllable of the second half-line. Richard Wilbur's poem "Junk" closely mimics the Old English alliterative line:

Haul them off! Hide them!

                The heart winces

For junk and gimcrack

                for jerrybuilt things

And the men who make them

                for a little money.

When poets reprise the Old English line they invariably are seeking a strong physicality that is suited to the subject at hand. It is a clanging, hammering line that commands attention. (3)

Poets are fond of sounds for the sake of sounds. Wright, for instance, imitates the actual sound of the mourning dove when he writes "*coo coo.*" The notion that a name imitates a sound so that there seems to be a similarity between the meaning of the word and the sound the word makes is called onomatopoeia. Words such as "buzz," "hiss," "whoop," seem to echo the sense of the word in the sounds they make. Onomatopoetic words are fun to use, as they are lively words that delight the tongue. We can feel it when the basketball announcer exclaims, "He stops, he pops, it drops." Not only is the rhyme memorable but "pops" is a remarkably strong little word to portray the athlete getting the shot off. When that shot goes through the hoop cleanly, it is a "swish" and another bit of onomatopoeia.

As with alliteration, poets tend to use onomatopoetic words for definite effects. A surfeit of such words may turn the poem into a comic strip where loud words are the only words spoken. Then again the poet may pull it off as Edgar Allan Poe does in his famous, onomatopoetic set piece "The Bells." Here is the first stanza of that poem:

Hear the sledges with the bells—

   Silver bells!

What a world of merriment their melody foretells!

   How they tinkle, tinkle, tinkle,

      In the icy air of night!

   While the stars that oversprinkle

   All the Heavens, seem to twinkle

      With a crystalline delight;

> Keeping time, time, time
> In a sort of Runic rhyme,
> To the tintinabulation that so musically wells
> From the bells, bells, bells, bells,
> Bells, bells, bells—
> From the jingling and the tinkling of the bells.

Poe clearly relishes the onomatopoetic feel of certain words, "tinkle," for instance, just as he uses the power of repetition to mimic the ringing effects of the bells. The word "bell" becomes a bell as it sounds within the poem. The most surprising word in the stanza, "tintinabulation," echoes Poe's intent for it means "a jingling or tinkling sound as of bells." Onomatopoetic words tend to be one syllable but there are—as "tintinabulation" shows—exceptions. (4)

Poe also uses end-rhyme: One-syllable words rhyme with two-syllable words as in "night / delight;" words rhyme on their penultimate syllable as in "oversprinkle / twinkle;" monosyllabic words rhyme head-on as in "wells / bells." Poe thus varies his end-rhymes and is representative in the intriguing stanza form, the varying line lengths, and the use of end-rhyme of much nineteenth-century poetic practice. One reason the twentieth century lost interest in rhyme was because the nineteenth century did so much with it. The first stanza of Longfellow's poem "Hawthorne," about the great fiction writer, shows how much could be achieved with the simplest of rhymes:

> How beautiful it was, that one bright day
> In the long week of rain!
> Though all its splendor could not chase away
> The omnipresent pain.

The hankering for rhyme and the common identification of poetry with the presence of end-rhyme ("If it doesn't rhyme, it isn't a poem.") stem from poems by the likes of Longfellow in which the concision, finality, expressiveness, and aural pleasure of rhyme (note how the alternating line lengths match the alternating rhymes) make an indelible impression. The poem is inconceivable without its rhymes. (5)

Other major poets of the nineteenth century such as Browning and Hardy (who indeed wrote into the twentieth century) juggled rhymes with relentless dexterity. Both poets enjoyed toying with stanzas as a way of keeping rhyme fresh. Browning uses very short stanzas:

> Be a god and hold me
> > With a charm!
> Be a man and fold me
> > With thine arm!

> "A Woman's Last Word"

and long-lined stanzas:

> Here you come with your old music, and here's all the
> > good it brings.
> What, they lived once thus at Venice where the merchants
> > were the kings,
> Where Saint Mark's is, where the Doges used to wed
> > the sea with rings?

> "A Toccata of Galuppi's"

and five-line stanzas:

> And all day long a bird sings there,
> > And a stray sheep drinks at the pond at times;
> The place is silent and aware;
> > It has had its scenes, its joys and crimes,
> But that is its own affair.

> "By the Fireside"

and six-line stanzas (also using two rhymes):

As for the grass, it grew as scant as hair
> In leprosy; thin dry blades pricked the mud
> Which underneath looked kneaded up with blood.
One stiff blind horse, his every bone a-stare
Stood stupefied, however he came there:
> Thrust out past service from the devil's stud!

"Childe Roland To the Dark Tower Came"

Typically a Browning stanza is not enjambed; it is a unit unto itself and often the stanzas are numbered as if they were chapters of a book. Rhyme seeks conclusiveness and Browning enjoyed that challenge as he created various rhyme schemes that produced various aural satisfactions. In his poems Browning creates many decisive personalities; rhyme was a natural aspect of that decisiveness. Browning would have been lost without exclamation marks; his characters are forever mouthing off. That they do so in rhyme has little to do with everyday speech but much to do with a passionate, careening expressiveness as in the first four lines of the first stanza of "Soliloquy in the Spanish Cloister:"

Gr-r-r—there go, my heart's abhorrence!
> Water your damned flower-pots do!
If hate killed men, Brother Lawrence,
> God's blood, would not mine kill you!

One rhyme is quite elementary—"do / you"—while the other is more complex—"abhorrence / Lawrence." The rhymes along with the overall vigor of the sounds insist powerfully. The speaker—whoever he is—is no pushover.

Later in the nineteenth century in the work of Thomas Hardy the conclusiveness of rhyme takes on a fatalistic, almost cosmic aspect. Hardy builds upon the fact that rhyme joins words that otherwise might not be joined. It is thus a great incitement to the poet's imagination since words are suggested in the search for rhymes that otherwise might not appear in the poet's mind. Rhyme socializes words as it suggests new relationships among them. The decisiveness of rhyme as it thumps the last word of the line appears to have a fated aspect: words that were strangers to one another ("abhorrence / Lawrence") chime irrevocably. It is the irrevocable aspect of rhyme that deeply influenced Hardy. Rhyme, after all, is a sort of determinism. Once the rhyme is decided upon only certain words are possible and all other words are discarded. Hardy's poetry revels in the tension between the narrowness of rhyme ("rain / pain," "day / away") and the freedom that lies within the range of choices. The result is ingenuity and intensity as rhyme fuels Hardy's sense of the simultaneous pathos and bravery of human lives, of constrictions and of the paths taken within those constrictions. Here is a stanza from a late Hardy poem "The Best She Could":

> Sunlight goes on shining
> As if no frost were here,
> Blackbirds seem designing
> Where to build next year;
> Yet is warmth declining:
> And still the day seems to say,
> "Saw you how Dame Summer drest?
> Of all God taught her she bethought her!
> Alas, not much! And yet the best
> She could, within the too short time
> Granted her prime."

The weave of the end-rhymes is compounded by the presence of a species of internal rhyme as a word within a line rhymes with the word ending the line—"day / say," "taught her / bethought her." For Hardy, rhyme is an obsession that takes ever-new forms: Hardy may have invented more stanza forms than any other English language poet. He welcomed the constraints of rhyme because for him they chimed with the constraints of life. Life wasn't infinitely open; there were endings and disappointments and regrets, and the finality of rhyme spoke to human finitude. The aural satisfaction of rhyme has an almost grim quality in Hardy as it speaks so often to entrapment and limitation. The rhymes ring like nails while Hardy implacably pounds his statements home. (6)

Twentieth-century poets have not abandoned rhyme by any means but they certainly have modified it. Essentially, they have moved in the direction of what is known variously as half rhyme, slant rhyme, near rhyme, or pararhyme. In this type of rhyme the stressed syllables agree but the vowel sounds do not. The extent of agreement varies from full consonance where both the preceding and final consonants match as in "tap / top" to the echoing of the final consonant "map / top" to the joining of similar but not identical sounds "lake / top." Many poets wanted a subtler and more haunting soundscape than that of end-rhyme. End-rhyme for the sake of end-rhyme came to seem too thumpingly obvious to modern poets. The world wars, depressions, genocides, and weapons of destruction that marked the century had little to do with the confidence that once went with rhyme. The decisive habits of thought that went with rhyme were based in many ways on largely unchallenged assumptions about what a poem was. The events of the twentieth century—what is a poem in the face of the Holocaust?—have challenged those assumptions powerfully.

Given the experiences of the twentieth century, it seems just to cite Wilfred Owen, first of all, in regards to the deliberate use of half rhyme. Owen died in World War I and his use of half rhyme is strongly influenced by his wartime experiences. Here is the first stanza of "A Terre":

> Sit on the bed. I'm blind, and three parts shell.
> Be careful; can't shake hands now: never shall.
> Both arms have mutinied against me—brutes.
> My fingers fidget like ten idle brats.

Owen uses full consonance to end his lines as he provides a strong feeling of rhyme but withholds the certainty of frank end-rhyme. Often Owen is writing about things that have gone wrong in ghastly ways, where men are killed and maimed amid confusion and darkness. The approximation of half-rhyme, the slightly out-of-kilter feeling it generates, perfectly suited Owen's artistic goals as he aimed to present a world that made little sense to the average soldier but to which the soldier somehow had to adapt in order to survive. Here is another Owen stanza, this time from "Exposure:"

> Sudden successive flights of bullets streak the silence.
> Less deathly than the air that shudders black with snow,
> With sidelong flowing flakes that flock, pause, and renew;
> We watch them wandering up and down the wind's nonchalance,
>> But nothing happens.

Again the half-rhymes have an anxious, uncanny quality while the final, abbreviated, unrhymed line virtually mocks rhyme. Owen sought to physically register anguish and he succeeded.

The predilection for half-rhyme that runs throughout modern poetry has resulted in a subdued sort of music. To the assertiveness of rhyme, half-rhyme suggests the more casual consolations (and frustrations) of proximity and the wider net of similarity. Many poets have excelled at half-rhyme; we cite the American poet Stanley Kunitz as an example of what has been wrought. Certainly he is a master of this mode. Here is the final stanza of "River Road":

> Lord! Lord! who has lived so long?
> Count it ten thousand trees ago,
> five houses and ten thousand trees,
> since the swallows exploded from Bowman Tower
> over the place where the hermit sang,
> while I held a fantail of squirming roots
> that kissed the palm of my dirty hand,
> as if in reply to a bird.
> The stranger who hammers No Trespass signs
> to the steghorn sumac along the road
> must think he owns this property.
> I park my car below the curve
> and climbing over the tumbled stones
> where the wild foxgrape perseveres,

I walk into the woods I made,
my dark and resinous, blistered land,
through the deep litter of the years.

Kunitz seeks a reflective, searching tone for a poem that looks back at
"That year of the cloud, when my marriage failed." In his hands the resources of half-rhyme, alliteration, consonance, and assonance seem
endless. The care with which he crafts his line endings speaks to the
patience of a practiced artist as he deftly employs a register of sounds
from full rhyme ("perseveres / years") to a single, final sound ("trees /
roots") to sheer proximity ("made / land"). Overall the sounds create
a feeling of spirited ruefulness. Things went askew yet the experience
was real and Kunitz confronted it. As in Wilfred Owen (though in a
very different context) half-rhyme captures a sense of disjunction and
approximation. (7)

The nuances of sounds are a sort of wonderland for our ears. It is in regards to sound that poets are artificers in the root sense of that
word—makers of art. Sound is a physical fact and how poets shape, meld,
blend, mute, finesse, echo, and trumpet sound is one of the primal pleasures of poetry. We end with a poem by the American poet Robert Francis entitled "Overhearing Two on a Cold Sunday Morning":

We left our husbands sleeping,
Sun in our eyes and the cold air
Calling us out, yet not too cold
For winter to be rehearsing spring
At ten o'clock in the morning.

Like harps the telephone poles hum
And the glass insulators dazzle.
We left them warm in bed dreaming
Of primavera, dreaming no doubt
Of fountains, fauns, and dolphins.

Chickadees dance on the wind. They
Are young, our husbands, especially
As they lie sleeping. Sometimes
We imagine we are older than they
Though actually we're a little younger.

We have come up into the upper light.
We have come out into the outer air.
We could almost for a moment forget
Our husbands. No, that is not true.
Never for a moment can we forget them.

Soon we will go back to them and shout
"This is a beautiful day!" Or if
They are still sleeping, whisper it
Into their ears or on their lips.
We do not often leave them sleeping.

Although the whole poem is a delight, the second stanza stands out
for us as a virtual epitome of various sound devices that poets use. We
wish only to call attention to how Francis moves in that stanza from
sound to sound—from the *s/z* sound to *d* and then to *f* while bringing
in a dash of *s/z* and *d* into the final line. Without the benefit of overt
rhymes the stanza strongly impresses itself on our minds. In its off-
hand way it recalls that bravura English poet Gerard Manley Hopkins
who in the latter part of the nineteenth century created poetry of astonishing rhythmic and auditory freshness. Hopkins and such artistic
successors of his as Dylan Thomas pulled out all the stops regarding
sound. The lessons of their work are evergreen, for the vibrancy of
sound is irresistible.

SOUND
In the Classroom

1. Every poem has a soundscape of vowels. Take a short poem and chart all the vowels in the poem line by line. Are there any patterns? Is there a preponderance of one vowel sound? Is there a balance overall among the variety of vowels?

2. Find some examples of alliteration. Is it used for similar effects in different poems or does the occasion for using alliteration vary from poem to poem? Do you ever encounter alliteration in daily life?

3. Read some of the Old English of *Beowulf* or read an alliterative translation of that poem (see chapter Bibliography). Also read "The Seafarer" by Ezra Pound. What relationship is there between alliteration and the physical environment in which the poems take place?

4. List ten onomatopoetic words. Write a poem that incorporates at least five of those words.

5. As regards sound, end-rhyme has taken up a lot of attention, understandably so. Read some poems that have end-rhyme. How does end-rhyme affect other aspects of the poem such as syntax and rhythm? What pleases you about rhyme? Is there anything that displeases you? Find some poems from different centuries that use a tight rhyme scheme, such as the rhymed couplet. Given that the rhyme scheme is the same, are there differences among the poems concerning matters such as syntax and rhythm?

6. Read more poems by Thomas Hardy. Does he always use rhyme? Does he favor any particular rhyme scheme? Do the words he chooses for his end-rhymes surprise or do they seem predictable? What makes the rhymes effective?

7. Look for more poems that use half-rhyme. Thom Gunn is one master of this technique as in his poem about a tattoo artist, "Blackie, the Electric Rembrandt." That poem is in half-rhymed, spatial couplets. What effect does the series of half-rhymed couplets have?

SOUND
Five-Day Lesson Plan

Day 1   The first day focuses on consonance and assonance.

- Identify and recite the major vowel sounds of the English language.
- Assign groups of students a vowel sound.
- Give each group the same poem from their literature anthology.
- Ask each group to identify their vowel sound every time it appears in the poem.
- Every group then reports their findings to the class.

(The class does one poem at a time.)

- Class Discussion Questions:
- Are there clusters of similar vowel sounds?
- Is any particular vowel sound dominant in the poem?
- Are there end-rhymes in the poem?

Repeat this exercise using the same poem and the same procedure for consonants and diphthongs.

Day 2   This day begins the focus on alliteration and onomatopoeia, the intentional repetition of sound.

- Read Richard Wilbur's poem, "Junk," which is based on Old English alliteration. Students copy the poem into their poetry notebook.
- Students now write their own alliterative lines about some "junk" in their lives in their poetry notebook.

Day 3   Having been introduced to alliteration, the students can now examine the concept of onomatopoeia. The teacher begins by listing a few examples of onomatopoeic words on the board. The teacher then lists as many onomatopoeic words as the students can think up.

- Identify examples of onomatopoeia from your literature anthology.
- Create a group poem using as many onomatopoeic words as possible. Write the poem on the blackboard as it progresses.

With the group poem, each student in the class adds one word at a time to the poem.

Day 4   This day is devoted to half-rhyme.

- Identify half-rhyme in an entire poem by Wilfred Owen. Students write the poem in their poetry notebook.
- Examine a poem by a poet such as Thom Gunn who uses a broader range of half-rhyme than Owen does. Compare his use of half-rhyme with Owen's. Students write down their response in their poetry notebook.

Day 5   Bring in poems that are rich in sound qualities. Have the students identify the elements of the soundscape of the poems.

Beyond the Week

- Students choose a favorite poem that appeals to them in terms of sound. Have them identify the sound qualities that they admire in this poem. Students write their responses in their poetry notebook.

SOUND
Bibliography

Poems

"Meditation on Song and Structure" by Charles Wright from *Black Zodiac*, Farrar Straus Giroux, 1997; "Domesday Song" by W. H. Auden from *Collected Poems*, Random House, 1976; "Junk" by Richard Wilbur from *New and Collected Poems*, Harcourt Brace, 1988; "A Terre" and "Exposure" by Wilfred Owen from *Collected Poems*, New Directions, 1964; "River Road" by Stanley Kunitz from *The Poems of Stanley Kunitz 1928–1978*, Little Brown, 1979; "Overhearing Two on a Cold Sunday Morning" by Robert Francis from *Collected Poems 1936–1976*, University of Massachusetts Press, 1976.

Alliterative *Beowulf* translations include *Beowulf: An Imitative Translation*, translated by Ruth Lehmann, University of Texas Press, 1988; *Beowulf*, translated by Michael Alexander, Penguin Books, 1973; and *Beowulf*, translated by Edwin Morgan, University of California Press, 1964. For a recent, non-alliterative translation see *Beowulf: A Translation and Commentary* by Marc Hudson, Bucknell University Press, 1990. See also "The Seafarer" by Ezra Pound in *Translations*, New Directions, 1963.

"Blackie, the Electric Rembrandt" is in Thom Gunn's *Collected Poems*, Farrar Straus Giroux, 1994.

Prose

Further discussions of sound can be found in *A Prosody Handbook* by Karl Shapiro and Robert Beum, Harper & Row, 1965, and *Western Wind* by John Frederick Nims, Random House, 1974. *Sound and Form in Modern Poetry* by Harvey Gross, University of Michigan Press, 1964, provides a historical overview of the latter part of the nineteenth century and the first half of the twentieth.

3

Line

Summary

Poems are written in lines. In metered poetry the line is the sum of x number of rhythmic units. In free verse the lengths of lines are determined by a variety of intentions such as ending lines where syntactic units end, running lines across syntactic units, stopping lines to coincide with punctuation, and using line lengths to imitate physical effects. How quickly or slowly a free-verse poem proceeds depends a good deal on whether lines are enjambed (run on) or not, how long the lines are, and how much variation there is among the line lengths. There are some poems that are neither metrical nor free verse, they are syllabic: The poet counts the number of syllables in a line and uses a pattern based on syllable counts. A haiku is an example of a poem organized according to the number of syllables per line.

Unlike prose, which travels automatically across the page until it hits the right margin and then dutifully returns to the left margin, poetry moves across the page in lines that typically end well short of the right margin. The length of these lines is carefully considered by the poet because the line is the bearer of rhythm. The accents, sounds and pauses all consort within the propulsive line that moves steadily forward in time. Poetry always has been an oral art and the bards and reciters who once spoke and chanted their poems in Greek and Latin and Gaelic and Spanish and Russian (among many languages) used the line to help them keep time with a musical accompaniment, to keep track of rhythms (so many accents or syllables to a line), and to

41

provide a rule of thumb in organizing and memorizing a poem that could be thousands of lines long. The line was (and remains) the staple of the poem just as the sentence is the staple of prose.

The beauty of lines is that they are infinitely flexible. They hold all number and manner of syllables and accents; they can be of the same length or vary in length; they can begin at the left margin or somewhere else on the page; they can enact any array of syntactic arrangements; they can be built into stanzas of various lengths; a line can run onto the following line ("enjambment" is the poet's word) or end with a period that coincides with the end of the line. For poets the line has an intensely physical quality because each line is shaped according to the dictates of rhythm, syntax, and meaning. Each line of a poem has a tangible weight, pace, and presence. (1)

In metrical poetry the number of accentual-syllabic units per line dictates where the line ends. A pentameter line (five weak/strongs), for instance, ends with the fifth metrical unit. Thus, although the rhythmic texture of each line of a Shakespearian sonnet varies a good deal, each line has the same number of metrical units—five. By adhering to the same number of units, the poet is keeping faith with his or her reader. The poet proposes a standard and maintains it and that faithfulness is part of the aesthetic satisfaction of the poem.

Beyond the counting of rhythmic units, the poet who is writing in meter is particularly concerned with two aspects of the line. One is where the pauses (termed "caesuras") will fall within a line. Our breath capacity is such that it is hard to speak longer lines (such as pentameters) without some pause. Also, punctuation of any sort within a line of any length results in some degree of pause. How decisive the pauses are depends on what the poet's purposes are. As pauses slow the line down, they have all sorts of possibilities in terms of emphasis. They are minute silences within the soundscape of the line. When Hamlet realizes that he has been poisoned he says:

> Heaven make thee free of it! I follow thee.
> I am dead, Horatio. Wretched Queen, adieu!

The emphatic pauses after "it" and "Horatio" correspond with emphatic feelings as Shakespeare packs four powerful sentences into two lines. The shattering of a life is felt in the pronounced pauses: All the unimpeded eloquence is done. The slighter pauses after "dead" and "Queen" slow that line down further. The reader feels Hamlet's agony in its painful deliberateness. (2)

Compare this with some lines Hamlet speaks to Laertes a bit earlier in the scene:

> If Hamlet from himself be ta'en away,
> And when he's not himself does wrong Laertes,
> Then Hamlet does it not, Hamlet denies it.

In the first and second lines of this excerpt there is no internal punctuation whatsoever. When we speak these lines we notice that we pause slightly after "himself." Shakespeare uses the caesura we take to get our breath to reinforce Hamlet's self-awareness. It is an emphasis we physically experience. Compare this effect with the more decisive pause the comma affords after "not" in the third line. In that line Hamlet sums up his experience and the definite, punctuated caesura highlights the brisk finality of his logic.

In the three lines above, the caesuras fall in the same place (after the third metrical unit) but they don't have to. The sense, syntax, rhythm, and punctuation of a line dictate the caesura so that when Claudius says "And in the cup a union shall he throw" we feel the syntactic pause after the second metrical unit ("the cup"). Although there are only so many places the caesura may fall within the line, the shadings of the caesura are remarkably expressive. How much the poet writing in meter varies the pause within each line helps determine the overall feeling of a poem or passage. A master metrical hand such as Thomas Hardy uses pauses for maximum expressiveness. In the following stanza from "During Wind and Rain" Hardy employs virtually every aspect of caesura:

> They change to a high new house,
> He, she, all of them—aye,
> Clocks and carpets, and chairs
> On the lawn all day,
> And brightest things that are theirs ....

> Ah, no; the years, the years;
> Down their carved names the rain-drop ploughs.

Line four has no pause; the second and penultimate lines have three strong punctuated pauses; the final line has a slight natural pause for breath after "names;" the third line has a punctuated caesura after "carpets." The stanza as a whole forces the reader to experience the intensity of the passage of time by continuously varying the pace of the lines. As human beings, our perception of time stops and starts; we notice this and that now and then. Hardy captures this fragmentary, wayward, emphatic aspect along with the inexorability of time in the final line—just barely pausing, unpunctuated, relentless. It is the longest line in the stanza and thus enacts, in its way, the stubborn enormity of time.

Whereas caesuras speak to the issue of the degree of pause within a line, enjambment speaks to the degree of pause at the end of a line. The pause may be decisive as when a line ends with a period (and hence no enjambment) or it may be almost unnoticeable as when a line of a word or two runs onto the next line without intervening punctuation. In any case, lines that run on promote the natural flow of a poem's rhythm. When the contemporary metrical poet Norman Williams writes in his poem "Skonoke's Barber Chair" that he ("I" in the poem)

> Trundled down as regular as church
> Each Saturday to take my place
> On that plush red leather, grimed
> By the backside printer's ink
> Of its patrons from across the street ...

the enjambment works to engage the reader in the undifferentiated whole of the experience. There is no getting away from the haircut just as there is no place to pause at the end of lines: The dutiful momentum of routine rules utterly. By definition enjambment is propulsive, as the reader will register only the tiniest pause at the end of the line before proceeding to the next one. If there is no punctuation, there is no decisive pause between lines. Enjambment thus may work to make the reader feel all manner of movement—be it pell-mell or delicate. (3)

Another poem by Williams illustrates how noticeable enjambment can be in contradistinction to lines that end with punctuation. The poem is entitled "Plovers":

> Tramping, in early spring, up Higbee's hill
> Through twice-melted and refrozen crust,
> I envy my young daughter's thoughtless skill
> At staying atop the drifts. In a field of frost—
> Bedraggled Queen Anne's lace and beggar's tick,
> Near an unpruned apple tree whose center bough
> Has split, we come on northern plovers, black
> And white, whirling in the mid-March sun, as though
> To praise and celebrate the cloudless day.
> It is, I think, a ritual display,
> A means to claim a mate or nesting place.
> My daughter's mind is somewhere else: dumbstruck,
> She stumbles up, arms wide, as though to take
> Some chosen bird into her small embrace.

Williams uses enjambment throughout the poem, but it seems particularly effective in lines seven and eight. It is in these lines that the poet and his daughter see the birds. In both lines there is a punctuated pause late in the line and then a movement onwards that carries the reader a bit more strongly forward for having taken the pause. In its understated way, the enjambment speaks to the flight of the birds and the wakening of feeling the sight of the birds causes. The pace of the meter seems to be slightly quickened. It is a small thing in the overall economy of the poem, but then a poem is the sum of many small attentions.

Enjambment and caesura speak to the ever-changing rhythmic feel of lines. Some poems in meter promote a further degree of variability by using different line lengths within the same poem. Such poems are termed "heterometric" (see the Hardy stanza above) as they mix different line lengths. One of the oldest examples in English of this sort of poem is the ballad. Here is the first stanza of the ballad "Chevy Chase," a poem commemorating a battle fought in 1388:

> God prosper long our noble King,
> Our lives and safeties all!
> A woeful hunting once there did
> In Chevy Chase befall.

The shift from four units ("tetrameter") to three units ("trimeter") that occurs twice in each stanza of a ballad has a tripping yet abrupt quality that is suited to the ballad's story-telling intent. The shorter second and fourth lines of the stanza act to succinctly define some narrative aspect, at once tersely summing up and hurrying the tale along. The tautly lilting, slightly off-center cadence of the ballad is mesmerizing, and poets and songwriters still use it routinely as in the following stanza from John Betjeman's "The Arrest of Oscar Wilde":

> I want some more hock in my seltzer,
> And Robbie, please give me your hand—
> Is this the end or beginning?
> How can I understand?

Betjeman takes metrical liberties (as in the second line of four units) but the intent of the form is unmistakable: A story is being told succinctly and memorably. The ballad form is narrow in scope but the opportunity it provides for teaming rhythmic decisiveness with narrative terseness explains its longevity. (4)

Songs too are often heterometric. The song sung in Act II, scene v of *As You Like It* is a marvelous example:

> Who doth ambition shun,
> And loves to live i' the sun,
> Seeking the food he eats,
> And pleased with what he gets,
> Come hither, come hither, come hither.
> Here shall he see

No enemy
But winter and rough weather.

The first four lines with their three weak/strong units ("trimeter") are intensified by the fifth line, which places a degree of stress on the *come's*. The rhythm is then tightened in a sprightly couplet of two units to the line before ending with a trimeter line. The contrasting couplet asserts a deft, swift touch which in turn makes the conclusion seem the more fully conclusive. (5)

Beyond the distinctly aural tradition of songs and ballads, there are poems in which the poets consciously resort to heterometric lines. Two lines, for instance, of Hamlet's speech to Laertes in the play's final scene (lines 237 to 263) are not full pentameter lines. Here the brevity of the two lines ("This presence knows," "Sir, in this audience") seems a nod to the tension in the scene as if Hamlet could not quite fulfill the obligation of courtly decorum. He is—in his fashion—in a hurry. A superb modern example of the heterometric poem is Robert Frost's "After Apple-Picking." Most of the lines are pentameter but a number of lines are dimeter (two weak/strong units), a few lines are trimeter, and one line is monometer (one unit). The poet is "overtired" from apple-picking. He has had enough of his endeavor; he is "drowsing off," and he dreams, of course, of apples. The shorter lines counter the certainty of the full lines as if to say that things are not all they seem to be; they are not so predictable. The sameness of the motion of picking many apples is mimicked in the regular pentameters but it is purposely curtailed at times, again as if to say that there is more to humanity than regularity, that the spirit can bear only so much exactitude. The poem is a masterful instance of form expressing content. The heterometric lines surprise; they are perfectly metrical yet unpredictable in their line lengths, and by working against completion ("the picking is over and done"), they suggest that the mind is not so quiescent: In dreams the experience is far from over.

Throughout his life Frost wrote in meter and he was fond of making gibes at poets he called "free versters." He liked to compare free verse to playing tennis with the net down—no difficulty, thus no art and no fun. From Frost's point of view, that of a man who relished the struggle it took to make the regular stress of meter feel natural, free verse was loafing: There was no strain, no opposition. (He said, "I like to drag and break the intonation across the meters as waves first comb and then break stumbling on the shingle.") Free verse lines made the rules up as they went along, a sort of indifferent cheating to Frost's mind. One must say in free verse's defense that it is not about predetermined structure. It is about process. It values the tension between certainty—the poem will move forward some way or another—and uncertainty—how it moves depends on the tone and intent of the particular poem. Metrical lines display great variety within a set pattern. Because free verse lines are not determined, they are open to the play of local circumstances: Every time a free verse poet ends one line and begins another a choice has been made that was not a wholly predictable choice. The free verse poet intends each line break (where the line ends) to be expressive. It may be modestly expressive; it may be quite demonstrative. It depends on the poet's intentions. All in all, a good free verse poem is like one, complete motion: One can dissect the stages of the motion (like analyzing how a player shoots a free throw), but what the poem aims for is the overall effect of the motion. Where the metrical line insists on its completeness, the free verse line enjoys its incompleteness. How long will the next line be? Where will the line break occur? What will the connection be between one line and another? How enjambed? Such guessing is part of free verse's charm.

Free verse lines are indeterminate in length but hardly artless. Although the gradations and variations among free verse lines seem infinite, a few recognizable categories assert themselves. They are ways of breaking lines that occur time and again and indicate definite predilections as to how the poem proceeds. Perhaps the most common inclination of free verse lineation (a term used to denote the writing of free verse lines) is the phrasal or syntactic approach. The poet breaks lines at the appropriate syntactic juncture. Thus Jane Kenyon writes in "The Three Susans":

> Ancient maples mingle over us, leaves
> the color of pomegranates.
> The days are warm with honey light,
> but the last two nights have finished
> every garden in the village.

The line breaks follow clear syntactic divisions; for instance, Kenyon completes the verb phrase "have finished," then enjambs to the next line. The word that dangles at the end of line one is the exception that proves the rule. As a phrase it belongs with line two but in terms of expressiveness—vulnerable and by itself, like a leaf in autumn—it makes good sense to put the word at the end of the first line rather than the beginning of the second. Since the length of lines is not to be taken for granted in free verse, one of its chief pleasures lies precisely in this sort of sensitivity and alertness. (6)

Shaun Griffin's poem about Robert Lowell also follows the syntactic-phrasal format:

A Metered Vision

> We asked to be obsessed
> with writing, and we were.
>   Robert Lowell

You fell from the back seat
of a New York cab
with eyes so intense
that nothing, save death, could enter.
Was it the lens of the lithium,
or were you speaking to us
that day we learned
the shrill comfort of your silence.

References to Thoreau and thorazine
were scattered like dice
among the women,
the poets, and the family
who almost endured
your sleepless nights to the end.

In your arms, a lone
metered vision gathers still.

The lineation here perfectly suits the grave, plain pace of the elegy. The poet does not want to call attention to the line breaks and the poem proceeds unobtrusively as it observes the series of natural syntactic breaks. There is nothing especially to notice until the word "lone" in the penultimate line. There, as in Jane Kenyon's poem, the slight variation in format works expressively: "a lone" is alone at the end of the line. It is a very light, glancing moment for there is no stop at the end of the line and it is thus an enjambed line. The lineation enacts ("What a poem is is essentially what it does.") a quietly telling moment.

Sometimes poets seek to break down the line further by narrowing the natural, syntactic segments of sentences. Consider this passage from the beginning of a poem by Donald Hall about John Keats and Fanny Brawne entitled "For An Exchange of Rings":

> They rise into mind,
> the young lovers
> of eighteen-nineteen:
> As they walk together
> in a walled garden
> of Hampstead, tremulous,
> their breathing quick,
> color high, eyes lucent,
> he places the floral
> ring with its almondine
> stone on her finger.

The brief lines here evoke a feeling of great attentiveness and care: Everything is being scrutinized—not out of finickiness but love, for every distinct aspect of the story is precious. Each small phrase ("the young lovers," for instance) wants to be acknowledged for its own worth. The scale of the lines echoes against the implied immensity and cruelty of time. Keats will die in a mere two years; this love will come to little. The lengths of the lines emphasize this fragility. When Hall enjambs lines, the words "floral" and "almondine" emphasize the poignance and doomed sensuality of the relationship. It is exquisite poetry—deeply sensitive without being at all mannered.

Following the natural syntactic breaks is far from the only way to construct free verse poems. Indeed, the poet can work to great effect by working against the natural breaks. If the poet wishes to emphasize a degree of edginess, uncertainty, the sheer spasmodic energy of life, then fracturing lines across syntactic phrases makes good sense. One master of this approach is Robert Creeley. The opening stanzas of "The Cracks" show Creeley's artistry:

> Don't step
> so lightly. Break
> your back, missed
> the step. Don't go
>
> away mad, lady in
> the nightmare. You
> are central,
> even necessary.

In the first stanza Creeley won't let the reader rest, the enjambed lines keep moving the reader forward—just as the unnerving subject matter may make the reader wish to warily pause. Creeley uses lineation to implicate and immerse the reader in the poem. The scale of the poem may be small but there is no escaping it once one starts reading. When in the second stanza Creeley pauses at the end of a line with a comma, it is ironic, as if to say, "Well, now you are in a nightmare of uncertainty. Sure, pause and relax." By refusing the natural line breaks, Creeley creates his own out-of-kilter, cross-purposes momentum that is perfectly suited to his unsettling intentions.

Creeley's intent is very close to what we call the mimetic aspect of free verse lineation where the poem mimes some physical action. Free verse is very good at this imitative physicality. A droll example are these lines by Gerald Barrax from his poem "Slow Drivers":

> ... they bait
> your fury
> and impatience across double lines
> into blind

curves

making you wait

wait

wait

wait

The purpose is clear: You are made to experience the awful tedium of being stuck behind a slow driver. In Barrax's words, "you must be getting on, getting on" but you can't. The tautness and tension of the situation is captured in the short lines. You feel tense; you feel imprisoned: when will this poem end? How many "wait's" must I endure? The lineation is as merciless as those slow drivers.

The only limit on the mimetic aspect of free verse is imagination. It can range anywhere. A beautiful example is this excerpt from Li-Young Lee's poem "Braiding":

We sit on our bed, you

between my legs, your back to me, your head

slightly bowed, that I may brush and braid

your hair. My father

did this for my mother,

just as I do for you. One hand

holds the hem of your hair, the other

works the brush.

While the rhythm is that of an easy, natural cadence, the lineation serves to press the insistent, physical actuality of hair braiding. By enjambing virtually all the lines, Lee propels the poem forward in a mimetic fashion: one motion leads to another motion, the process of the braiding is steady and ongoing. The reader senses how the narrative of generations is itself a sort of braiding. The poem is about a physical action (like Barrax's) and the poem uses lineation to create (as Barrax does) a physical sensation. The various line lengths emphasize that the labor is not mechanical but organic. The moments that make up the lines describe an action but they are not exactly equivalent. (7)

A number of the poems cited in this chapter emphasize short lines. The reader, recalling Walt Whitman, may wonder about the long line and indeed there is a vigorous tradition of free verse poems that use a markedly long line. In his poem "Praises" Thomas McGrath praises vegetables:

The vegetables please us with their modes and virtues.
                                        The demure heart
Of the lettuce inside its circular court, baroque ear
Of quiet under its rustling house of lace, pleases
Us.
    And the bold strength of the celery, its green Hispanic
Shout! its exclamatory confetti ...
                            O and the straightforwardness
In the labyrinth of Cabbage, the infallible rectitude of Homegrown
    mushroom
Under its cone of silence like a papal hat—

The long line is expansive and inclusive. It lends itself to full-lunged praise and lament (see Allen Ginsberg's "Kaddish"), declamation, a passion for relating all manner of events and leaving nothing out. The long line is like an expandable piece of luggage: The feeling that drives the poem can make it as big as it chooses. McGrath wants to emphasize the riotous energy of the vegetable world and the long line allows him to impart some of the feeling of that energy. As an animate presence, the line literally surges across the page. (8)

Jim Harrison similarly uses the long line to give a sense of huge—and in this case—miscellaneous energy at the end of his "A Domestic Poem for Portia":

                            The male dog, a trifle
stupid, rushes through the door announcing absolutely nothing.
He has great confidence in me. I'm hanging on to nothing today and
with confidence, a sureness that the very air between our bodies,
the light of what we are, has to be enough.

It takes breath to get through long lines and when one reaches the last line of Harrison's poem its relative shortness stands as a sort of reward, a graceful assertion that rests on the energy the long lines contain. Unlike McGrath, Harrison returns to the margin for each line with dogged (excuse the pun) persistence. Harrison is more engaged with determination than with the sprawl McGrath gleefully invites. Both poets belong to the tradition of the long line which asks what is fullness to us human beings? What is the whole of an experience? What is satiation? What is relentlessness? The long line asks and in its passionate, full-lunged way seeks to answer such questions. (9)

The free verse tradition (for it is, after all, well over a hundred years old) does not count syllabic accents the way meter does, but it is hardly indifferent to them. The free verse line is alert to accent as it retards, smooths, or speeds up the tempo of a line. Accent is part of the texture of the free verse line. A burst of monosyllabic adjectives ("a brisk, dour, salt wind") is going to intensify a free verse line whereas a spate of unaccented "of's" and "the's" is going to loosen the line. There is, however, a type of free verse poem that scants accent in favor of syllables. It is called "syllabic verse" and its organization is based on syllable counts—so many syllables to a line. This is certainly an artificial arrangement given that English is not French or Japanese, but not a wholly perverse one. Syllabic verse imposes a standard that is arbitrary and to a degree nonsensical, then it sees what happens to the poem within those confines. It makes the poet search for words in a place the poet is unaccustomed to searching—the number of syllables in words. What occurs in the work of the best-known exemplar of syllabic verse, Marianne Moore, is a sense of structure that allows the poet's perceptive chattiness to seem at once effortless and highly determined. Look at the first stanza of her "Critics and Connoisseurs":

There is a great amount of poetry in unconscious
    fastidiousness. Certain Ming
      products, imperial floor-coverings of coach-
    wheel yellow, are well enough in their way but I have seen something
      that I like better—a

mere childish attempt to make an imperfectly ballasted animal
    stand up,
similar determination to make a pup
  eat his meat from the plate.

There are three more stanzas of this poem and they replicate the syllable counts of each of the lines in the first stanza: fourteen syllables in
the first line, eight in the second, twelve in the third, and so on. The
stanzas look the same to the eye with their pattern of indentations,
and the same degree of rhyme is observed as in lines seven and eight.
For Moore, the rules she has invented serve to structure her conversational flow. It is a deliberate art for what seems a rather prosy and almost garrulous voice. The contrast between artifice and talkiness is
delicious, and the rhythm Moore creates is all her own as the poem
rattles on yet periodically contracts. Reading her stanzas is a bit like
standing in a boat when there is a strong swell—a sort of steady un-
steadiness.

Just as poems combining different metrical line lengths are called
"heterometric," poems that proceed by lines of various syllable counts
may be termed "heterosyllabic." Similarly, poems that maintain the
same syllable counts from line to line are isosyllabic. Here are the
opening lines of Hayden Carruth's "Loneliness: An Outburst of
Hexasyllables":

Stillness and moonlight, with
thick new fallen snow. I
go to the hollow field
beneath the little ridge
of spruces. The snow lies
on the trees, drapery
white and unmoving. I
cannot see any light
from here, no farmhouse, no
car moving through darkness.

The effect is utterly different from Moore's. The poet uses the syllabic line not to highlight the degree of artifice as Moore does but to downplay it. The count is a steady obligation; the poet honors the obligation. Loneliness is more than a random mood here: The syllabic structure makes it a physical entity. Six syllables per line is not many. The poem feels taut and careful, yet as it proceeds it builds a wary momentum. The poem is subdued in tone and treads very lightly. It is hushed and, indeed, syllabic verse seems one way to turn the volume down a bit on the accentual nature of the English language. It's not that the accents go away but that the syllabic count says in effect to the accents, "You don't matter as much as you are accustomed to mattering." This alternative approach frees Carruth to pursue stillness and silence and solitude with a form (a poem whose lines are all six syllables) that is relatively soundless and transparent.

This quiet quality of syllabic verse is prominent in the tradition of English language haiku. The original syllabic scheme of the Japanese haiku is five syllables in the first line, seven in the second, and five in the third. English language haiku follow this form and sometimes other conventions such as the way a Japanese haiku will allude, however lightly, to a season of the year. The haiku form is a discipline in a number of ways: The syllabic counts must be observed, there is no room to develop the topic, syntax is bound to be tricky given the brevity of the poem. The popularity of the haiku form lies precisely in this degree of difficulty: Each syllable counts for so much that it forces the poet to ponder language in a new way. To use an analogy, it is like being a child with a few small coins in one's pocket. The coins are very finite, they are of small worth, and yet they matter greatly. The poet speaks very carefully but with zest too (like the child putting the coins on the counter) as in the following two haiku:

> August's soft downpours—
> Kitchen voices hum next door—
> Who hears the gutter?

Under the elm log
One antenna in, one out,
The slug lifts its head.

Although there are very genuine differences among the metrical, free verse, and syllabic verse lines, the line's physical presence is a constant. The line materializes time: It lasts for so long and then there is another line that lasts only for so long. Compared to the sheer volume of daily language, any line of a poem—even a relatively long line—is brief in scope and duration. There is an enduring modesty and strength in the poetic line; like a reed it is slim but powerfully supple. (10)

LINE
In the Classroom

1. Consider the following seven lines from Randall Jarrell's poem "Lady Bates":

The lightning of a summer

Storm wakes, in her clay cave

At the end of weeds, past the mock-orange tree—

Where she would come bare-footed, curled-up-footed

Over the green, grained, rotted fruit

To eat blackberries, a scratched handful—

The little Lady Bates.

In terms of physical presence, which line feels weightiest? Why? Is it necessarily the longest line? Which line is most memorable? With what physical qualities is its memorableness connected?

2. Longer lines, whether in metered verse or in free verse, have caesuras in them, pauses that help shape rhythm and poetic purpose. Read some poems from an anthology that covers the history of English-language poetry and locate caesuras. Do there seem to be particular purposes for the caesuras? What about the "medial caesura," the balanced pause in the middle of a line ("The wise man's passion, and the vain man's boast") that is common in the poetry of such eighteenth century poets as Jonathan Swift and Alexander Pope? How often do these poets use the medial caesura? How do contemporary, free-verse poets use caesuras? Are there any points of comparison concerning the caesura among different eras?

3. An excellent way to learn about enjambment is to read poems aloud. After a poem has been read aloud twice, read it aloud a third time, sentence by sentence, and have the class write the poem down in their poetry notebooks as it is being read. Read the poem aloud one more time and then have the students turn the sentences into lines. Discuss the students' versions of the poem's lines. How do the versions differ from one another and from the original poem (to be handed out at this point)? To what degree can you hear enjambment?

4. Listen to a recording of an African-American ballad such as "Stagolee." After hearing it a few times, write down a few stanzas. Then write your own ballad about some recent incident in your community.

5. Listen to the radio, tapes, CD's. Write down the lyrics of a recorded song and bring them to class for discussion. Are the lyrics rhythmically steady in the weak/strong tradition or do the lines vary rhythmically? Are the lines all the same length or do they vary? The blues tradition tends to be isometric: All the lines are the same lengths. Listen to some blues recordings and write down a stanza. Is it isometric? Do the lines form a triplet? Write your own blues poem. See Langston Hughes's "The Weary Blues" and Nikki Giovanni's "Mastercard Blues" for further extensions of the blues poem.

6. Using Jane Kenyon's *Otherwise: New and Collected Poems*, look at some poems specifically in terms of enjambment. What do the enjambments accomplish? What happens if the enjambments change?

7. Lineation lends itself to miming physical action. Write a poem using the lines to recreate a particular physical activity such as running a cross-country course or bouncing a ball down a basketball court.

8. Allen Ginsberg, a contemporary successor to the Whitman tradition, was a great exponent of the long line. Read "Howl" and "Kaddish" and examine the relationship between what is said and the line lengths. How do the two work together? Could the poems work as successfully in shorter lines? What are the differences in regard to line between the two poems? Ginsberg considered "Kaddish" a "litany." What qualities distinguish Ginsberg's litany?

9. The long line is a great incorporator and includer. Write a poem about the day's experiences in long lines. Try to catch specific feelings, sensory details, and locales. Let your various thoughts from the day into the poem also.

10. Discuss syllabic verse in terms of poems that vary syllable counts and poems that maintain the same syllable count from line to line. Write poems that are heterosyllabic (different syllable counts in lines), isosyllabic (same syllable count in every

line), and a haiku. Compare the poems in terms of the differing demands that the forms make. For instance, how does the concision of the haiku affect what is being said?

LINE
Five-Day Lesson Plan

Day 1   Give students a free verse poem written out like a prose paragraph. Ask the students to lineate the poem.
- Ask the students to first think about the poem as a whole.
- Then ask them to lineate the poem according to elements of line, such as rhythm, enjambment, and syntax.
- Have a number of students present their versions of the poem using overheads to present the poem.
- Discuss the versions. Students should be able to speak to the reasons behind their version.
- Ask the class to reach consensus on one version.
- The teacher then distributes the original poem.
- Students compare the class consensus version with the original poem.
- Have students compare in their poetry notebook their personal version with the original.

Day 2   Have students analyze a free verse poem, looking at enjambment and punctuation only. This can be presented either as a class discussion or as group work.
- Hand out another poem by the same poet. Pick two examples from the poem where enjambment and punctuation affect the poem. Ask students to explain how.

Day 3   The teacher brings in examples of short-line and long-line free verse poems. Discuss with the class how the poems differ in terms of syntax, tone, and rhythm. Based on the examples provided, students choose which approach they prefer and write a poem of their own.

Day 4   This day deals with syllabics.

- Teacher brings in examples of poems written in various syllabic forms.
- Students then identify the different structures of the syllabic poems to tell one form from another (count syllables).

- Counting syllables is an artificial device. How does this counting of syllables help the poet organize his or her material?
- Ask students to choose a simple, direct topic such as dogs, hamburgers, sneakers, cars. Ask them to choose a syllabic form and write a poem about the subject in syllabics.

Day 5 This day is devoted to the reading of student poems aloud and commenting on the poems in terms of what it was like to write in syllabics. Students can present their poems on overheads as well. The discussion can lead to issues of revision.

Beyond the Week

- Ask students to choose a contemporary poem and write an essay response to how the poet uses line.

LINE
Bibliography

Poems

"Skonoke's Barber Shop" by Norman Williams from *The Unlovely Child*, Alfred A. Knopf, 1985; "The Arrest of Oscar Wilde" by John Betjeman from *John Betjeman's Collected Poems*, John Murray, 1979; "After Apple Picking" by Robert Frost from *Complete Poems*, Holt Rinehart and Winston, 1949; "The Three Susans" by Jane Kenyon from *Otherwise*, Graywolf Press, 1996; "For an Exchange of Rings" by Donald Hall from *Old and New Poems*, Ticknor and Fields, 1990; "The Cracks" by Robert Creeley from *The Collected Poems of Robert Creeley 1945–1975*, University of California Press, 1982; "Slow Drivers" by Gerald Barrax from *From a Person Sitting in Darkness*, Louisiana State University Press, 1998; "Braiding" by Li-Young Lee from *Rose*, BOA Editions, 1986; "Praises" by Thomas McGrath from *Selected Poems 1938–1988*, Copper Canyon Press, 1988; "A Domestic Poem for Portia" by Jim Harrison from *Selected and New Poems 1961–1981*, Dell Publishing, 1982; "Critics and Connoisseurs" by Marianne Moore from *The Complete Poems*, The Macmillan Company/The Viking Press, 1980; "Loneliness: An Outburst of Hexasyllables" by Hayden Carruth from *Collected Shorter Poems 1946–1991*, Copper Canyon Press, 1992; haiku are from "The Vinalhaven Sequence" by A. David Cappella.

"Lady Bates" by Randall Jarrell from *The Complete Poems*, Farrar Straus Giroux, 1969. For a compilation of blues lyrics see *The Blues Line: A Collection of Blues Lyrics*, compiled by Eric Sackheim, Schirmer Books, 1975.

Prose

Robert Frost's prose can be found in the Library of America volume *Collected Poems, Prose, and Plays*, 1995. For a discussion of haiku see *Zen and Japanese Culture* by Daisetz T. Suzuki, Princeton University Press, 1959.

4

Syntax

Summary

Since each word in a poem is influenced by considerations about rhythm and sound, the issue of how to order those words within sentences is not as straightforward as it is in prose. Indeed, poets formerly inverted regular word order solely to satisfy the demands of meter (by putting verbs before nouns or adjectives after nouns). Though nowadays poets rarely use inversion because it feels artificial, they do use every other aspect of syntax available to them in terms of complex sentences, simple sentences, and phrases. How poets mix these aspects depends on the purposes of the particular poem. What all poets have in common is the awareness that they do not have to follow one path, such as the declarative sentence, over and over again. Every time a sentence or phrase is constructed, the poet faces an expressive possibility.

Syntax is the way in which words are arranged within sentences. As it represents a conditioned aspect of our lives, we tend not to think about it very much. Verbs follow subjects the way night follows day. At one time or another we probably all have been told when writing prose to vary our syntax. Strings of sentences with identical syntactical structures tend to be boring. Syntactic variety keeps us alert to the play of structural possibilities: Sentences can begin with different parts of speech, for instance. (1) Similarly, we may have been told to always use complete sentences though when we reflect

65

upon this advice we notice that there are all manner of sentence-like units that do not conform to the world of the subject (the topic) and the predicate (what is being said about the topic). "Sure" and "Gee whiz!" and "Get trucking" and "No dice" are all complete, meaningful units. There is life beyond the typical subject-predicate patterns, especially in the spoken flow of conversation where sentences tend to blur into phrases and other sentences. (2)

For poets, syntax is an expressive opportunity. What choices the poet makes concerning syntax are not only going to determine the tone of a poem (elegant or knotty or in-your-face, for example) but also what we like to call the poet's vision, by which we mean how the poet sees the world and articulates those perceptions. Syntax is world-view, and how the poet chooses to deploy syntax tells us a good deal about the poet's attitudes about life and language. To read, for instance, Emily Dickinson is to fall into a world where syntax is continually jolted, as the exclamatory phrase takes precedence over the dutifully complete sentence. It is unsettling yet exhilarating. Dickinson rejected the suasive voice of calm sentence following calm sentence for a staccato, interjectory feeling. She is closer to a shaman imparting visionary intuitions that proceed in fragmentary leaps than the fluent, professional poets her age revered. Her syntax is part of her re-definition of the means of poetry. To charges of choppy and inelegant syntax she might have responded, "Yes and forceful, passionate, and startlingly alive, also." (3)

For the poet syntax is both a challenge—how to structure sentences and phrases so that they enforce the poet's vision—and a basic responsibility—there is no avoiding syntax. For example, one of the greatest challenges a poet can set for her- or himself is to write a poem in one sentence. Such a poem self-consciously celebrates the confines of syntax, even as it revels in the structural riches of syntax. Consider Eleanor Wilner's poem about Helen Keller and Ann Sullivan, "Of a Sun She Can Remember":

> After they had been in the woods
> after the living tongue woke Helen's

hand, afterwards they went back
to the little house of exile, Annie and
Helen, who had lived in the silent
dark, like a bat without radar in
the back of a cave, and she picked up
the broken doll she had dismembered
that morning in her rage, and limb
by limb, her agile fingers moving
with their fine intelligence over each
part, she re-membered the little figure
of the human, and, though she
was inside now, and it was still dark,
she remembered the missing sun
with a slow wash of warmth
on her shoulders, on her back—
as when you step shivering out of
a dank shade into the sun's sudden
balm—and as the warmth spread,
it felt like the other side of water,
and that is when she knew how
light on water looks, and she put
her outspread hands into the idea
of it, and she lifted the lines of light,
cross-hatched like a web, out of
the water, and, dripping, stretched
the golden net of meaning in the light.

The syntax of this poem is a "golden net of meaning" in its own right. Wilner refuses to fragment experience: It must be a whole as Helen Keller came to experience the life of her senses as a whole rather than a violent jumble of frustrations. The poet begins the poem firmly with the time-situating preposition "After" and proceeds through a series of "and's" to her conclusion. The poem defies the conventional admonition about the run-on sentence, for there is nothing lurching or awkward about the pace of the poem. Each "and" clause is given a goodly amount of space to add its particular segment to the story of Helen's awakening. "Here," all the "and's" say as if in unison, "experience does hang together." In the democracy of the "and" clauses, one clause is not superior to another; all aspects of living are knit together. The calm, unhurried syntax mirrors the discovery and healing that were set in motion by the unobtrusive "After." The poem is a remarkable achievement on Wilner's part, but the reader knows she didn't write a 28-line poem in one sentence for the sake of showing it could be done. The syntactic form of the poem is at one with the story the poem tells of Helen Keller's re-membering and awakening. "What is the benefit of all this putting things together that syntax does?" an impatient student of the English language might ask. Wilner's poem is one answer. In its patient way, syntax, as it joins moments together, subdues isolation. (4)

On the other hand, as poetry honors every aspect of expression, the poet may well choose to emphasize the syntactic force of isolation. Here is David Ignatow's poem "Self-Employed":

> I stand and listen, head bowed,
> to my inner complaint.
> Persons passing by think
> I am searching for a lost coin.
> You're fired, I yell inside
> after an especially bad episode.
> I'm letting you go without notice
> or terminal pay. You just lost
> another chance to make good.
> But then I watch myself standing at the exit,
> depressed and about to leave,
> and wave myself back in wearily,
> for who else could I get in my place
> to do the job in dark, airless conditions?

The syntactic structure of subject-predicate is unrelenting. One declarative follows another in lock-step sentences that impart their information succinctly and end without any flourish. The syntax gives the reader a claustrophobic and—to quote from the poem itself—"airless" feeling. Only with "But then" does Ignatow change his structure and that change is the turning point of the poem. After all the sentences beginning with pronouns, the presence of "But" seems a grace note, as if to say, "A degree of thoughtfulness remains." The compassion proferred by the final sentence is, to be sure, ironic as it notes "dark, airless conditions." Still, the reader feels that the more complex sentence structure of the compound clauses creates a different emotional tenor. The poem relents a bit as it allows a broader syntactic scope for the feelings. That the feelings are dark ones helps create the brusque poignance that is the poem's ending. (5)

One thing the poet must grapple with in using syntax is that in poetry there are no rules about syntax. There is no voice saying, "There must be a predicate for every subject." How to effectively use this freedom? Alberto Ríos in his poem "What a Boy Can Do" shows how precisely various syntax can be:

> February, and the wind has begun
> Milk cartons moving along the curb,
> An occasional wrapper, Baby Ruth.
>
> The young tree bends in a hoeing.
> Cirrus clouds, sparrows, jet trailings:
> Each puts a line on the sky. February
>
> Kites, too, their shapes: the way three
> Boys have taken their baseball fields
> Into the air, flying them on strings.
>
> When I flew my kite I shouted, louder,
> Anything, strong, boy wild and rocks:
> February was here. I was helping.

Ríos uses a variety of sentence structures to keep his reader alert to the physical presences that animate his poem. Most notably he introduces nouns at the beginnings of sentences but does not follow them with predicates. The poem begins with a noun that is allowed to exist in its own right without a predicate—as well it should as the poem's subject. Another noun that is the poem's living force takes the predicate: "the wind has begun." Twice more in the poem Ríos puts nouns at the beginnings of sentences: "Cirrus clouds, sparrows, jet trailings" and "Kites, too, their shapes." It is as if Ríos is saying, "These things exist in their own right. They do not need verbs to complete themselves. As presences they are already complete." The last stanza contains the poem's only complex sentence as the poem moves away from the facts of the nouns to the narrator's participation. The two short declaratives of the final line solidify and proclaim the actualities of February and the boy. Syntactically they are truly final notes: pungent and terse. As Ríos has avoided such short declarative sentences, they are all the stronger for being unique.

Within a short poem Ríos consciously modulates his syntax. He does not want sameness. After all, he is celebrating the forceful vagaries of the wind and the narrator's spirit. A poet, however, may choose to work in one syntactic structure throughout a poem. Indeed, the poet may choose to gut the syntactic core of English language sentences—the subject-predicate relationship. This occurs in Ted Kooser's "Notes on the Death of Nels Paulssen, Farmer, at the Ripe Old Age of 93":

> A harvest
> of nail parings,
>
> a wagonload
> of hair—
>
> over his ashen
> fields,
>
> no dust
> in the air.

No predicates in this death. In his title Kooser refers to his poem as "Notes" and the couplets are content to offer their verb-less actualities. Kooser, nonetheless, as far as the poem is concerned, creates a complete sentence. The dash after "hair" implies the spreading of a physical lifetime over "ashen / fields" without directly stating it. It is one of those marvels of punctuation that poets use (similar to Ríos's colons) to create expressive syntaxes. A verb would mar the stillness, the near-eternity of the scene. The poem pays homage to its subject not by recounting how Nels Paulssen did this and that but by testifying metaphorically to the reality of his life and death. As a farmer his life has been the stuff of harvests and wagonloads; in death the mute abundance of actuality still reigns. Simple syntax allows Kooser to register both the weight of death and a sense of the sturdy tenacity of many years. (6)

Syntax—as the poems we have cited illustrate—is protean, yet as it is part of poetry and as poetry is a human enterprise, syntax inevitably has changed over the centuries. In this light, the British poet and critic Donald Davie's generalization about syntax seems tenable, namely that "in the seventeenth and eighteenth centuries poets acted on the assumption that syntax in poetry should often, if not always, carry a weight of poetic meaning; in the nineteenth and twentieth centuries poets have acted on the opposite assumption, that when syntactical forms are retained in poetry those forms can carry no weight." Another way of saying this is that previously poets were involved heavily in making discriminations, judging, arguing, proposing notions, examining hierarchies, and making all manner of contrasts and comparisons in their poetry. Poetry was forthrightly an instrument of thinking. To read, for instance, Alexander Pope's "Essay on Man" is to enter a realm where syntax facilitates judgment:

> Two principles in human nature reign;
> Self-love to urge, and Reason, to restrain;
> Nor this a good, nor that a bad we call,
> Each works its end, to move or govern all:
> And to their proper operation still,
> Ascribe all Good; to their improper, Ill.

The balancing of clauses here is a principle of its own as it is a form of the weighing and pairing of concepts that Pope favors. (7) Syntax comprises the rational skeleton of Pope's judicious thoughts. Similarly, when William Blake, a very different poet from Pope, writes in "The Human Abstract"

> Pity would be no more
> If we did not make somebody Poor;
> And Mercy no more could be
> If all were as happy as we.

Blake is balancing clauses the way Pope does. It is less elaborate than Pope but the instinct to judge among behaviors is the same. In "In a Mirtle Shade" Blake uses an an orderly, decorous syntax to indict the rationalizing excesses of orderliness:

> Why should I be bound to thee
> Oh my lovely mirtle tree?
> Love, free love, cannot be bound
> To any tree that grows on ground.

Blake wrote on the verge of the Romantic era that ushered in the poetry of the modern world. By the end of twentieth century, syntax for some poets had, indeed, become weightless. The following lines are from the beginning of the poem "The Room" by Mark Strand:

> I stand at the back of a room
> and you have just entered.
> I feel the dust
> fall from the air
> onto my cheeks.
> I feel the ice
> of sunlight on the walls.
> The trees outside
> remind me of something
> you are not yet aware of.
> You have just entered.

Syntax as a tool of discrimination and judgment is not a factor here. Syntax has become a ghost. Strand writes in complete sentences but the utter plainness of the syntax disavows any interest in making complex statements. The poet is consciously playing in one key; he does not want to make connections. His narrative is flat yet tactile, simple yet mysterious. The sentences feel hard-won and constricted. Things stand on their own; they do not hang together. Each perception is solitary. (8)

   Strand's simple syntax makes a metaphysical statement. It is quite possible, however, to liberate syntax in the sense of dispensing with complete sentences and letting the energy of phrases take on a life of their own. Whereas Strand cultivates an intentionally flat affect, David Henderson in his poem about the great jazz trumpeter Lee Morgan generates powerful momentum by unleashing a basic structure—adjective-noun phrases. Here is "Lee Morgan":

> *fly by night*
>> black galaxy
>>> friendly galaxy
> fly by night
>
>> black space/light beams
>> fly by night
>
> dance with sphere monk
> in the club baron manhattan island
> fly deep into night towards the light
> good smoke
> sings the horn
> metal glass under capricorn sky
>
> fly by night
> lee morgan trilling on the ceiling
> sphere monk dancing round the horseshoe bar
>
> ghetto jazzbeaus
> slick trumpeteers
> jericho jammin
> ass-kicking

good timing
hard bopping
good lovin
slick be bop blues and ghetto dues
so tough and tight
and beau

the white bars
cross our blue bodies
behind us glow the red lights
the black night

Particularly in the "ghetto jazzbeaus" stanza Henderson replicates some of Morgan's fierce, sweet, unremitting energy as the phrases keep on coming. Henderson's lines exemplify a whole line of expressiveness that did not exist in pre-modern poetry, just as jazz did not exist in pre-modern music. A well-turned, complete sentence is a fine thing but so is the force of direct physical experience.

Syntax on the page is influenced by the syntax that comes out of our speaking mouths. Many poets of the Beat school that surfaced in the 1950s and strongly influenced American poetry sought to make the page mirror the mouth. Allen Ginsberg, for instance, noted that many American poems gravitated to an "average-daily talk short breath." The syntax of various American speeches is a whole topic unto itself but poets do listen to how people speak and they play it back in poems. It may come out of their own mouths as in Leo Connellan's poem "Boxing":

He'd snap his right up
to smash cheek while it
was his left to the jaw nerve
like the Asp's tongue, one dart;
and to take him all you had to
do was trip his rhythm, change
his feet movement any way
you could, stamp on the floor,

duck, any way.... you change the
feet and his plan was gone. You
had him. But you had to step in
and do it! I seen one time a
guy hesitate after throwing him
off good and it was over.

Or it may come out of the mouth of someone in a poem as in Gary Snyder's "Hay for the Horses," when an old-timer speaks about his life:

"I'm sixty-eight," he said,
"I first bucked hay when I was seventeen.
I thought, that day I started,
I sure would hate to do this all my life.
And dammit, that's just what
I've gone and done."

The great Irish poet W. B. Yeats once noted that "the abandonment of syntax testified to a failure of the poet's nerve, a loss of confidence in the intelligible structure of the conscious mind and the validity of its activity." Yeats's contention is worth pondering. One may agree with it or one may say that "the intelligible structure of the conscious mind" is not very valid at all, that the intelligible is the conceptual and that concepts have little place in any poetry that desires to be true to the particular shapes of experiences. Neither Pope's brisk serenity nor Blake's taut serenity may seem relevant to an age that largely abhors an art of conscious judgments. In either case, what we wish to stress is that the reader and writer of poetry needs to consider the possibilities that syntax offers. As Eleanor Wilner's poem lovingly illustrates, it is possible to engage syntax in all its connecting glory. And it is just as possible to minimize or suspend syntax and let fragments speak for what is fragmentary as T. S. Eliot did in "The Waste Land." Whether at its extremes or in its vast mid-range of declarative sentences, adroit syntax furthers eloquence. (9)

SYNTAX
In the Classroom

1. Syntax depends on context. Syntax that is appropriate to one situation may not be appropriate to another. Look at poems that speak to different occasions (an elegy and a lyric, for instance). Do the syntaxes differ? If so, how and why?
2. Try to write down some verbatim conversation. What does it look like? Does it have complete sentences, fragments, run-ons? Write a poem that consists of a conversation.
3. Read some poems by Emily Dickinson. Are the poems constructed with complete sentences? How would you characterize her syntax? How is syntax crucial to her art?
4. Based upon your reading of Eleanor Wilner's poem, write a poem that is one sentence long.
5. Write a poem that consists of short, declarative sentences. Think before you write about what sort of situation would lend itself to such a syntactical approach.
6. Based upon your reading of Ted Kooser's poem, write a poem without verbs. Again, think about what sort of situation would lend itself to such a syntactical approach.
7. Spend time reading some of Alexander Pope's poetry. What are the advantages of Pope's measured clauses?
8. Read some poems by Mark Strand and observe his use of syntax. Is there a relationship between syntax and the subjects of his poems? What is the relationship between syntax and tone in Strand's work?
9. Using your knowledge of syntax in poems, write a poem of your own that uses syntax expressively. Try combining different sorts of syntax.

SYNTAX
Five-Day Lesson Plan

Day 1 To focus on syntax is to focus on how words in a sentence are put together. The teacher brings in a poem, reads it, and the students write it in their poetry notebook. Students examine the poem sentence by sentence in terms of syntax.
- Are the structures of the sentences the same? If not, how do they differ?

Teachers can then repeat the exercise with more syntactically complex poems.

Day 2 Based on the previous day's class discussion of syntax, have students choose a poem that they are revising and examine it in terms of syntax. Ask them to consider sentence length and structures of sentences. Ask them if all of the sentences begin in the same way as, for example, a verb following a noun. Lastly, ask students to revise their poem from the point of view of its syntax.

Day 3 Look at examples of contemporary poetry in which simple declarative sentences predominate. How do you respond to the repeated syntactical structure? What does the poet gain by repeating a sentence structure? Are there drawbacks to the repetition of declarative sentences?

Day 4 Read a poem from the eighteenth, nineteenth, and twentieth centuries and examine them in terms of their syntax. Write a comparison/contrast essay discussing the differences in syntax among the poems.

Day 5 Continue with the work of Day 4.

Beyond the Week

- Sentence structures appear in many varieties. Have students write down in their poetry notebooks examples of different sentence structures in poems that they read.

SYNTAX
Bibliography

Poems

"Of a Sun She Can Remember" by Eleanor Wilner from *Reversing the Spell*, Copper Canyon Press, 1998; "Self-Employed" by David Ignatow from *Selected Poems*, Wesleyan University Press, 1975; "What a Boy Can Do" by Alberto Ríos from *Teodoro Luna's Two Kisses*, W. W. Norton, 1990; "Notes on the Death of Nels Paulssen, Farmer, at the Ripe Old Age of 93" by Ted Kooser, *Sure Signs*, University of Pittsburgh Press, 1980; "The Room" by Mark Strand from *The Story of our Lives*, Atheneum, 1973; "Lee Morgan" by David Henderson from *The Low East*, North Atlantic Books, 1980; "Boxing" by Leo Connellan from *Short Poems, City Poems 1944–1998*, Hanover Press, 1998; "Hay for the Horses" by Gary Snyder from *Riprap and Cold Mountain Poems*, North Point Press, 1990.

Prose

Donald Davie's volume about syntax and poetry is *Articulate Energy*, Routledge and Paul, 1955.

5

Grammar, Punctuation, and Capitalization

Summary

As conscientious users of language, poets cherish the clarities that grammar, punctuation, and capitalization promote. Poets are perfectly willing, however, to flout prescribed usages if it is necessary to the artistic success of the poem. If a poet is being ungrammatical or ignoring standard punctuation or is not using capital letters where capital letters seem to be called for, it is safe to say that the poet has a good reason for doing what she or he is doing. Notions of correct usage emphasize comprehension and poems want to be comprehended but that comprehension must occur on the poems' own terms.

More than one student while reading passages from John Milton's long poem *Samson Agonistes* has asked us more or less facetiously in what language the poem is written. These students have pointed out that if they handed in sentences such as Milton's, there would be red correction marks all over their papers. Here is a by no means atypical sentence from that poem in which Samson is recounting some of his exploits:

That fault I take not on me, but transfer
On Israel's Governours, and Heads of Tribes,
Who seeing those great acts which God had done
Singly by me against their Conquerors

Acknowledg'd not, or not at all consider'd

Deliverance offerd: I on th'other side

Us'd no ambition to commend my deeds,

The deeds themselves, though mute, spoke loud the dooer;

But they persisted deaf, and would not seem

To count them things worth notice, till at length

Thir lords the Philistines with gather'd powers

Enterd Judea seeking mee, who then

Safe to the rock of Etham was retir'd,

Not flying, but fore-casting in what place

To set upon them, what adavantag'd best;

Mean while the men of Judah to prevent

The harrass of thir Land, beset me round;

I willingly on some conditions came

Into thir hands, and they as gladly yield me

To the uncircumcis'd a welcom prey,

Bound with two cords; but cords to me were threds

Toucht with the flame: on their whole Host I flew

Unarm'd, and with a trivial weapon fell'd

Their choicest youth; they only liv'd who fled.

We can sympathize with those students who felt that Milton deserved to be taken to task for writing such a monumental run-on sentence. Not many teachers would let Milton get by with that "Mean while" nor would they stand for the way he slings semi-colons and colons around. "One colon per sentence, Mr. Milton," a teacher might inform him. "And what (a teacher might go on to say) about that artificial word order, Mr. Milton? 'Acknowledg'd not?' No one speaks or writes that way. What sort of syntax is that?"

Times of course change and much as many of us would like to feel that the rules of prescriptive grammar, punctuation, and capitalization are immutable, the many social factors at work on language indicate that immutability is hard to come by. For his part, John Milton was an explainer; characters in Milton's poems are forever relating what happened to someone or interpreting what someone thought or did or commenting upon actions and motives and beliefs. In Milton everything is connected; nothing just happens out of the existential blue. Milton's fondness for going on and on, along with the requirements of meter, led him into some formidable intracacies. He had no intention of overturning the notions of grammar; on the contrary, Milton is hyper-grammatical. If the grammar of a language "is an account of the language's possible sentence structures, organized according to certain general principles," then Milton is a grammarian's grammarian for his poems are virtual laboratories of sentence structures. And if grammar reflects world views, Milton's certainly speaks for a Puritan outlook that treasured the resources of human reason (and argument) while acknowledging God's omnipotence. All of which is to say that Milton was writing in English and if we have grown uncomfortable with his version of English, the loss is ours because one of the pleasures of a poet's style is how the poet manipulates grammar and punctuation. (1)

Indeed one definition of the poet might be as an explorer of sentence structures. In everyday use we commandeer grammar; it is "part of our daily linguistic survival" in which we attempt to make ourselves understood. Perhaps we pride ourselves on grasping various niceties of grammar such as "that" and "which" or "who" and "whom," but such distinctions are not ends in themselves: they exist to facilitate comprehension. Poets are in the business of questioning what comprehension constitutes; they write poems not to assert what is already known but to locate the mystery and vibrancy that dwell in the most mundane or exalted, delicate or indelicate situations. Accordingly they stretch the limits of comprehension; Milton called *Paradise Lost* an "adventrous Song." His attempt to "justifie the wayes of God to men" was a self-conscious effort to push limits.

The sorts of comprehension poetry offers differ from other sorts of comprehension. Milton was well aware that there were centuries of theological explanation of the story of Adam and Eve. This did not deter him from writing his poem, for a poem brought to bear resources of language, rhythm, sound, and grammar that affected people very differently from the way a prose commentary would affect them. Grammar in Milton's sentence-shaping hands testified to the "enormous creative power of language." His elaborations stretched the very horizons of what a sentence in a poem was. If at times his lines seem torturous, we must remember that there are risks that go with stretching limits.

Modern poetry has continued this adventurous, risk-taking tradition in regard to grammar, punctuation, and capitalization. Here is a poem by the American Objectivist poet George Oppen entitled "Street":

Ah these are the poor,
These are the poor—

Bergen street.

Humiliation,
Hardship …

Nor are they very good to each other;
It is not that. I want

An end of poverty
As much as anyone

For the sake of intelligence,
'The conquest of existence'—

It has been said, and is true—

And this is real pain,
Moreover. It is terrible to see the children,

The righteous little girls;
So good, they expect to be so good.…

Like Milton, Oppen is very attentive to punctuation. Muriel Rukeyser's remark that "Punctuation is biological" makes splendid sense when reading Oppen. One feels a careful mind searching among actualities and feelings and then a sifting of them. The voice is grave

and attentive, pausing deliberately: "It has been said, and is true—"
The comma after "said" is a rhythmic comma that deliberately slows
the line's pace. Similarly, Oppen is sensitive to grammatical possibilities. A sentence containing "nor" typically displays parallelism.
Oppen, however, elects an unbalanced construction: "Humiliation, /
Hardship ... / Nor are they very good to each other; / It is not that."
The ellipses seem to indicate that the sentence is a fragment as each
noun takes a whole line to itself—but then a complete, simple sentence appears after the semi-colon. As far as the long sentence is concerned that constitutes the bulk of the poem, it feels chiseled and taut
despite its length. Again, the proportions of the sentence are skewed
as the first clause is much longer than the second. One feels that the
sentences are being scrutinized the way the poem's subject is being
scrutinized. The little miracle of Oppen's poem is how much feeling
he introduces within the framework of a "Bergen street" that is not
described in any detail. (2) The care we give to grammar is a model for
the care Oppen shows towards his subject; his poem is the opposite of
the dismissive, glib remarks that often are made about "the poor." (3)

Oppen quite consciously regards the possibilities of grammar as it
influences the construction of sentences. Most poets simply use
grammar the way they breathe or walk; it is part of their being. Much
research over the past half-century shows that we acquire language
without troubling ourselves with terms and rules. A kindergartner already possesses a complex grammatical system. What makes poetry
unique in regard to grammar, punctuation, and capitalization is that
the poet uses them for artistic ends. For poets, the common notion of
grammar as a series of prescriptive don'ts—don't split an infinitive,
don't end a sentence with a preposition, don't join sentences with a
comma, don't use fragments—is irrelevant. The poet's artistic aims
determine the grammar. (4) Whether the poet writes "It is I" or "It's
me" depends on the poem's context. It isn't that poets are especially
eager to commit solecisms (grammatical slip-ups); rather, it's that
they are bound to respect the way different people use the language.
The realities of usage are part of the lifeblood of the language. Poetry,
after all, is not just a written art; it is a spoken one, too.

There is, for instance, a world of nuance at the end of Naomi
Shihab Nye's "The Use of Fiction" (see chap. 14) when the narrator

replies to the boy who has spoken carefully to her: "It was I." The correctness of her grammar is decisive. She isn't showing off; instead, she is affirming the community of respectfulness that prizes care and precision. The irony—that she was not the one whom the boy saw and that our perceptions can fail us—makes the affirmation all the stronger. On the other hand, when Yusef Komunyakaa begins "Soliloquy: Man Talking to a Mirror" with these lines—"Working night shift / panhandling Larimer Square / ain't been easy"—he is forthrightly taking into account who is speaking the poem. The wry taunt of many high school English students —"Ain't ain't English"—is held up in Komunyakaa's poem to the merciless light of reality. Correct usage is a social propriety—but what of those outside the borders of propriety? Are their lives one, long "mistake?"

That poets scrutinize usage isn't as surprising regarding grammar as it is regarding punctuation. Punctuation seems ironclad. There had better be a period at the end of each sentence and there had better be a capital letter when a new sentence begins. It's the law—and poets flout it. Here is "Continuum: a Love Poem" by Maxine Kumin:

> going for grapes with
> ladder and pail in
> the first slashing rain
> of September   rain
> steeping the dust
> in a joyous squelch   the sky
> standing up like steam
> from a kettle of grapes
> at the boil   wild fox grapes
> wickedly high   tangled in must
> of cobweb and bug spit
> going for grapes   year
> after year   we two with
> ladder and pail stained
> with the rain of grapes
> our private language

Kumin's absence of punctuation hearkens to the physical reality of the poem. She addresses the sense of continuum, of something that goes on and on. How better to portray that than by turning the poem itself into a continuum? Punctuation makes necessary distinctions so things don't blur and tangle and confuse. Kumin, however, seeks to praise the blur of "year / after year." She enumerates the elements of the experience quite succinctly but she refuses to distinguish among the elements. It is the sense of the whole that concerns her, and her decision to forsake punctuation recognizes the power of punctuation. Kumin uses spaces to indicate groupings of words but the flow of the experience is unhindered: the years do not pause. **(5)**

Poets—as John Milton illustrates—use punctuation as they see fit. Robert Frost, for instance, uses the dash as slight pause in speech or action, as a way of indicating that speech has broken off, as an informal link to an enumeration or clarification, as a mark (typically following a comma) to indicate an appositive, and as a manifestation of a rhythmic break (again following a comma). **(6)** It is always interesting to see how specific poets punctuate; how comma-conscious, for example, a poet is in any given poem. Does the poet separate adjectives—"big, ugly, sullen dog" or not—"big ugly sullen dog?" Does the poet favor certain punctuation marks? What does that preference have to do with the poet's art? We should respect Oscar Wilde's remark to the person who asked him what he did on a certain morning. "Well," Wilde replied, "I put a comma in—and then I took it out." Since poetry is a rhythmic art and since punctuation tangibly affects rhythm, every punctuation decision affects the poem's cadence. Similarly, the intensity of punctuation—the semi-colon versus the comma, for instance—affects how we read the poem. Poems stand or fall according to such details. Certainly, the rules of prose punctuation inform the punctuation of poetry, but as T. S. Eliot observed, "verse, whatever else it may or may not be, is itself a system of punctuation, the usual marks of *punctuation* [sic] themselves are differently employed." **(7)**

A reader may well wonder then what to make of the vagaries of capitalization within poems. Why—to ask the most common question—do some poems capitalize the first word in a line and others do not? In fact, the convention of capitalizing the first word of a line was not firmly established until the late fifteenth century when William Caxton became the first printer of books in England. The capitalizing of the first word in a line hearkens to the roots of the word "verse" (from the Latin "versus") which refers to the furrow a plow or hoe makes in a field. One row in a field turns back to another row ("versus" literally means "turning") and the lines of a poem were likened to such rows. The beginning of a "row" in a poem was noted by a capital letter. Indeed a poem typically returns to the left margin so that the lines are uniform the way the rows of a field are uniform. This may seem far-fetched but it is a convention to which the majority of poets have subscribed over centuries. They like how the capital letter declares a new line; how it increases the sense of the line as a distinct, rhythmic unit; and how it promotes a uniformity that gives the poem a decidedly polished look. No vagaries need apply.

Many poets do not adhere to this convention. A look at any contemporary anthology of poetry shows that a lot of poets simply observe the rules of capitalization: the first letter of the first word of a sentence is capitalized. As far as they are concerned there is no special reason to capitalize the first word of each line. They prefer to see the poem move down the page unimpeded by a surfeit of capital letters. "Let the poem be," they say, in effect. Rita Dove's poem "Sunday Greens" is a fine instance of this approach to capitalization:

> She wants to hear
> wine pouring.
> She wants to taste
> change. She wants
> pride to roar through
> the kitchen till it shines
> like straw, she wants
>
> lean to replace
> tradition. Ham knocks
> in the pot, nothing
> but bones, each
> with its bracelet
> of flesh.

The house stinks
like a zoo in summer,
while upstairs
her man sleeps on.
Robe slung over
her arm and
the cradled hymnal,

she pauses, remembers
her mother in a slip
lost in blues,
and those collards,
wild-eared,
singing.

It is easy to understand why Dove did not want to capitalize at the beginning of each line. The poem is casual and weary: Capital letters would indicate a degree of formality that goes against the poem's informal grain. The return to the margin in "Sunday Greens" is not a clarion of any sort; it is more like a quiet obligation. To call attention to that return would misrepresent the emotional tenor of the poem. (8)

It is not a huge step from not capitalizing the beginnings of lines to not capitalizing anything in a poem. Kumin prefers the lower case in her poem as she wishes to avoid distractions of all kinds. This attitude toward capital letters in poetry has become common and was pioneered by E. E. Cummings in the 1920s. Sometimes Cummings used punctuation, sometimes not; sometimes he used a smattering of capital letters for proper nouns (though not for his own name) and at the beginnings of some lines. He resolutely spelled the first-person singular pronoun with a lower case letter: "i had an uncle named / Sol who was a born failure [...]" While there was nothing inherently startling about Cummings's poetry, which tended toward droll observation and wry romanticism, his typography made the reader reconsider the conventions of upper- and lower-case letters. Reading a Cummings poem is like seeing a familiar scene from a different angle: Though we recognize the view, everything seems changed. Certainly, Cummings did not challenge conventional typography for the mere sake of challenging it;

rather, he sought to promote a sort of lower case view of life that was opposed to pretensions of all sorts. His poetry emphasizes a basic aspect of artistry, namely that whether artists endorse or vary a convention, they have a sure sense of why they have done what they have done. Nothing is done unquestioningly because that is the way it has always been done. This is not to say that poets go around looking for carts to kick over. It is to say that all poets have their traditions; what a poet does within traditions is part of the signature of the poet's art. (9)

Grammar, Punctuation, and Capitalization
In the Classroom

1. Once a reader accepts Milton's style, there is a genuine pleasure in seeing how far the poet could push grammar and still be writing sentences. Find a sentence in Milton as long as or longer than the lines we have cited. In terms of grammatical units, how does Milton build the sentence? What effect on you does such a lengthy sentence have?

2. As an Objectivist, George Oppen relished direct, literal language. Objectivism was defined as the attempt "to think with things as they exist" and, indeed, Oppen is a thinker. Does the thinking that a poet does differ from the thinking a problem solver does? Is the sort of thinking that occurs in a poem such as Oppen's logical? If so, how? (Remember that grammar is intimately connected with logic.)

3. Adrienne Rich's well-known poem "For the Record" is about outsiders. Do grammar and punctuation have an expressive role in that poem?

4. Identification of parts of speech is an excellent way to focus on how a poet uses a certain grammatical element in a poem. Choose a poem in your notebook and write down all the verbs in it. Do they have anything in common as verbs? What tenses are they in? If there are shifts in verb tense, why do they happen? Consider other parts of speech in the poem, for instance, all the adjectives. Does each noun have an adjective in front of it? Do some nouns have more than one adjective? Is there a thematic relationship among the various adjectives?

5. Find other poems that have no punctuation in them. What purposes does the absence of punctuation seem to indicate?

6. Look at how various poets use a punctuation mark such as the dash. Emily Dickinson, for instance, made liberal use of it. How do different poets use it?

7. Examine a favorite poem from the point of view of punctuation and rhythm. How does punctuation affect rhythm in the poem?

8. Read some poems by contemporary poets that have capitals at the beginning of each line and some poems that don't. Do you notice any differences in tone between the two groups of poems that speak to the presence or absence of capital letters?

9. How does Cummings's typographical inventiveness affect you? Cummings often used parentheses in his poems. How do those parenthetical statements work in his poems (as, for instance, when he ends a poem with parentheses)?

Grammar, Punctuation, and Capitalization
Five-Day Lesson Plan

Day 1   Closely analyze the punctuation of poem that exhibits a wide range of punctuation marks. Carefully consider each punctuation mark in the poem, not as a strictly grammatical decision but as an artistic decision. Do you agree with all of the punctuation decisions that the poet has made?

Day 2   Give students a poem without any punctuation or capitalized letters and ask them to punctuate and capitalize it. Compare students' versions. Show students the poet's version and discuss.

Day 3   Ask students to write a poem without punctuation. Have them discuss how the absence of punctuation affects what they have to say.

Day 4   Capitalization can be expressive for poets. Poets for instance used to capitalize important abstract nouns such as truth, beauty, and love. Ask students to look at a poem that they have written in their poetry notebook and consider all aspects of capitalization. Students should be able to articulate why, for instance, they have or have not capitalized at the beginning of lines. Are there any words in the poem that would benefit from being capitalized or not capitalized (a la E. E. Cummings)?

Day 5   E. E. Cummings was one of the pioneers of typewriter poetry. He used "spaces" within lines and to vary margins. How is the look of a Cummings poem integral to what the poem is about?

Now, ask students to take a poem they have written and reconsider their decisions about margins and spacing. Have them rewrite the poem accordingly. Does this reworking make the poem more or less effective on the page? Why?

Beyond the Week

- After you have read some of Milton's lengthy sentences and figured out what the subject of the sentence is and who is doing what to whom in the sentence (i.e., what is exactly going on in the sentence), try writing a Miltonic mini-epic of a few pages. Take any situation that features some sort of hero or heroine.

Grammar, Punctuation, and Capitalization
Bibliography

Poems

"Street" by George Oppen from *The Collected Poems*, New Directions, 1975; "Soliloquy: Man Talking to a Mirror" by Yusef Komunyakaa from *Neon Vernacular*, Wesleyan University Press, 1993; "Continuum: a Love Poem" by Maxine Kumin from *Selected Poems 1960-1990*, W. W. Norton, 1997; "Sunday Greens" by Rita Dove from *Thomas and Beulah*, Carnegie Mellon University Press, 1986.

Prose

Quotes about grammar and language are from *The Cambridge Encyclopedia of Language* by David Crystal, Cambridge University Press, 1987. For a discussion of William Caxton see *How Poetry Works* by Philip Davies, Penguin Books, 1986.

6

Word Choice

Summary

The integrity of any poem resides in large part in the quality of its word choices. Every word in a poem should be able to justify itself as to why it is there and not some other word. Since sound and rhythm are integral to each word in a poem, the reasons for choosing one word over another may be complex. Many poets never pick up a thesaurus because they feel there are no synonyms, that for the purposes of poetry no two words are equivalent. "Small" is not "little" and neither one is "tiny." Poetry is a precious lens that focuses our responsibilities concerning language. To read a poem or to write a poem is to try to see words more clearly and fully.

Language, both written and spoken, is a distinguishing human attainment. Other creatures communicate intricately and skillfully but they do not have words. Occasionally we reflect on this fact when someone expresses something well or we are in a situation where we are at a loss for words. Most of the time words are so much change in our pockets and purses. Like coins we use them daily but we do not stop to examine each one as to its particular qualities. Most words we use we know so well that an examination would be pointless. Words are like earth and sky—a given of existence.

Poetry does examine words. As the art of language, it is, in fact, obsessed with words in their own right. The poet's responsibility—which represents a basic human responsibility—is to "stand by words." The phrase comes from the American poet, novelist, and essayist Wendell Berry, and by it Berry means that useful, pleasing language is precise language. He notes that, "The idea of standing by one's word, of words precisely designating things, of deeds faithful to words, is probably native to our understanding."

Berry is broaching an ancient human notion here, that of *decorum*. That word does not mean being on one's best manners 24 hours a day but being appropriate to the situation. Thus, slang is not a bad thing; it is simply appropriate to slangy, casual situations. Similarly some occasions demand terseness; others demand exhaustiveness. Sometimes we just want to "shoot the breeze," as we say in English. (1) Concerning poets, Berry writes: "The first aim of the propriety of the old poets ... was to make the language true to its subject—to see that it told the truth." Words for the sheer sake of words become tiresome. Words have obligations in the sense that we do not use them idly. We choose them and our choices are influenced by many factors. We are responsible for our words. (2) When we are not responsible for our words, all sorts of mischief occur. There are lies, evasions, confusions. There is glibness, abstraction, sloppiness, condescension, obfuscation. We stop believing in language and we stop believing in the people who are using the language.

When, for instance, a government lies to its citizens, when it uses language to cover up practices it does not want its citizens to know about, when it surrenders to language that is thoughtless, vicious, cynical, reckless, those men and women who are representatives and employees of that government are acting irresponsibly. (3) For not only are they often attempting to circumvent the truth, they are debasing language. Evasion produces euphemism, language that does not want to address the situation at hand and that seeks an inoffensive way out. Euphemism is the result of fear and contempt. "What did he or she mean by that?" we ask afterwards and shake our heads. How can a totalitarian regime call itself a democracy? How can a bomb be labeled a device? Misrepresentation through language is as old as the human race. It is an issue that will never go away. (4)

Poets have a special responsibility. No one is calling them up on the phone to check a speech or ad campaign. It is not that sort of responsibility. Poets, as practitioners of the art of language, are the constant testers of language. In a good poem every word rings startlingly true. Every word in the poem knows what it is doing there. In addition to choosing the best words, the poet is responsible for the economy of language—not too many words, not too few words. The economy must be appropriate to the situation: A haiku about a fleeting moment is not an epic about a decade-long war. Different scales of action and feeling impose different economies of language but the responsibility of the poet is the same—to choose the right words. (5)

Ezra Pound noted of writers that "when their very medium, the very essence of their work, the application of word to thing goes rotten, i.e., becomes slushy and inexact, or excessive or bloated, the whole machinery of social and individual thought and order goes to pot." These are strong words. Are they true? Consider what has happened to societies that praised writing that was written to adhere to a party line such as the inevitable victory of world communism. Those writers were rewarded for looking the other way, for being callous, for saying only what was approved to be said. What happens to language when poets become sycophants and flunkies? If the poets sell out language, then who will protect it? The bureaucrat, the worker worried for his or her job, the politician? Who will stand by words?

Poets are responsible for words in many ways. They are responsible for how the words they use in a poem sound, for how those words connect rhythmically, for all the meanings and overtones those words possess, for the different kinds of words they use, for the precision of the words. Responsibility, however, should not be construed as joyless. Writing a good poem is not a day at the beach but it is not a matter of burdens either. The impulse of poetry lies in the steady joy of language. However tragic the occasion (as in Borowski's poem about Birkenau in Chapter 8), the poet's stubborn love of language impels the poet. This love is not blind adoration; it is open-eyed. It seeks to make words equal to the occasion, whatever that occasion might be.

Poets first of all relish words as words. Words are presences and poets have endless feelings about them. One knows a poet by her or his vocabulary—not according to how big it is but according to how expressive the words are. Laure-Anne Bosselaar is a native of Belgium who is fluent in four languages. Here is her poem "English Flavors":

I love to lick English the way I licked the hard
round licorice sticks the Belgian nuns gave me for six
good conduct points on Sundays after mass.

Love it when 'plethora', 'indolence', 'damask',
or my new word 'lasciviousness,' stain my tongue,
thicken my saliva, sweet as those sticks—black

and slick with every lick it took to make daggers
out of them: sticky spires I brandished straight up
to the ebony crucifix in the dorm, with the pride

of a child more often punished than praised.
'Amuck,' 'awkward,' or 'knuckles,' have jaw-
breaker flavors; there's honey in 'hunter's moon,'

hot pepper in 'hunk,' and 'mellifluous' has aromas
of almonds and milk. Those tastes of recompense
still bittersweet today as I roll, bend and shape

English in my mouth, repeating its syllables
like acts of contrition, then sticking out my new tongue—
flavored and sharp—to the ambiguities of meaning.

The poet's delight in words speaks for itself. What is especially remarkable is how Bosselaar responds to words with her senses. She can
taste them and smell them; in her mouth she rolls, bends and shapes
them. To learn a new word is to have a new experience, as each word
has a particular savor and tingle: "honey" and "hot pepper" and "almonds and milk." To choose words is to draw upon the memory not
only of the intellect ("What does that word mean?") but of the senses
also. (6) For the poet, no word is merely neutral. Each word as it is longer or shorter, as it is composed of such-and-such vowels and consonants, as it comes from one language through others, as it is in current
usage or out of fashion, as it has slang overtones or does not, as it feels
in one's mouth, as it has personal associations is a whole world unto it-

self. Think, for example, of the care we devote to choosing the names we bestow upon our children (to say nothing of pets and boats): "Elizabeth" is not the same as "Betty" and neither one is "Beth." (7)

Bosselaar's poem ends wisely with the acknowledgment that beyond the physical nature of words there are "ambiguities of meaning." For all their demonstrative texture and presence, words are pointers to actualities. As they exist in time and evolve and mutate over centuries of often rough handling, all sorts of meanings accrue to them. A "club," for instance, is, among other things, a bat or stick used to hit a ball, a figure on a playing card, and an association. How did one word get such various meanings? Indeed, every word has an etymology that is its history, and that history is a story (once "history" and "story" were interchangeable words). The poet savors these histories because they offer the poet the chance to use the word so that the wealth of the word's past is available to the poem. For instance, in the poem "The View from an Attic Window" Howard Nemerov describes trees that "received the appalling fall of snow." Nemerov is using the word "appalling" in its root sense, that of making something pale: the snow literally whitens the trees. The line is all the richer for how the present-day definition of the word—"to fill with dismay"—also registers on the reader.

The poet can make us re-experience words because the poet can put us in touch with a word's origins. Inside each word are things and qualities: to govern is to steer or pilot, to journey is to make a day's travel, to obey is to give an ear to. In "The Miser" Mona Van Duyn writes of a thief who steals newspapers from houses. At the poem's end the thief "has accepted utterly the heart's conditions." He has "been happy." There is no more common adjective than "happy," yet the word's core, the "hap" that is chance, resonates in the poem, for the thief is one who has come to accept how chancy his and all existences are. As he reads newspapers full of "murders, wars, bankruptcies, jackpot winnings," he confronts the "haps" of life. The thief's happiness is much more than the glow of some passing well-being. It is a state of awareness. (8)

Just as much as etymological knowledge can be used to let words glow with meaning, so words can be defused. Haki Madhubuti does this in his poem about the poet Gwendolyn Brooks. He writes:

... she knew that walt disney
was/is making a fortune off
false eyelashes and that time magazine is the
authority on the knee/grow.

The origins of the word "Negro" have to do with the color black, not
anatomy. This is precisely Madhubuti's point as he mocks journalistic
authority by mocking a word. His wry, sad, caustic, and zany
"knee/grow" testifies not only to how words can be manipulated according to who has power in a society and how identity is reflected in
words but also how for all the thingness of words, people will see what
they want to see in them. For some people "Negro" might as well be
"knee/grow." (9)

The word choices we have stressed thus far are unequivocal ones.
Meanings, however, as Bosselaar notes, are the stuff of "ambiguities,"
of equivocations. Not only do words often have multiple meanings
but those meanings depend greatly on the context. There is a relevant
story here that is well known in England for it concerns the last person
to be executed in that country. Derek Bentley and his friend Christopher Craig were cornered by the police after a robbery. Bentley sur-
rendered but Craig, who had a gun, did not. A police sergeant told
Craig to give up his weapon. Bentley told Craig to "Let him have it."
Craig shot and killed the policeman. Did Bentley's words mean
"Hand the weapon over?" or did they mean "Shoot the policeman?" In
any case, Bentley died because of those words.

Certainly this is an extreme example of how ambiguous words can
be. For their part, poets purposefully allow for ambiguity. The beauty
of ambiguity for poets is that there does not have to be a choice: Different meanings can exist at the same time. Thus when John Haines
writes of a wild child at the end of his poem "Watching the Fire" that
"he wears a necklace of fangs/and cries softly for flesh and blood"
the double meaning of "cries" cannot be avoided. The child weeps
and the child calls out. The ambiguity suits the mood of the
poem—pensive and brooding and conflicted. Haines's ambiguity
drives a whole line but sometimes the poet will simply let the double nature of a given word reverberate on its own. W. D. Snodgrass
does this at the end of "Winter Bouquet" where he notes that the

dry seeds he scatters "drift / across the neighbors' cropped lawns like an airlift / of satyrs or a conservative, warm snow." "Conservative" is one of two adjectives; it is more modest grammatically than Haines's single, strong verb. The word's meanings exfoliate without any of the narrative push Haines provides: the seeds conserve life; they are a material, dry snow rather than a fleeting, wet one and hence cautious and conservative. In addition the poem takes place in peacetime, which is contrasted to wartime. The very era in which the poem occurs has a conservative, stay-at-home tinge. The point is not to tease far-fetched meanings from a word but to reckon upon the richness of language. Poets are engaged in sounding the depths of words. As a word choice Snodgrass's "conservative" is daring and apt. (10)

The critic William Empson once noted that "ambiguity is a phenomenon of compression." A poet such as Walt Whitman who is busy naming and cataloging the world around him has no particular concern for ambiguities. His poems have all the time in the world to expound upon whatever Whitman notices. Emily Dickinson, on the other hand, may seem perversely ambiguous. Not only language but grammar itself becomes ambiguous in her hands. She takes the sense-making inclinations of language and, like a sculptor, reassembles, compresses, and fuses them according to her own lights. Whole poems of hers are one, mere quatrain, such as #1144:

> Ourselves we do inter with sweet derision.
> The channel of the dust who once achieves
> Invalidates the balm of that religion
> That doubts as fervently as it believes.

One could question many of Dickinson's word choices. How, for instance, is "achieves" being used? Sniffing out Dickinson's word choices is time well spent, but a poem, of course, is more than the sum of its word choices. For Dickinson ambiguity is an art—not because her word choices are fuzzy (they are crisp and decisive), but because ambiguity is Dickinson's text. For the workaday world there is no such thing as the oxymoronic "sweet derision." Derision is derision, but for Dickinson no word automatically excludes other words. Her art is in part to detonate words, to bend them, to fray them, to stand them on their heads, to re-situate them. Exactly what, a nineteenth century Amherst lawyer accustomed to carefully interpreting language may have asked, is "sweet derision?" We might answer something to the effect that it is our conventional religiosity—but Dickinson's phrase says infinitely more than any gloss. Poets challenge how words typically make sense—not out of self-conscious perversity but out of a desire to push words so that language may query our habitual and often thoughtless usages. As Dickinson builds a context for word choices in her poem, a sense of why this word is being used as opposed to that word, why she uses "sweet" rather than "sour," "ridiculous," or "plaintive," a quickening occurs. Our certainty is no longer so certain. **(11)**

How hard the poet pushes each word choice depends on the poem. Many poems have language that is quite plain; simplicity of language makes the reader almost forget about the words, as when Robert Frost describes a little calf and her mother: "It's so young / It totters when she licks it with her tongue." The pleasure of the language lies in its fresh, sensory, uncomplicated observation. On the other hand, many poems are brisk riots of words, as in the first stanza of Frank O'Hara's "The Spirit Ink":

> Prince of calm, treasure of fascinating cuts on my arm,
> an x ill-aims its roguish atonal bliss of "ment"
> and hatted is the viper whose illness I hated having to puke,
> April in the lavatory trouble, inside the air he deceives.

Between transparent clarity and lexical overdrive lies the terrain of most poems. Robert Lowell's well-known "For the Union Dead" is a good instance of this middle ground. The poem has many solid, unremarkable adjectives and nouns that evoke an actual world: "broken windows;" "barbed and galvanized fence;" "orange, Puritan-pumpkin colored girders." At the same time some adjectives are edgy and deeply suggestive. The Massachusetts Statehouse, for instance, is "tingling"—more a poet's word to describe the effect of excavations than an engineer's. At the poem's end Lowell writes that "giant finned cars nose forward like fish; / a savage servility / slides by on grease." Lowell's word choices register great breadth in a small space. The cars are indeed "finned" according to Detroit's designers, but Lowell has chosen to call attention to this detail because the poem conjures up the world of "cowed, compliant fish." As for "savage servility," it hearkens to Dickinson's "sweet derision;" the poet appends to a quality or action a strongly physical word. This sort of combination—yoking an objective, physical word to a more subjective word—is a signature of poetry as poets shade, slant, color, qualify, and vivify nouns. The "vigilance" of Colonel Shaw in Lowell's poem is an "angry wrenlike" vigilance; we are made to feel it, for poetry seeks to make us actively experience states of mind and prevent us from "gliding through an abstract process" (see Chapter 9). (12)

When we talk about adjectives and nouns we are talking about grammatical categories. Poets have decidedly strong feelings about the parts of speech. Not every noun, for instance wants an adjective. Far from it. Poets are respecters of nouns in and of themselves; the integral strength of the noun can never be discounted summarily. Lowell, for instance, uses the word "ditch" twice in "For the Union Dead," neither time with an adjective. The painful, unmitigated starkness of the noun is what the poem calls for: A ditch is where Colonel Shaw and his troops were buried. As for adjectives, Lowell uses them in ways that recall the words of the Polish poet Adam Zagajewski who has noted that "the adjective is the indispensable guarantor of the individuality of people and things." In Zagajewski's evocative words "A world without an adjective ... is as sad as a surgical clinic on Sunday." Adjectives are social creatures; as they speak to the discriminations we make about a thousand and one things, they differentiate. It is up to the poet to figure out how much differentiation she or he wants: no adjectives at all, one, two, three, even four? How much description is called for? Is the particular poem immersed in the world of social perceptions about clothes and manners and vacation destinations or does it partake of unqualified solidities? (13)

Along with what Zagajewski calls the "solid bow of a noun" comes "the moving, ubiquitous arrow of a verb." Indeed poets treasure strong verbs as they show that life is active rather than passive. Things continually happen; feelings continually pulsate. In Lowell's poem "frayed flags / quilt the graveyards of the Grand Army of the Republic." The flags "quilt"; they form a pattern; they are homely and seem homemade; they adorn; they do much more than simply exist even though as material objects they have no life of their own. The poem is studded with active verbs: "wince," "suffocate," "rise," "nose," "slides," "sticks." (14) Lowell, however, does not reject state of being verbs. Of Colonel Shaw the poet observes "He is out of bounds now": the indifference of time has vanquished the valiant soldier. Although there are many reasons why this poem has been singled out as one of the finest American poems of the twentieth century, Lowell's forceful and exquisite sense of word choice certainly is one of the keys to the poem's success. The poem haunts and disturbs as the Union soldiers memorialized in statues "doze over muskets / and muse through their sideburns ... "

As it engages our sense of play, the freedom of word choice is not a chore but a delight. When we read a poem we want to be alive to the poet's word choices, for however inevitable they may seem, they were once part of the boiling flux of the first draft. The poet may use slang or obsolete words; the poet may load the poem with active verbs or the poet may reduce the whole role of verbs and focus on the stillness of objects; the poet may pursue etymologies, ambiguities, simplicities. The final product is the result of many choices; the poems we write honor our human ability to make credible, imaginative, and engaging choices. In "For the Union Dead" Lowell pays homage to our human freedom as he writes of Colonel Shaw that "He rejoices in man's lovely / peculiar power to choose life and die." The choices we make about words reflect our intuitions and obligations as we are "the servants and masters of language." As we stand by words, we strengthen the language that binds us to one another. (15)

WORD CHOICE
In the Classroom

1. Write down three different social situations. What sort of language is appropriate for each situation? Cite some actual words that would be relevant for each situation.
2. We have many different roles in society. We are members of families, schools, teams, religious bodies, communities, nations. Choose two important roles in your life. How do you use language as a member of these two groups? Give examples.
3. Give instances from history where governments and leaders have misused language.
4. Cite examples of euphemism that you have encountered.
5. Select a poem that is notable for its economy of language. Give specific examples from the poem in which a few words say a great deal.
6. One of the simplest pleasures of language lies in enjoying the words we speak simply as words. Choose some words that you like and write them down. Share favorite words aloud. What are the factors that make some words more attractive than others?
7. How do you feel about your own names? Do you like having your name abbreviated? How do you feel about your middle name?
8. Look up some of your favorite words in an etymological dictionary and write down the histories of the word. Have the meanings of the words changed over time?
9. Research the etymological bases for such words as "good," "sad," "nice," "great," and "fine." Now that you know the etymological bases of these words, do you think that they are used properly in everyday speech?
10. Give an example of an ambiguity of language that you have experienced. Was the ambiguity intentional or not?
11. Based on your reading of poems, cite some examples of interesting, unexpected combinations of words. What effect did these combinations have in their contexts in the poems? Were any of the combinations synesthetic (combining two senses as in "green howl")?
12. Make two columns, one for objective, physical nouns (rock, comb, dog) and the other for subjective, abstract, state-of-mind adjectives (sad, peculiar, idealistic) and list ten words that are

appropriate for each column. Create combinations based on the two lists. Choose your favorite combination and use it in a sentence. Reverse the list and choose subjective nouns and physical adjectives.

13. Take a noun. Put one adjective in front of it, then two, then three. What happens to the noun each time that you add an adjective? Is there a point where you start to lose feeling for the noun or does the noun seem to become stronger? Look at some poems and note how adjectives are used. Do certain poems seem to call more for adjectives than other poems? How so?

14. Write down three simple verbs of action, such as "walk," "run" and "talk." Using a thesaurus, look up each action verb and find five synonyms. Use all fifteen words in sentences and be prepared to discuss the differences in meaning among the synonyms.

15. Choose a poem. Read it a number of times and then provide a commentary concerning the word choices in the poem. Indicate why you think certain word choices are effective.

WORD CHOICE
Five-Day Lesson Plan

Day 1   Read aloud a poem to all students for them to write into their poetry notebook. Then ask students to choose from the poem five words that interest, intrigue, and generally seem pivotal to them. Next use the dictionary to define all aspects of each word: meaning, etymology, syllabication. This information should be copied into the poetry notebook. Even though some words may be common, it is important to remember that poets are aware of the various connotations a given word will have.

Once students have defined their words, they discuss as a class what words they chose and why they chose them. The teacher keeps a list of words on the blackboard as the discussion proceeds. After the discussion, students write a sentence or two in their poetry notebook about how each of the words the student originally chose matter to the poem. For homework, students are assigned another poem to read and from which they choose five words.

Day 2   List words from the assigned poem on the board. Students then present to the class the words they chose and why they chose them. The rest of the class will ask questions after each presentation.

Read a new poem to the class for them to write into their poetry notebook. Then divide the class into groups and ask each group to come up with a list of pivotal words for the poem.

Day 3   Groups share their word choice selections as a class and discuss the choices. Class reaches consensus about the pivotal words for the poem.

Students then examine a poem in their notebook that they have written and identify five words that are pivotal to the poem and three words that are less important. Students then write a sentence or two about why the words are more or less important. Pair students and have them share their poem and read their word choice explanations to one another. The listener responds orally to the reader's explanations. The reader takes notes on the listener's responses.

Day 4   The teacher chooses students to put their poems up on the overhead and discuss their word choices. After each student has explained his or her use of words, the rest of the class asks questions regarding word choice. This at-large discussion is essential to allow students to talk about what words they use to create specific intentions and feelings in their writing.

Day 5   Students rework their poem given their new perceptions about word choice. After that, they write an accompanying explanation (minimum of a paragraph) of what changes they made in word choice and why.

Ask students to identify two poems in their notebook by other writers where word choice specifically impresses them.

Beyond the Week

Students share the two poems they have identified and discuss as a class the word choices the poets have made.

Students examine drafts of published poems with an eye for word choice decisions. The various drafts of many well-known poems (e.g., *The Waste Land* and "Howl") exist in book form and are fascinating to consider.

WORD CHOICE
Bibliography

Poems

"English Flavors" by Laure-Anne Bosselaar from *The Hour Between Dog and Wolf*, BOA Editions, 1997; "The Miser" by Mona Van Duyn from *To See, To Take*, Atheneum, 1973; "Gwendolyn Brooks" by Haki Madhubuti from *Directionscore*, Third World Press, 1971; "Watching the Fire" by John Haines from *The Owl in the Mask of the Dreamer*, Graywolf Press, 1996; "Winter Bouquet" by W. D. Snodgrass from *Heart's Needle*, Alfred A. Knopf, 1959; "The Spirit Ink" by Frank O'Hara from *The Collected Poems*, University of California Press, 1995; "For the Union Dead" by Robert Lowell from *Selected Poems*, Farrar Straus Giroux, 1977.

Prose

Standing by Words by Wendell Berry, North Point Press, 1983; *ABC of Reading* by Ezra Pound, New Directions, 1960; *Seven Types of Ambiguity* by William Empson, New Directions, 1966; "In Defense of Adjectives" by Adam Zagajewski from *Two Cities*, Farrar Straus Giroux, 1995.

7

Details

Summary

It is a commonplace of art that excellence lives not in some
grand concept but in the details. Poetry is no exception. Many a
poem creates in twenty or so lines a little world and for that
world to take shape so quickly and so fully, details must be provided that are not only convincing as knowledge about a time
and a place but also convincing emotionally. The poet tries to
choose among the myriad of details about any moment or place
or era or feeling those details that go to the heart of the matter.
The degree to which the simplest details—a name on a coffee
mug, the make of an automobile, a hair-do— can reverberate in a
poem is both startling and reassuring. Just as every picture tells a
story, every detail can speak about a life or many lives.

The American poet Ellen Bryant Voigt said it succinctly when she
wrote in her poem "The Last Class" that "A poem depends on its details." The details of a poem are witnesses to the truth of whatever experience the poem relates. If they feel genuine, if they have the ring
and bite and flavor of reality, we can believe the poem. A poem is a
simulacrum made out of words that exists on paper (or in our memories or on a computer screen) but it pulls all manner of actualities into
its created world. If there are no details, if the poem is a haze or a mush
of declarative feelings (e.g., "I love you so much. / You are my Truth. / I
feel good when I am with you." etc.), then all the sincerity in the world
is not going to make the poem convincing. Details are the confluence
of observant intelligence, apt feeling, and thematic sense: Does a par-

111

ticular detail belong in the poem or doesn't it? How much detail over all does the poem need? How do the details affect the pace of the narrative? How exact should the details be? Do I want to say "Baltimore Orioles" or "baseball team," "a polyester, green and purple tie" or "a gift from an aunt," "an old car" or "a Plymouth Duster with bad ball joints, no heater, and a dashboard dented from Bubba Henley's exuberant drumming"? Intuitively and critically the poet wrestles with such questions. Detail is credibility. Whether the setting is a Civil War battlefield or the girls' room in a high school, the reader must be convinced.

This convincing involves more than reading up about something or recalling (for those old enough to recall) the Top 40 from 1965 and then piling up a hill of details in the poem. A poem must not only be factually convincing; it also must be emotionally convincing. Consider Gjertrud Schnackenberg's poem "Thanksgiving Day Downstairs, 1858" from her poem in sixteen sections entitled "19 Hadley Street":

> Thanksgiving afternoon, and Charlotte waits
> On one foot, then the other,
> In the doorway: her mother
> Eyes the great platters she decorates
>
> With sugared grapes, while cousin Jed debates
> With Pa, slavery and war.
> Through the buffet's glass door
> The patterns painted on white dinnerplates,
>
> Blue willow-trees, blue, half-hidden estates,
> Are delicate, and shine.
> She's old enough, at nine,
> To set the table that accommodates
>
> The tall uncles Pa sometimes imitates
> To make Ma laugh and scold.
> Charlotte needn't be told,
> She knows, she'll whisper to her schoolmates

How each year Aunt Jerusha celebrates
  By drinking sherry
  And blushes red to see
Bachelor Moody, hat in hand, opening the gates.

Detail works here to create a perfectly poised credibility. Characters are named, a setting is evoked, historical reality makes its presence felt. The poet seeks to distill the essence of an occasion as a young girl experiences it. Detail, after all, depends on point of view. Ask three people about an event and each person is likely to pick out different details that caught that person's eye (or other senses). For instance, Aunt Jerusha's celebrating with a glass of sherry is predictable and pleases the little girl, whereas to an adult it might seem an old, not very interesting story. That a war is coming within a decade that is bound to shatter all predictability is a gist that shivers within the poem's careful tableau. Details—"sugared grapes," "blue willow-trees," "tall uncles"—anchor feelings that are more implied than stated. Each detail feels precious as it resists the blankness of the long ago and forgotten past. The reader feels that these lives were actually lived. (1)

Schnackenberg's poem is at once history that is a shared historical reality—each year Americans celebrate this holiday on the last Thursday of November—and personal history, something each person in America experiences as he or she celebrates (or does not celebrate) the day. Since human beings belong to many different worlds—social, economic, political, and religious, among others—details can resonate in many directions. Greg Pape's "A Job on the Night Shift" hauntingly blends the details of a workplace with the feelings and memories of a worker:

He is the prince of tin cans
here on the nightshift.
His job is to pick up
what has fallen, to crawl
among the constant gears
beneath the conveyors
that carry the regiments

of cans, the peaches
jostling under the gloved hands
of women who joke or curse
in Spanish under the nightlong
surging of engines.
He stops and leans
on his dolly to stare
at the fluent hands of the women
as they sort the fruit.
So many peaches the hands
fly over, so many nights,
so many voices hushed
or lost, so many peaches,
so many nights, nights
that carry him south
on the road to Magdalena
where the shadows hunched
over fires in oil drums
are dead men, uncles, brothers.
And the children run
in the night streets,
coils of firecrackers
snapping at their heels.
He can almost see their faces
but the foreman touches
his shoulder and orders "move it."
So he moves it
loaded with fallen cans
out the back door of the cannery
to his station under the stars
and yellow bug lights.
His job is to salvage
what he can. He has

a tool for straightening them
and a tank of cool still water
to wash them in, a tank
of water where the yellow lights
float among the power lines
and the stars, and when he bends
to his work over the water
there is the prince of tin cans.

The actuality of the factory is rendered convincingly. It is a world of "gears" and "conveyors," "of women who joke or curse / in Spanish under the nightlong / surging of engines." These details provide a setting for the poem that feels accurate but not too particular. Such a presentation allows Pape to move in and out of his character's feelings effortlessly. The poem's final sentence epitomizes this carefully modulated movement. Most of the nouns in that sentence do not have adjectives; the crucial exception is the "cool still water." The simple, tactile quality of the water summons up a clarity that has no industrial purpose: it is just water. It just is. The reader easily can imagine the "yellow lights," "the power lines / and the stars" as they are reflected in the tank of water. The job the man does is not much of a job but the man is a human being with an inner life and his dignity. That the man is "the prince of tin cans" is moving, pathetic, and strangely noble—all at the same time. What is noted in the very first line of the poem, we are made to experience in the course of the poem. The conclusions resound within the imaginative connotations of the word "prince," even as the poem has stripped those aristocratic, glamorous connotations away. (2)

The two poems we have looked at thus far are almost painterly in terms of how the poets use detail—a touch here, a touch there. In such relatively short poems each detail concisely contributes to the poem's narrative. In somewhat longer poems, poets can immerse the reader in the details of an experience and let those details speak for themselves as they create an environment. The beginning of C. K. Williams's "The Regulars" does this masterfully:

In the Colonial Luncheonette on Sixth Street they know everything there
    is to know, the shits.
Sam Terminadi will tell you how to gamble yourself at age sixty from
    accountant to bookie,
and Sam Finkel will tell you more than anyone cares to hear how to
    parlay an ulcer into a pension
so you can sit here drinking this shit coffee and eating these overfried
    shit eggs
while you explain that the reasons the people across the street are going
    to go bust
in the toy store they're redoing the old fish market into—the father and
    son plastering,
putting up shelves, scraping the floors; the mother laboring over the white
    paint,
even the daughter coming from school to mop the century of scales and
    splatter from the cellar—
are both simple and complex because Sam T can tell you the answer to
    anything in the world
in one word and Sam F prefaces all his I-told-you-so's with "you don't
    understand, it's complex."

Where he needs to enumerate, as in the work it takes to transform the
old fish market into a toy store, Willliams does not stint. Mostly, however, he trowels one modest detail upon another because "The Regulars" already know all the details in the world. The irony is that all
that hard-earned knowledge melts down into "one word" and it is not
a very descriptive or enlightening word. Familiarity breeds contempt
as the integrity of each detail of life is subsumed by the overbearing
mind. As far as "The Regulars" are concerned, things don't exist on
their own; they are pieces to be moved around in a mental calculus of
simplicity and complexity. Details exist to be manipulated, details are
the fodder of explanations, and yet the poet, as he creates the environment in which "The Regulars" live, shows that details have a stubborn life of their own. These guys are strictly from "The Colonial

Luncheonette on Sixth Street"—not from a fern bar that serves carafes of wine or from a fast food franchise. Their rational defining does not stop them from being definable. One of the strengths of the poem is how Williams sympathizes with his characters even though the joke in many ways is on them. (3)

The degree to which we are defined by physical, geographical, and spiritual identities is haunting. Our every motion seems to proclaim our individuality, and yet each one of us is easily subsumed into a few large facts about gender, race, nationality, and economic position. Since social identity is an assemblage of external details, which details come forward and how they are perceived by others and ourselves makes a world of difference for each of us. Toi Derricotte's "St. Peter Claver" speaks to the hazards of perception:

Every town with black Catholics has a St. Peter Claver's.
My first was nursery school.
Miss Maturin made us fold our towels in a regulation square
    and nap on army cots.
No mother questioned; no child sassed.
In blue pleated skirts, pants, and white shirts,
we stood in line to use the open toilets
and conserved light by walking in darkness.
Unsmiling, mostly light-skinned, we were the children of the
    middle class, preparing to take our parents' places in a
    world that would demand we fold our hands and wait.
They said it was good for us, the bowl of soup, its
    pasty whiteness;
I learned to swallow and distrust my senses.

On holy cards St. Peter's face is olive-toned, his hair
    near kinky;
I thought he was one of us who pass between the rich and
    poor, the light and dark.

> Now I read he was "a Spanish Jesuit priest who labored for
>   the salvation of the African Negroes and the abolition
>   of the slave trade."
> I was tricked again, robbed of my patron,
> and left with a debt to another white man.

Derricotte lays out the details so fully in the first stanza that the presence of the narrator is barely apparent. The child is put into a world of strict details, of "Miss Maturin" and "blue pleated skirts, pants, and white shirts." The child is made to feel that this world is who the child is. The force of the details is so powerful that even the child's senses are secondary. To say "Saint Peter Claver's" is to summon a presence that seems to exist in its own right. A child is a small thing compared to a church that traces its origins back over many centuries.

Yet even within this world of assertive definitions, there are ironies and ambiguities and Derricotte's narrator confronts a major one in the second stanza: Her patron saint was not who she thought he was. "On holy cards St. Peter's face is olive-toned, his hair / near kinky," details that lead to a supposition that turns out be false. The details of color—"light-skinned," "pasty whiteness," "olive-toned"—are noted very particularly and yet, "I was tricked again." Indubitable details may not be indubitable; the poem seems in many ways a parable. (4)

In Debra Nowak's poem "Bliss," the details of identity are almost larger than life. The school children who confront them do not want to confront them but they have no choice. Here is the poem:

> In the musty corner-basement room in Wayzata Junior High,
> Mr. Schulte's ready to sing. A hot directionless spring.
> Old canted windows tipped wide open. Twenty-six butts
>
> Stuck to textured orange plastic seats. Sweaty bangs
> Stick to my wide smooth forehead. 7th grade math.
> The year they call math "new" and we no longer bother
>
> To erase. The fat record arm humps round the dizzy
> Black plate. Mr. Schulte sings opera. He's a dead-ringer
> For Gomer Pyle, who's a good singer, too, when he's not

Talking like a big dope to little Opie on Mayberry.
Still, it seems pretty pathetic he's chosen us to sing to,
Even if we get out of math. He's a six-foot tenor canary.

He's unreasonably happy. We can't comprehend his motives
Or the Italian. We see his slack-jawed soul fluttering
Beyond finger-smeared windows,

Knock its big stubborn head against glinting glass.
Embarrassed, we hide behind bewildered hands.
Doubled-over notes blurt "This Stinks!!!".

Freedom rings. Dan Johnson, shortest boy in seventh grade,
(Not counting Bobby Ford The Midget), dispenses
A get-moving shove out the dumbfounded door.

Schools, as they are closed worlds, are veritable circuses of details. Everything is telling, be it the décor, a notebook, how math is taught. Most of the details can be assimilated because the students judge and thus tame them. The students try to do that with their opera-loving math teacher, when they write "This Stinks!!!". Those three exclamation marks register a world of adolescent indignation. The sum of the scene, however, is greater than the myriad details of windows and seats, and the bittersweet title registers a state of mind that can neither be avoided nor entered. The students "can't comprehend his motives / Or the Italian." For all the surfeit of actuality, there is a quality of the human soul that is dumbfounding. As in Derricotte's poem, the presence of details does not lead to tidiness; we may think we know and then find out we do not know, or we may not want to know, or we may be just plain puzzled.

The scope of details in a poem depends on how wide the poem's lens is. Nowak's poem is typical in that it focuses on a scene at a certain time. It is inclusive as it notes the entire classroom. The lens of a poem, however, may zoom in at any time and capture in detail any aspect of a situation. In Belle Waring's poem "Ending Green" a woman gets on a bus and the driver (shades of Mr. Schulte) is singing:

he smacks the note, then teases it,
rallies the feeling, then shaves it into whittles,
carries falsetto, tumbles low—
now ringing, now throaty, now grave.
Now he is pitiless with it. Then forgives.
Then lets it fade.

This attentiveness brings the woman in the poem back to life in the sense that she lets go of the thoughts in her head (leaving her fiancé) and latches onto the zest of what is going on in front of her eyes and ears. Such devoted description is an act of love in and of itself that puts the world of fiancés and social obligations in the shade. Mere moments—a bus driver singing—may contain gulfs, prairies, and heights of energizing detail. Part of the students' uneasiness in Nowak's poem stems from their being captives; Waring's narrator is free to relish an unbidden actuality. (5)

Belle Waring's careful, adoring, playful intentness speaks to a deep source of our fondness for description, what the poet Richard Wilbur called attention to when he titled a poem "Love Calls Us to the Things of This World." That poem is about angels who are "rising together in calm swells of halcyon feeling." For all the rapt, spiritual presence of the angels, the poem's next-to-last stanza begins with a "Yet":

Yet, as the sun acknowledges
With a warm look the world's hunks and colors,
The soul descends once more in bitter love
To accept the waking body, saying now
In a changed voice as the man yawns and rises,

"Bring them down from their ruddy gallows;
Let there be clean linen for the backs of thieves;
Let lovers go fresh and sweet to be undone,
And the heaviest nuns walking in a pure floating
Of dark habits,

keeping their difficult balance. "

As it acknowledges at once a "warm look" and "bitter love," Wilbur's poem achieves a fine equilibrium. The acceptance of the details of this world is the acceptance of finitude and the acceptance of finitude is the acceptance of mortality and transience. "The world's hunks and colors" are enchanting, yet the details—those "ruddy gallows"—are intractable. To describe this world fully, to not flinch, requires a "difficult balance." To put in only the positive details is to court sentimentality; to put in only the negative ones is to court despair. (6)

We choose to end this chapter with "Break of Day," a poem by Galway Kinnell that uses unremarkable details to render an experience in all its fullness. The poem is deeply attentive, painfully so, to everyday circumstances. It speaks unapologetically from that "bitter love" Wilbur evokes and never takes its eye away from what is occurring:

He turns the light on, lights
the cigarette, goes out on the porch,
chainsaws a block of green wood down the grain,
puts the pieces into the box stove,
pours in kerosene, tosses in the match
he set fire to the next cigarette with,
stands back while the creosote-lined, sheet-
metal rust-lengths shudder but manage
to lure the *cawhoosh* from inside the stove,
which sucks in ash motes through holes at the bottom
and glares out fire blaze through cracks around the top,
all the way to the roof and up out through
into the still starry sky starting to fade,
sits down to a bowl of crackers and blue milk
in which reflections of a 40-watt ceiling bulb
try to drown, eats, contemplates
an atmosphere containing kerosene stink,
chainsaw smoke, chainsmoke, wood smoke, wood heat,
gleams of a 40-watt ceiling bulb in blue milk.

Kinnell ends the poem with a hallmark of detail—a simple list. That it reverberates with so much feeling speaks to the power of poetry to invest the things of this world with a hard-won eloquence. (7)

DETAILS
In the Classroom

1. Schnackenberg's poem echoes, in its quietness and precision, many of the shorter poems of Edwin Arlington Robinson. Read some of Robinson's poems such as "Richard Cory" and "The Tavern." How does Robinson use detail to convey, in not many lines, a sense of a life or a place? How does meter affect details in Robinson's work? Does it seem to call more attention to them or does it work to downplay them?

2. Locate other poems that occur in the workplace. The two anthologies edited by Nicholas Coles and Peter Oresick that are cited in the chapter bibliography are a good place to begin. How do different poets communicate what different workplaces are like? To what degree do the poets use detail? Write a poem about a work experience you have had.

3. A strength of C. K. Williams's poem is that he clearly knows the environment his characters are in. Write a poem about some people who come to the same place again and again: They may know each other, as with some high school students who meet at a hangout after school, or they may not, as with people who go to a laundromat each week. Remember that the details of the environment are as important as the details about the people.

4. Write a poem that registers a misperception. How did the misperception come to happen? What consequences did it have? Was it anyone's fault? Think about how Toi Derricotte creates a detailed (but not exhaustive) setting in her poem.

5. The passage from Belle Waring's poem seizes a moment and enumerates the fullness of what is there. Write a poem that focuses on a moment when someone is doing something—making a pie crust or playing the drums or driving a car on a freeway—and detail as fully as you can all that is happening in that moment.

6. Richard Wilbur has been praised as a poet of great poise and spirit. His poems range widely in subject, from the myth of "Merlin" to the stark actuality of "On the Eyes of an SS Officer." Based upon your reading of a number of Wilbur poems, how does he use detail to convince the reader of the truth of his observations?

7. To convey a sense of what life is like for another human being is a great challenge to a poet. Try to write a poem that looks (as Galway Kinnell does) at one person on one morning of that person's life. Use detail to show what the person is doing with his or her time. Try to convey actualities of the person's experience—not ideas about the person.

DETAILS
Five-Day Lesson Plan

Day 1   Detail is rooted in being attentive. Often, we forget or just don't notice exactly what is going on around us. Begin with everyday activity. Ask students how much detail they remember of their trip into school this morning. Have them list ten details that they observed on their trip to school this morning. Now, while they are sitting in class, ask them to note one detail from this class for each of their five senses.

Have students share their observations as a class. Have them pick one detail, their own or someone else's, and use it to respond to the following prompt, " I had never noticed, _____ but … "

Day 2   No two poets use details in the same way. Read some poems by three different contemporary poets. How do the poets use detail in their work? Do details carry emotion in their work? How?

Day 3   Have students choose a poem that is about a person. Focus on how details used in the poem can give a sense about a person's life. Ask the students how the poet links details with one another to give you that sense. (Is syntax a factor here?)

Days 4 & 5

Point of view often dictates observation. For this 2-day exercise, ask students to choose one scene, event, or incident (such as a couple breaking up) and write two poems, each from a different point of view. Each poem should have a set of details that reflects a particular point of view.

Beyond the Week

Ask students to write a poem that describes and evokes a work of visual art. Ask them to think about using all of their senses, about point of view, about how details carry emotions, and about what makes the work of art special.

DETAILS
Bibliography

Poems

"The Last Class" by Ellen Bryant Voigt from *The Lotus Flowers*, W. W. Norton, 1987; "Thanksgiving Day Downstairs" by Gjertrud Schnackenberg from *Portraits and Elegies*, David R. Godine, 1982; "A Job on the Night Shift" by Greg Pape from *Black Branches,* University of Pittsburgh Press, 1984; "The Regulars" by C. K. Williams from *Selected Poems*, Farrar Straus Giroux, 1994; "St. Peter Claver" by Toi Derricotte from *Captivity*, University of Pittsburgh Press, 1989; "Ending Green" by Belle Waring from *Dark Blonde*, Sarabande Books, 1997; "Love Calls Us to the Things of This World" by Richard Wilbur from *New and Collected Poems*, Harcourt Brace, 1988; "Break of Day" by Galway Kinnell from *3 Books*, Houghton Mifflin, 1993.

The anthologies edited by Nicholas Coles and Peter Oresick are *For a Living: The Poetry of Work*, University of Illinois Press, 1995, and *Working Classics: Poems on Industrial Life*, University of Illinois Press, 1990.

8

Metaphor

Summary

As far as poetry is concerned, metaphor is the most scintillating
move a poem can make, for it changes one thing into another
without any prefaces or summaries or apologies. We use metaphor on a daily basis and for better or worse, as we shout out
someone's nickname or refer to a public figure or invent a metaphor on the spot to describe what something was like, we tend
not to think twice about it. Certainly in poetry metaphor and
simile (a metaphor with "like" or "as" appended) hold great
power and deserve to be treated respectfully. How much metaphor is used in any given poem and how a metaphor is handled in
a poem depend on how extensive the poet wants the metaphor to
be. Metaphor can range from the assertive zinger of "x is y" to a
leisurely presentation of as many details as the poet chooses to
load into the "y" that tells about some "x." In any case, metaphor
speaks for the subconscious mind. It is verbal lightning.

Metaphor comes from the Greek word *metaphora* which is composed of two parts: *meta* meaning "over" and *pherein* meaning "to
carry." The classical Western tradition of writing about metaphor, of
which Aristotle is the progenitor, has focused on the mechanical element in this derivation. When we say, "Joe is a pig," the quality of pig-
gishness is carried over to define Joe. For Aristotle, metaphor is "a
departure from the ordinary means of language." Terence Hawkes
goes on to note in his book about the history of metaphor that for Aristotle "metaphor is a kind of dignifying, enlivening ingredient, a set

of 'unfamiliar usages' which 'by the very fact of not being normal idiom' can ... raise the diction above the level of the commonplace." For Aristotle, metaphor exists in contradistinction to everyday, ordinary, prosaic speech. Everyday speech is objective whereas metaphor is subjective. Aristotle does not dismiss metaphor. Indeed, he considers a facility in its use to be a mark of distinction. In his *Poetics* he writes that "This [metaphor-making] is one thing that cannot be learned from anyone else, and it is the mark of great natural ability, for the ability to use metaphor well implies a perception of resemblances." To perceive resemblances is an instance of intellectual acuity: "It is from metaphor that we can best get hold of some thing fresh" (*Rhetoric*).

All well and good, and yet there is something terribly condescending in the tradition typified by Aristotle. Doesn't metaphor play "an enormous role in shaping [our] everyday understanding of everyday events," as the authors of a book about metaphor entitled *More Than Cool Reason* note? Isn't a metaphor an act of "transformation" (to use the British writer Jeanette Winterson's word)? Joe becomes piggish when we say, "Joe is a pig." He has been changed because our perception of him has changed. We know that Joe has not taken up residence in a barnyard. That is not the point of metaphor. Metaphor is a way of structuring experience. "Joe is a pig" is as relevant as "Joe has brown eyes and has mastered three word processing programs." Metaphor uses details; it perceives connections between sensory modalities (as psychologists like to put it) and draws inferences. We use it daily as it helps us conceptualize life. It is part of ordinary human talk. "Poetry through metaphor exercises our minds so that we can extend our normal powers of comprehension" (*More Than Cool Reason*). This is one reason people have turned to poetry for millennia, because metaphor is at the heart of the poetic enterprise. (1)

Alas, in the words of Lakoff and Turner, "The Literal Meaning Theory [Joe is not really a pig. Metaphor is just a decorative way of commenting on Joe's eating habits.] has for two thousand years defined meaningfulness, reason and truth so as to exclude metaphor and other aspects of ... 'imaginative rationality.'" By excluding "metaphor from the domain of reason ... poetry and art [have been relegated] to the periphery of intellectual life—something to give one a veneer of culture, but not something of central value in one's every-day endeavors" (*More Than Cool Reason*). This is a serious charge yet the uneasiness and fears so many people feel towards poetry substantiate the accusation. Poetry's relegation to the periphery of the life of the mind is certainly understandable when one looks back at Aristotle who noted that the ability to make metaphors can't be learned from others. Just the way some people can hit a baseball or whistle in key, some people can come up with utterly convincing metaphors. There is no accounting for it. It is uncanny—and what is uncanny makes people nervous. (2)

Yet if something is a somewhat unusual gift, does that mean we reject all aspects of it because each of us cannot expertly do it? Do we all stop playing baseball because we aren't going to make the Hall of Fame? Of course not. Kids (and adults) like to play ball. People like to use metaphor. It is "at the center of human concern [for] we live in a world of metaphors of the world out of which we construct myths. We make the world up ... as we go along, and we experience it concretely" (Hawkes). Metaphor, as it is transformative, extends language and, as Hawkes notes, "since language is reality" metaphor expands reality. (3)

To confront the place of metaphor in our daily lives and in poetry is to confront the disconcerting truth that as one particular society at one particular time we—amid the welter of so many definitive circumstances—nonetheless invent ourselves. "There is a Creator who is our father," we say, but some say that Creator is a mother and others say that it is the sun or an animal-spirit. Instinctively we resort to metaphor to extend the resources of language, and the truth that metaphor gives us feels unconditional. Yet, as it is a socially influenced perception, metaphor is emphatically conditional. "Jews are devils, " anti-Semites have said for centuries. How many people have nodded their reasonable heads in ready agreement as if to say, "It goes without saying." (4)

We experience life so deeply as a matter of physical givens—we breathe, we sleep, we eat—that it is second nature to feel that whatever comes out of our mouths are givens also. Yet to say "There are carrots in the garden" is not the same thing as saying "Women are angels." This is not to return to the segregation of metaphor as figurative, hence not literal, language. Rather it is to suggest that metaphor-making is instinctual and because it is instinctual it is not to be taken for granted. A metaphor is a weapon of sorts as it proposes transformation. This is a heady power and like any such power it is to be savored and scrutinized. Our ability to make metaphors is part of our human outlook; metaphors, as Lakoff and Turner put it, "are conceptual not linguistic in nature." Metaphor-making is as definitively human as tool-making.

Consider the phrase "the Cold War." This signifies the atmosphere of distrust and hostility between the United States and the Soviet Union that lasted for over 4 decades. Those in the Soviet Union were—as tabloids in America delighted in calling them—"Reds." In fact the tabloids asserted that all communists were Reds. But did each communist see him or herself as the same metaphorical Red? Was the Cold War the cause of all wars in all countries? Did objective statesmen make decisions based on mere, subjective metaphors? One could consult the histories of "Camelot" and "Tricky Dick" and the "Iron Maiden," among other metaphors. The point here is that the endemic nature of metaphor has very large consequences. As a phrase, "the Cold War" is acutely descriptive. Such acuity makes it easy to substitute a metaphor for the complexity of a reality. That is why, in part, we look to metaphor. A metaphor may come to seem not so much language describing a reality as a reality with a life of its own. Metaphor is the servant and metaphor may be the master. The danger was summarized well by Isaiah Berlin when he wrote that "to take such expressions so literally that it becomes natural and normal to attribute to them causal properties, active powers, transcendent properties, demands for human sacrifices, is to be fatally deceived by myths." (5)

The place of poetry and the place of metaphor in a society are intertwined. Metaphor is not a special faculty that is dusted off every now and then. "Poetic language differs from 'standard' language not in kind, but only in degree" (Hawkes). Thus as Lakoff and Turner define it, "Poets are artists of the mind." If we dismiss metaphor, we dismiss the generative vitality of the human mind. If we dismiss poetry, we dismiss the possible genius of that vitality. (6)

If there ever was a poet who was aware of the power of metaphor and who reveled in its strength, it was Emily Dickinson. Born into a family and world in nineteenth century America where all the powerful metaphors belonged to the men—suns, gods, kings—she fashioned a poetry that bears witness to the transformative nature of metaphor to feel and conceptualize every inch of life anew. In her hands one feels that metaphor is very much a weapon. To not live a second-hand, timid life one must probe every old metaphor and fearlessly imagine new ones. Every metaphor is an assertion—yet women were not supposed to be making assertions. (7)

Virtually every poem of Emily Dickinson's is a new definition of some notion or feeling or moment or encounter. If life, as in the conventional metaphor, is a book, it is the task of the poet as Dickinson saw it to rewrite every word of that book, to test every definition and propose truer ones. She sees a snake—" ... a whiplash / Unbraiding in the sun" (from #986). That metaphor is snaky-ness defined, as is the feeling she gets from meeting a snake—" ... a tighter breathing,/And zero at the bone." To encounter a snake is to encounter something very foreign to us human creatures. To get that feeling onto the page so that the utter strangeness of the snake is not lost demanded of Dickinson that she find new words. This newness was her abiding joy, for in those words she experienced (as we her readers experience) the novelty of such a thing existing. To the degree that habit and purpose may tend to deaden us, metaphor may enliven us as it proposes new and stirringly sensate definitions.

In some ways Dickinson was the most open person who ever lived, for all of life was hers to originally experience and define. Nothing was too small (insects) or too large (God). Yet the experience of definition was not a Sunday stroll. Many of her poems are stark confrontations. Metaphor-making is a physical rigor, because the whole weight of conventional society sits behind each self-satisfied, socialized metaphor ("Women are angels"). Each and every day Dickinson felt that weight. She refused to turn away from it. "Struck was I, nor yet by lightning"; "Dying! To be afraid of thee"; "Bereaved of all, I went abroad"; "Remorse is memory awake"; "Because I could not stop for Death": These are first lines of Dickinson poems and they stand as heralds of what she must undergo in the course of writing the poem. Whereas the socially approved authors of her time (both male and female) felt free to spout their opinions and perceptions within the safe confines of steadfast meter and accepted metaphor, Dickinson chose to test her perceptions. Why write a poem, one can imagine her asking, if not to test perceptions?

Hence a Dickinson poem, as it goes about its metaphor-making, often proceeds by fits and starts. Metaphors don't fall smoothly into the poet's aproned lap; like the snake they may startle. The poem is a series of encounters, turnings that become further turnings. Here is #875:

> I stepped from Plank to Plank
> A slow and cautious way
> The Stars about my Head I felt
> About my Feet the Sea.
>
> I knew not but the next
> Would be my final inch—
> This gave me that precarious Gait
> Some call Experience.

For Dickinson the physical world is inherently metaphorical. Whereas symbols are congealed metaphors (in Dickinson's era hearth, for instance, symbolized home), every physical presence possesses qualities that may summon resemblances. A plank is a plank for Dickinson but it is also a metaphor for the way she must walk. Stars and the sea are stars and the sea but they are also signs of height and depth. It is the phrase "Precarious Gait" however that is pure Dickinson—perfectly actual and metaphorically resonant. The definition comes in the last line with the wry attestation that "Some"—not the poet—"call Experience." The world of other people remains but how decisively is the poem hers!

#889 begins with a definition:

> Crisis is a Hair
> Toward which the forces creep
> Past which forces retrograde
> If it come in sleep

To suspend the Breath
Is the most we can
Ignorant is it Life or Death
Nicely balancing.

Let an instant push
Or an Atom press
Or a circle hesitate
In Circumference

It—may jolt the Hand
That adjusts the Hair
That secures Eternity
From presenting—Here—

We say typically "hangs by a hair," "a hair's breadth," "decided by a hair." By leaping into the definition in the first line, Dickinson is using metaphor to assert her ability to create worlds of her own. She draws upon conventional metaphor only to use it for her own purposes. She evokes plausibly referential worlds but she does not have to overly define the references (for example, "forces"). Metaphor is—for all its presumptuous clarity—ambiguous, as any one thing (a pig or a hair) possesses many qualities. "Which ones am I to take?" the reader wonders. The poem exists not to reassure the reader ("This quality, dear reader, is the approved one.") but to provoke the reader. Dickinson is a very great provoker, as she continually makes things happen ("To suspend," "Let an instant") while letting the context percolate (What "Crisis" is this?). She is at once serious and playful, prone to persist and dally ("Or," "Or"). Above all, she is a poet who takes the invitation to create metaphors at its full value: Each genuine metaphor is a new world, a new thought and perception and feeling—for poetry is not linear. It is omni-directional. Dickinson used metaphor to claim a world of her own devising. Whereas Whitman simply assumed the physical world and brought it into the spaciousness of his free verse, Dickinson wrote in short lines that scrutinized the physical world. The contrast is remarkable and one feels that it is in part a contrast between the domains of men and women in the nineteenth century. Dickinson understood that metaphor is poetry's most explicit and magical key. To transform one thing into another is to call the world of settled facts and opinions into question. Whereas Whitman loved to evoke the sheer energy of life in all its varieties, Dickinson chose to confront the seeming solidity of life. Whereas Whitman spoke for the self and the force of identity, Dickinson wrote (#288), "I'm Nobody! Who are you?" (8)

Metaphor remains for many women a particularly crucial aspect of poetry. For her book of retellings of fairy tales published in 1971, Anne Sexton chose the title *Transformations*. Fairy tales of course represent a metaphorical domain already; fairy tales are the realm of transformation, of pumpkins that become coaches and frogs who turn into princes. Sexton decided to update the fairy tales, to subject them to the withering light of modern times. As she writes: "Without Thorazine / or benefit of psychotherapy / Iron Hans was transformed." Sexton however did not write simply to debunk fairy tales. On the contrary, there is a deep yearning in her for the magic of fairy tales. The question Sexton is asking herself over and over is how do we keep the sense of magical possibilities alive in a world of daily papers and insurance policies? How does poetry stay alive?

Sexton's ingenious answer was to play both sides of the issue. In "Cinderella" she subjects the Cinderella story of rags to riches to pure sarcasm:

> You always read about it;
> the plumber with twelve children
> who wins the Irish sweepstakes,
> From toilets to riches.
> That story.

Our longing to believe in transformations becomes tawdry and trite. We are suckers for such stories. After all, it could happen to any of us. In retelling the Cinderella story Sexton mocks all the conventions of the magical world. For instance when the dove responds to Cinderella's implorings and gives her "a golden dress / and delicate little gold slippers, "Sexton notes it was "Rather a large package for a simple bird." Or when the prince wearies of trying the slipper on so many women, she writes, "He began to feel like a shoe salesman." The simile is comic; he is a prince. What startles is the mundane directness of the simile. It is a droll, brusque resemblance, a transformation in the opposite direction of fairy tales—instead of moving from low to high, we move from high to low. Sexton relishes metaphor's capacity to assert actuality. Reality keeps intruding as Cinderella's stepsisters had "hearts like blackjacks" and Cinderella, who must sleep on "the sooty hearth each night," "walked around looking like Al Jolson." When the dove pecks out the evil stepsisters' eyes: "Two hollow spots were left / like soup spoons." To the degree that fairy tales have gilded our longings for happy endings and just rewards, Sexton proposes the blunt magic of transforming metaphor as if to say "You want magic? I have it—but it is fearsome." She writes in "One Eye, Two Eyes, Three-Eyes" of a child that "she was as innocent as a snowflake." It is Emily Dickinson's inclination in a modern key, the summoning of the depth of feeling that lies dormant in each and every physical term. Conventions debase metaphor ("It was a Cinderella story"); new metaphors explode conventions. (9)

Metaphor takes courage because there is no place to hide in a metaphor. Because it is transformative, true metaphor allows us to get close to terrible things, to things we might not otherwise be able to approach. Consider Etheridge Knight's poem "Hard Rock Returns to Prison from the Hospital for the Criminal Insane":

Hard Rock / was / "known not to take no shit
From nobody," and he had the scars to prove it:
Split purple lips, lumbed ears, welts above
His yellow eyes, and one long scar that cut
Across his temple and plowed through a thick
Canopy of kinky hair.

The WORD / was / that Hard Rock wasn't a mean nigger
Anymore, that the doctors had bored a hole in his head,
Cut out part of his brain, and shot electricity
Through the rest. When they brought Hard Rock back,

Handcuffed and chained, he was turned loose,
Like a freshly gelded stallion, to try his new status.
And we all waited and watched, like a herd of sheep,
To see if the WORD was true.

As we waited we wrapped ourselves in the cloak
Of his exploits: "Man, the last time, it took eight
Screws to put him in the Hole." "Yeah, remember when he
Smacked the captain with his dinner tray?" "He set
The record for time in the Hole—67 straight days!"
"Ol Hard Rock! man, that's one crazy nigger."
And then the jewel of a myth that Hard Rock had once bit
A screw on the thumb and poisoned him with syphilitic spit.

The testing came, to see if Hard Rock was really tame.
A hillbilly called him a black son of a bitch
And didn't lose his teeth, a screw who knew Hard Rock
From before shook him down and barked in his face.
And Hard Rock *did nothing.* Just grinned and looked silly,
His eyes empty like knot holes in a fence.

And even after we discovered that it took Hard Rock
Exactly 3 minutes to tell you his first name,
We told ourselves that he had just wised up,
Was being cool; but we could not fool ourselves for long,
And we turned away, our eyes on the ground. Crushed.
He had been our Destroyer, the doer of things
We dreamed of doing but could not bring ourselves to do,
The fears of years, like a biting whip,
Had cut deep bloody grooves
Across our backs.

In terms of using metaphors, this poem is downright virtuosic. Like a
musician who is intent on registering all the notes within an octave.
Knight touches on the whole range of metaphor: from the nickname

of the prisoner to the casual slang of jail ("screw," for instance, meaning "guard" and "the Hole" meaning "solitary confinement") to an astonishing mix of similes. Sometimes in the poem metaphor is ennobling: The previously untamable Hard Rock had been not just another prisoner but "our Destroyer." At other times, metaphor is ghastly, as when Hard Rock is likened to "a freshly gelded stallion" whose eyes are "empty like knot holes in a fence." Then there are moments in the poem where Knight does not resort to metaphor, where instead he uses utterly direct language to convey the lobotomy: "the doctors had bored a hole in his head, / Cut out part of his brain, and shot electricity / Through the rest." Part of knowing when to use metaphor lies in knowing when not to use metaphor, when to let actuality have its forthright say.

As it makes one thing into another, metaphor may seem to have the ability to make the unbearable into the bearable. Metaphor in Knight's poem isn't about lying; it's about dignifying lives in a vicious, demeaning world. That is why, in a very un-prison-like phrase, the inmates "wrapped ourselves in the cloak / Of his exploits." And that is why Knight ends his poem with the simile of the "biting whip" that makes so very real the "fears of years." Who would say that those "deep bloody grooves" across the backs of African-American men in a racist society are merely metaphors? To the question of whether language can be found to describe the terrible impact of racism, Knight's poem answers in the affirmative. (10)

The awful history of the twentieth century is full of events before which language must pause and question its credentials. The Polish poet Tadeusz Borowski was arrested by the Gestapo and put to work at Auschwitz. This is his poem about the Birkenau concentration camp that was adjacent to Auschwitz (translated by Tadeusz Pióro, Larry Rafferty, and Meryl Natchez):

Night Over Birkenau

Night again. Again the grim sky closes
circling like a vulture over the dead silence.
Like a crouching beast over the camp
the moon sets, pale as a corpse.

And like a shield abandoned in battle,
blue Orion—lost among the stars.
The transports growl in darkness
and the eyes of the crematorium blaze.

It's steamy, stifling. Sleep is a stone.
Breath rattles in my throat.
This lead foot crushing my chest
is the silence of three million dead.

Night, night without end. No dawn comes.
My eyes are poisoned from sleep.
Like God's judgment on the corpse of the earth,
fog descends over Birkenau.

How to make us feel the experience—not to talk about it but feel it? This is metaphor's province and Borowski relies extensively on simile and metaphor to make the experience palpable. Physical evocation must have its place in such a poem and does ("It's steamy, stifling"), but only metaphor can move the experience into the realm of myth—myth that is actuality. What is the moon in the context of a concentration camp; what is fog; what is a constellation; what—most pressingly—is the import of human life where life is being systematically extinguished? "Sleep is a stone," Borowski writes. Is this decorative language, impractical language, unusual language? The concision of metaphor is almost unbearable and that is what language must be to render this experience. The mind reels and gropes (and the poet is an artist of the mind) and metaphor proposes new mindholds to approach the unspeakable. (11)

There is, as Aristotle noted, no accounting for the gift of metaphor. It seems to stem from the ability to feel intimately the qualities of things. Metaphor is certainly animistic. Nothing is mute as far as metaphor is concerned. To explore the truth of metaphor (and as any name-calling group of children knows, metaphor can be deeply cruel) is to learn to be comfortable with how changeable life itself is, how it is full of surprising, elating, and scary resemblances, and how metaphor is meaningfulness that vaults accepted definitions as it creates new ones.

METAPHOR
In the Classroom

1. Some athletes and entertainers have had nicknames that are very distinct metaphors. George Herman Ruth was "Babe" and "Bambino," Joe Louis was "the Brown Bomber," Elvis Presley was "the King." What do such nicknames imply about the person? To what personal qualities do such nicknames call attention? Is it common for women athletes and entertainers to have nicknames? Are there differences according to gender as far as nicknames are concerned? Find metaphors about people in magazines and newspapers then list them in your poetry notebook and analyze them for the kinds of qualities about the person that they convey.

2. To directly name an object for its qualities, real or imaginary, changes the object. We do this all the time within the context of our everyday world. For example, the cafeteria becomes "the frialator" or "the four star."

   Take a place like school, home, or work and create metaphors that transform the specific place into something else. School might be "the brain factory," or the guidance office might be "the confessional."

   By using real objects in the world, the poet can evoke emotional responses through metaphor. Take an experience in your life and create a physical metaphor for it by naming actual physical objects connected with the experience. A date, for instance, may be a car or a box of popcorn or a ticket stub. From this base create a poem rooted in metaphor.

3. Metaphors can be fashioned to work on various levels, and this is accomplished by expanding the degree of detail in the metaphor. How much metaphor to use depends on the situation. For example, "Joe is yappy as a dog" can easily become "Joe is yappy as a cocker spaniel," which can then become "Joe is yappy as a cocker spaniel in a bad mood."

   Begin with some basic metaphors and build them up, bit by bit, to see how the metaphor can be detailed. For example: His hair is a forest. His hair is a forest full of small creatures. His hair is a forest full of small creatures that make disturbing sounds at night.

4. In certain cases, metaphors are weapons. They have been used to stereotype, and they can prove deadly. Look up primary sources in American history to find metaphors that have been used to denigrate groups of people. What do these metaphors say about the society in which they were used?

5. Historical metaphors about personages, eras, and events reveal perceptions about realities. "The Gilded Age," "the Roaring Twenties," "Old Ironsides," "Flower Power," "the Greenhouse Effect," "Nuclear Winter," "Surfing the Net," all describe reality and take on a life of their own. Find metaphors for people, eras, and events from printed texts as well as non-print media. How accurate do these metaphors seem to you?

6. Poets in the nineteenth century were in the habit of evoking the great abstractions: Truth, Beauty, Justice, Hope. Take one of these abstractions (or use one of your own) and "metaphor it" with words from your world and experiences.

7. Consider the words that men and women use to describe each other. Is there a difference between the metaphors each sex uses to describe the opposite sex? In what ways do the sexes use metaphor?

8. Adrienne Rich's poem "Diving into the Wreck" offers an opportunity to extend work on metaphor through a close look at a contemporary poem. Copy Rich's poem into your poetry notebook. How does Rich use metaphor in this poem?

9. In her book *Transformations*, Anne Sexton uses new metaphors to explode the conventional fairy tale. Read traditional versions of the fairy tales that Sexton parodies. Form groups according to which tale particularly interests students. Have each group reread the fairy tale and Sexton's related poem. Compare the two versions. What aspects of the original fairy tale does Sexton poke fun at? Retell a fairy tale from a contemporary point of view.

10. Write a response piece that identifies and considers all the metaphors Etheridge Knight uses in "Hard Rock Returns to Prison from the Hospital for the Criminal Insane."

11. Tadeusz Borowski's poem deals with extreme human experiences. There are numerous poems about the Holocaust in *Against Forgetting*, an anthology edited by Carolyn Forché (see chapter bibliography). Copy some poems from Forché's anthol-

ogy into your poetry notebook. Do the poems use metaphor? It has been said that writing cannot convey the enormous suffering of the Holocaust. How do the poems say with words what some have felt cannot be said with words?

METAPHOR
Five-Day Lesson Plan

Day 1   Discuss movie titles as metaphors, for example, "The Terminator." First, define metaphor and simile and have a discussion of these concepts. With the class, make a list of movie titles (or TV shows, songs, or book titles) that are metaphors. Why give a movie a metaphorical title? Discuss how these titles are metaphorical.

The basis for metaphor is comparison. Have each student create a metaphorical title for a movie based upon his or her life. List these titles on the board and discuss them in terms of effective metaphors.

Day 2   The teacher brings in a sampling of poems with metaphorical titles. Since the title of a poem is a signpost that tells about the poem, have students read the poems and discuss how the titles are metaphors for the whole poem. Then examine how much metaphor the poet uses within each poem. Are there other metaphors in the poem that are aligned with the metaphorical title?

Day 3   Divide students into groups. Give each group a poem to examine in terms of how metaphor works within it. Each group reports out to the class, discussing specific instances of metaphor in the poem.

Days 4 & 5

Students draft a poem based upon their metaphorical title for the movie based on their life. Working in pairs, students will share their first drafts with a partner. Constructive criticism should focus on the use of metaphor within the draft.

Beyond the Week

Ask students to choose several current political or social situations that are in the news. Ask them to answer the following question: What metaphorical titles might be given to these situations?

METAPHOR
Bibliography

Poems

The Complete Poems of Emily Dickinson, edited by Thomas H. Johnson, Little Brown, 1960; *The Complete Poems* by Anne Sexton, Houghton Mifflin, 1981, includes *Transformations*; "Hard Rock Returns to Prison from the Hospital for the Criminal Insane" by Etheridge Knight from *The Essential Etheridge Knight*, University of Pittsburgh Press, 1986; "Night Over Birkenau" by Tadeusz Borowski from *Selected Poems*, hit & run press, 1990.

Against Forgetting: Twentieth Century Poetry of Witness, edited by Carolyn Forché, W. W. Norton, 1993.

Prose

Metaphor by Terence Hawkes, Methuen, 1972; *More Than Cool Reason* by George Lakoff and Mark Turner, University of Chicago Press, 1989. The quote from Isaiah Berlin is from "Historical Inevitability" in *The Proper Study of Mankind*, Farrar Straus Giroux, 1998.

9

Image

Summary

An image in a poem is language that evokes a vivid, sensory, concrete presence. The predilection for image arose around the time of World War I in opposition to the vagueness, generality, and abstraction that were the staples of much sentimental, nineteenth-century poetry. Twentieth-century poets, after all, were living in an age that emphasized the visual in terms of motion pictures and photographs and ads and the concrete in terms of the new fruits of the machine age. Whereas capitalized words such as Honor and Truth easily could be distrusted, the stubborn integrity of the image could not be denied. There was no world without that sheer, particular, physical presence. Everything (to paraphrase William Carlos Williams) depended on it.

The image holds a special place in the annals of twentieth century poetry. From the pre-World War I era up to the millennium, it has been a touchstone for many different poets. The reasons for this trust are not hard to find, for the image at once participates in the genius of the visual, for which the century of boldly colored painting, photography, movies, and electronic screens has had an enormous appetite, and rejects the dead weight of abstraction. The image is the bravery of visual precision: say what is seen and it speaks for itself. The image embodies the classic advice of writing teachers: show it, don't talk about it.

The image first was promoted as a cure for what ailed poetry in pre-World War I London, England. The ailments ascribed to poetry included sentimentality, vagueness, muddleheadedness, and emotional torpor. When Ezra Pound in a two-line poem likened a crowd in the subway to "petals on a wet, black bough," he was self-consciously proposing the inalienable values of concision and clarity. A poetry governed by the image presented (according to Pound) "an intellectual and emotional complex in an instant of time." And an instant was a sufficient amount of time; a poem did not have to natter on in search of immemorial truths. An alert image was a truth.

T. E. Hulme, a remarkable thinker who wrote at the same time and in the same place as Pound and who perished in World War I, evinced a similar dislike of generalities and conceptual thinking in poetry. Hulme insisted that "Images in verse are not mere decoration but the very essence of an intuitive language." Poetry was a "visual concrete language" that endeavored to "arrest you, and to make you continuously see a physical thing, to prevent you gliding through an abstract process." For Hulme poetry was "an affair of the body ... [and] to be real it must affect the body." The image—as it tautly related sensory experience—was a way to do that.

The insistence on the image spawned a brief movement that not unexpectedly called itself Imagism. A few anthologies were published containing brief poems of various merits. Since poems cannot be written to recipes of any sort—aesthetic, political or otherwise—such a movement proved self-defeating and evaporated in the years defined by the tragedy of World War I. The point about poetry, however, had been made. The horror of the war in fact reinforced the truth of Imagism, for the war was not only a matter of the physical nightmares of the front but also the home front horror of muzzy banalities that somehow were supposed to placate a generation that was dying on a scale no one ever had believed possible. On one hand, some poets actually in combat instinctively resorted to graphic, visual language, as in Isaac Rosenberg's "Dead Man's Dump" where "A man's brains splattered on / A stretcher-bearer's face" and "The dark air spurts with fire." On the other hand, the image was an antidote to the outright lies of wartime propaganda. That some poets sensed the importance of the image before catastrophe swallowed up so many seems uncanny. The image rejected the grandeur of humankind just as the war was proving how hollow that grandeur was. What remained was unrepentant physicality that arose from what Hulme called the "contemplation of finite things." Lice, rats, shrapnel, mud, poison gas called not for abstractions and poetic terms but a hard, precise language of the senses. (1)

One poet who also was in London and who had meditated on the lessons of Imagism was T. S. Eliot. Consider these lines from Eliot's "Preludes":

> And now a gusty shower wraps
> The grimy scraps
> Of withered leaves about your feet
> And newspapers from vacant lots;
> The showers beat
> On broken blinds and chimney pots,
> And at the corner of the street
> A lonely cab-horse steams and stamps.

Here is Pound's "intellectual and emotional complex in an instant of time." It is by no means a frozen instant: things are occurring. Nor is it an emotionally neutral instant. Eliot conveys an intense feeling of urban loneliness. What was remarkable about Eliot was his determination to let the scene speak for itself. He refused to provide a gloss or commentary, refused to connect the scene to any sort of conceptual moral, refused to inject his own opinions about how sordid and sad cities could be. He let it be in a way in which poets at the time were not accustomed. Using a simple syntactic structure ("And," "And," "And") he presented what seemed an actuality, though not of the journalistic sort. Here was an actuality delineated by poetry. (2)

While Eliot retained a predilection for the image throughout his career, he moved towards the inclusion of the image in an overall context. The image was as effective, if not more so, when contrasted with other modes of statement such as declaration and narration. In the generation that followed Eliot and that studied his work intensively, Robert Lowell is representative of how poets made the image part of the poem's strategic texture. (3) "Skunk Hour," a poem about extreme mental anguish that is set in a coastal Maine village, ends with these lines:

a mother skunk with her column of kittens swills the garbage
   pail.
She jabs her wedge-head in a cup
of sour cream, drops her ostrich tail,
and will not scare.

To the narrator's torment ("I myself am hell") Lowell counterpoints the calm, unswerving, mother skunk. To the narrator's inner turmoil Lowell contrasts the world of creatures that go about their business and take their nourishments quite literally where they find them. As an image the humble skunk is eloquent. The beauty of her existence in that instant is that she is not a symbol or an explanation or a moral. She is a skunk who "will not scare." The integrity of the image vouches for the integrity of the poem as the poet does not try to justify himself or make himself out to be better than he is. The poem is the stuff of dramatic actuality rather than special pleading, and the confidence Lowell placed in the power of image—choosing as he did to end the poem with an image—was rewarded. (4)

The value of the image, as Hulme and Pound saw it, lay in its objectivity. The image had a concise, verifiable life of its own. It was not a plaything or prop of the poet's to be trotted out to swell the poet's feelings. This sort of concrete clarity has fascinated poets in the twentieth century because even as the image fully broaches an instant of time, it speaks for timelessness. A complete image is a small eternity as it seems to hold all the motley forces of a moment in equipoise. This sort of image had long been a staple of Chinese and Japanese poetry and Ezra Pound evoked it memorably in the loose translations he published in 1915 under the title *Cathay*. These translations were based on notes given to Pound of an American scholar, Ernest Fenellosa, who was studying the Chinese poet Li Po in Japanese. This was a roundabout and often startlingly inaccurate way to get to the original poems but the English versions proved to have lives of their own. Fenellosa's notes gave Pound the chance to pursue one of his cardinal notions, that (in the words of the scholar Hugh Kenner) "a poem may build its effects out of things it sets before the mind's eye by naming them." (Kenner refers to this as the Imagist principle.) Pound's poems in *Cathay* verified an Imagism that stressed effort and energy: "It [did not] (in Kenner's words again) appease itself by reproducing what is seen, but by setting some other seen thing in relation."

> Blue mountains to the north of the walls,
>
> White river winding about them;
>
> Here we must make separation
>
> And go out through a thousand miles of dead grass.

These lines from Li Po's poem titled "Taking Leave of a Friend" exemplify the strength of the image. The descriptions in the first two lines have a lucid, straightforward quality as metaphor and actuality merge in the color adjectives. The moment is clarified in the third line where the occasion of the poem is made plain and then the moment is intensified and confirmed by the image of "dead grass." Once again we have "an intellectual and emotional complex in an instant of time." The final line sets "some other seen thing in relation." Through images Pound delineates a landscape and evokes powerful feelings. He is scrupulously careful about avoiding sentimentality as he uses the rather stiff phrase "make separation" to ward off any mistiness. As evocations these delicate yet firm lines are strongly sensory and confirm a tenet of Imagism, that the poem must be true to the life of the senses. (5)

Translation has been a sort of glass for twentieth-century American poets in which they have been able to see all sorts of sights. Pound set a course that has been traveled extensively. It is not our intent to go into the inexhaustible debates concerning the pros and cons of translation. We do want to note that American poetry throughout the century has been a good deal more than American poetry in that it has been influenced greatly by translations made by American poets from a myriad of languages. Although the syntaxes of other languages often have not lent themselves to transparent translations, the images from other poetries have come into English with often startling amounts of energy intact. This energy has not been lost on poets. (6)

Indeed poets such as W. S. Merwin, Mark Strand, Robert Bly, and James Wright, although strongly individualistic talents, have had in common a strong preference for what has come to be called "the deep image." According to Robert Bly, Imagism "was largely 'picturism.'"

Bly holds that "an image and a picture differ in that the image, being the natural speech of the imagination, cannot be drawn from or inserted back into the real world. It is an animal native to the imagination ... [and] cannot be seen in real life. A picture, on the other hand, is drawn from the objective 'real' world. 'Petals on a wet, black bough' can actually be seen." Thus for Bly the Imagists were misnamed because they did not write in images from the unconscious. In the words of one of Bly's explicators, James F. Mersmann, Bly has sought "images that writhe in the fogs halfway between deep and inarticulate passions and conscious thought." Pound's classical, objective viewpoint had no interest in writhing and fogs. Deep image poets, as they have translated particularly from modern Spanish poetry, have been entranced by images that arise from the unconscious and whose animal energies do not so much set "some other thing in relation" as, at once, unhinge and locate the poem. The deep image has a spiritual, non-social, and at times surreal quality. (7)

Thus, when Bly writes in "Snowfall in the Afternoon" about a barn in a snowfall, he feels that the barn is alive and "moving towards us now, / Like a hulk blown towards us in a storm at sea; / All the sailors on deck have been blind for many years." The simile of the hulk is very understandable in the context of the poem, but the image of the sailors in the last line is a stark assertion of the unconscious. To ask "what sailors?" is to avoid Bly's artistry. The energy of the image makes vivid the rather literary simile. In Pound's translation of Li Po the "thousand miles of dead grass" is naturalistic; it exists in a chronological, geographical context. In Bly's poem the sailors are called forth solely by the poet's imagination. The line feels hauntingly right because Bly has honored the force of his feelings. The strength of the image stems from what Pound and Hulme expounded about the clarity of "a physical thing." The intent of the image, however, is not so much to conclude and confirm, as Pound's petals did, but rather to pry open the emotional depths of a situation and let that emotional energy speak for itself.

The notion of the deep image testifies to the continued power of the image in American poetry. The reader need not categorize images to feel this power. James Wright, a poet who at his best was deeply affecting, trusted images in ways that are for his readers both salutary and challenging. Here is Wright's short poem "Rain":

It is the sinking of things.

Flashlights drift over dark trees,
Girls kneel,
An owl's eyelids fall.

The sad bones of my hands descend into a valley
Of strange rocks.

To the daylight mind, thinking about what chore it needs to do next, this poem may make ittle sense. To the mind that delights in the rich, ungovernable, earthy suggestiveness of images it makes a good deal of sense. In its way, Wright's poem is thrilling because it takes something that has been written about a countless number of times and feels it anew, the way when we are fully alive we feel something as if for the first time. His images testify to the eloquence of mute actualities and to the poet's imagination that shapes the common treasures of life into something new. The image is very much a gift and the poet is someone who is open to receiving gifts, who is not afraid of what is there in the world around him or her nor of the powers of the imagination.

IMAGE
In the Classroom

1. The graphic nature of war has prompted many poets to make notable use of image. Read poems by veterans of the Vietnam War, such as Bruce Weigl, Yusef Komunyakaa, and Michael Casey. How do images in the poems speak to you about the war?

2. Write down a series of images that visually define a place in your life. Do not title them. Read them aloud and see if classmates can identify the place. Which image was most informative? Why?

3. Choose a poem about an incident from history (an account of a death or an act of protest, such as Philip Levine's "On the Murder of Lieutenant Jose Del Castillo by the Falangist Bravo Martinez, July 12, 1936," Gwendolyn Brooks's "The Assassination of John F. Kennedy," or Amy Clampitt's "The Dahlia Gardens") about which you also can read historical material (see chapter bibliography). How do poets use images to get beneath the bare facts of history and make incidents dramatically compelling?

4. Read some poems about animals such as D. H. Lawrence's, Mary Oliver's, or Ted Hughes's (see chapter bibliography). What sorts of images do the poets use to convey the animal's particular being? Does image seem especially effective in writing about animals? Why or why not? Do the poets put themselves (in the form of the pronoun "I") into their poems about animals or do they leave themselves out? What difference does it make?

5. Billie Bolton's poem "To the Crossing" exemplifies how the senses inform images:

Silhouettes hurry in twilight backyards,
Shouts from doorways—come in, now ....

Not yet, we hide by the glimmer of lightning bugs,
Seek in the deep purple shadows.

Then, a ways off, the train whistle unfurls its warning;
We drop our game and take off running.

Down the driveway, past the maples
Bare feet slapping the warm sidewalk,

Skinned knees stretching.
We race against the whistle flat out to the crossing.

Gasping and sweaty we shout hello to the trainmen,
The engineer blows long on the whistle just for us—

We listen, blue notes filling our ears.
The train rushes on, its clicks fade to whirring crickets.

Write a poem that picks a moment and portrays what is there to all the senses in that moment.

6. Many translations from the Japanese and the Chinese have been made in the twentieth century such as those by Kenneth Rexroth (see chapter bibliography). Sample some of these translations. How do images in them embody the world of nature? What emotional qualities distinguish the images?

7. Spanish and South American poets such as Federico García Lorca, Pablo Neruda, and Antonio Machado have affected many recent English-language poets. American poets such as Mark Strand and Robert Bly have translated many such poets (see chapter bibliography). Are there any similarities you notice between original poems by Strand and Bly and translations by them? What is unique about the images in the poetry of a poet such as Lorca?

IMAGE
Five-Day Lesson Plan

Day 1   Write on the blackboard Ezra Pound's two-line imagist poem, "In the Metro." Discuss the mood this image creates about the metro. Ask students to write their own two-line imagist poem about a place.

Day 2   Pass these drafts of a two-line poem to the class. Give each student a poem written by another student but without the student's name. Have students redraft the poem. If a student feels the draft is perfect, have him or her explain in writing why every word belongs there.

Pass back redrafts to the author. Then, have the author respond by either redrafting this second version or, if there is no other work, begin another two-line poem.

Days 3 & 4

Images are sensory pictures. The teacher brings in a sampling of poems that have strong images in them. Students then identify the images in these poems. What senses are evoked in these images? How precise is the language that comprises the image?

Day 5   Ask students to look at a moment in their life and see (or hear, etc.) what images are in that moment. Draft a poem that incorporates these images.

Beyond the Week

Redraft the poem from Day 5 based upon input from the teacher or from peers.

IMAGE
Bibliography

Poems

"In a Station of the Metro" by Ezra Pound from *Selected Poems*, New Directions, 1957; "Preludes" by T. S. Eliot from *Collected Poems 1909–1962*, Harcourt Brace, 1963; "Skunk Hour" by Robert Lowell from *Selected Poems*, Farrar Straus Giroux, 1977; "Taking Leave of a Friend" by Ezra Pound from *Selected Poems*, New Directions, 1957; "Snowfall in the Afternoon" by Robert Bly from *Selected Poems*, HarperCollins, 1986; "Rain" by James Wright from *Above the River: The Complete Poems*, Farrar Straus Giroux and The University Press of New England, 1990.

D. H. Lawrence, *The Complete Poems*, Penguin, 1971; Ted Hughes, *New Selected Poems*, Harper & Row, 1982; Mary Oliver, *New and Selected Poems*, Beacon Press, 1992. Bruce Weigl, *Song of Napalm*, Atlantic Monthly Press, 1988; Yusef Komunyakaa, *Dien Cai Dau*, Wesleyan University Press, 1988; Michael Casey, *Obscenities*, Yale University Press, 1972.

"On the Murder of Lieutenant Jose Del Castillo by the Falangist Bravo Martinez, July 12, 1936" by Philip Levine from *New Selected Poems*, Alfred A. Knopf, 1991; "The Assassination of John F. Kennedy" by Gwendolyn Brooks is collected in the anthology *Of Poetry and Power: Poems Occasioned by the Presidency and By the Death of John F. Kennedy*, edited with an introduction by Erwin A. Glikes and Paul Schwaber, Basic Books, 1964; "The Dahlia Gardens" by Amy Clampitt from *The Collected Poems*, Alfred A. Knopf, 1997.

Women Poets of Japan, translated and edited by Kenneth Rexroth and Ikuko Atsumi, New Directions, 1977; *One Hundred Poems from the Chinese* by Kenneth Rexroth, New Directions, 1956; *One Hundred Poems from the Japanese* by Kenneth Rexroth, New Directions, 1955. *Neruda and Vallejo: Selected Poems*, edited by Robert Bly, Beacon Press, 1971; *Travelling in the Family: Selected Poems of Carlos Drummond de Andrade*, edited by Thomas Colchie and Mark Strand, Random House, 1986; *The Selected Poems of Federico García Lorca*, edited by Francisco García Lorca and Donald M. Allen, New Directions, 1955.

Prose

Speculations by T. E. Hulme, Routledge & Paul, 1936; *The Pound Era* by Hugh Kenner, University of California Press, 1971; *Robert Bly: When Sleepers Awake*, edited by Joyce Peseroff, University of Michigan Press, 1984. For an account of Imagism see *Imagism: A Chapter for the History of Modern Poetry* by Stanley Coffman, Jr., University of Oklahoma Press, 1951.

10

Architecture (Stanzas)

Summary

The lines of a poem and the spaces between lines constitute a poem's architecture. They form units that in turn form a whole. Sometimes a poem is written out all-of-a-piece without any spaces between lines. Many poems, however, use stanzas. Stanzas come in various lengths; sometimes a poem will maintain a constant stanza unit such as a quatrain throughout the entire poem and sometimes the stanza lengths will vary. It depends on the artistic aims of the poet for that poem, as different sorts of stanzas offer different possibilities. A couplet, for instance, doesn't offer the poet the room in which to maneuver that a ten-line stanza offers. In all cases, however, the stanza is a great organizer, focuser, and sequencer. Stanzas help to articulate the overall energy of the poem. The spaces between stanzas are as critical as the units themselves.

Poets use all sorts of words to describe how they make a poem. Often they speak of poetry in ways that recall the title of this chapter: they "construct," they "build," they "carpenter." Some poets use sculptural words; they "shape" the poem, they "form" it. Still others use kinetic words; for them the poem is a dance or a walk through a field or a crawl over uncertain terrain. Whatever analogy the poet prefers, a sense of how the poem hangs together is common to all of them. Poems are mysterious creations whose origins lie in the rich vagaries of inspiration, but they are, nonetheless, coherent creations. A

157

poem's lines relate to one another; they echo and interpenetrate and angle as they form "an intellectual and emotional complex." Donald Hall has written that the poem is multi-faceted. It is like a diamond. Every syllable and every word is a facet and there are relationships of sound and meaning among all the syllables and words. Mathematically this means that even a "tiny" poem generates thousands of facets. Light bounces off them in ever-unpredictable ways.

A diamond is an organic entity and also a processed one as the diamond is cut and polished. To our minds the finished poem should seem as incontrovertible as a diamond, yet we as readers and auditors always should recall that the poem is something that was fashioned. Without pushing any analogy too far—be it diamonds or houses or dance steps—what seems incontestable is that the poem is all of a piece. In that unified sense the most basic poetic architecture is the poem that is written out as one solid block of lines. The line is the basic unit of the poem and one line follows another in a one-stanza poem without any spatial pauses. The poem must say its piece all at once. To resort once more to analogy, such a poem is like a saxophone solo. The player is breathing but all you hear is one long cascade of notes. The poet is breathing but the lines are unbroken.
Consider Emerson Gilmore's poem "I Am Fifteen":

> Ronnie Twible is my first death:
> when I am too early
> at Rose Hill for his funeral,
> I go for ice cream
> then to the humid granite room
> where the corpse waits
> under muted yellow funeral-parlor lights.
> I sit behind the football team.
> Each player huddles alone,
> muscles drained, and weeps.
> Seeing the tears I'm embarrassed and look at my feet.
> Mr. McCarthy rises, says being so young
> at least all Ronnie knew was good.
> This doesn't change the powder on his mother's cheek

to anything less dusty than the death
I try to brush from my quivering lips after I kiss her.
Walking home through a field of razor grass, I throw up.

Why does the poet narrate the poem in one stanza? The poem is about the totality of the experience of "first death." The poem's title presents us with a factual statement, and the poem proceeds through a number of moments and encounters, all of which are lived under the palpable hand of death. There is no avoidance, no turning aside; above all, there is no rest. The narrator must endure the entire experience. An enormous amount is happening to him, but he cannot withdraw from this social experience of death that is also an intensely and bewilderingly personal experience as the poem ends with the narrator alone, vomiting in a field. The architecture of the poem—line fitted beneath margin-returning line—enforces and exemplifies what the poem is about. In its way the architecture makes us experience what the narrator goes through. We cannot take a time-out; life and death are right up against one another. The impact is visceral. (1)

Not every poem wants to be all-of-a-piece. Gilmore's poem treasures the terrible force of an experience; it compresses time into one, unremitting unit. When we reflect upon the architectural analogy, however, we recall that architecture is the art of solids and spaces. Walls create spaces. In their ways poems use stanzas to create spaces and break up the solidity of the poem-as-a-mass. The very word "stanza" comes from architectural parlance as it means "room" in Italian. As it has definite boundaries—two or three or however many lines—the stanza shapes space the way the rooms of a house do. It is also a room-like container—it holds words. As it also exists in time, lasting for so long and then ceasing, it adds another dimension to its existence. (2)

As human beings we love patterns and the stanza satisfies that craving for patterned order. Many poems use stanzas of uniform length. For instance, the stanzas all may be four lines long or "quatrains" in the terminology of poetry. This precision is pleasing and lulling. We can follow the poem from stanza to stanza and enjoy the poem's fidelity to a stanzaic pattern. As with meter, commitment matters. If the poet breaks the pattern, we assume there is an expressive reason for doing so. The uniformity of the stanza is a comfort, a reassurance, as the poem goes its languid or precipitous or cautious way.

Although poets have written poems in which one line is separated from another so that there is a uniform space between each line of the poem, the couplet or two-line stanza qualifies as the minimal stanzaic unit. Twentieth century poets have been particularly fond of the couplet as it enables them to use a pattern in which there are numerous spatial gaps—an open space after every two lines—which accordingly breaks the text into many units. Such couplets may rhyme or they may not. When encountering these spatial couplets, the reader may think of a series of photographs mounted in time or of motion pictures as the poem hurtles forward in time and one enjambed line leads into another line. William Carlos Williams, for one, was aware of the visual aspect of the spatial couplet in his poem "At the Ball Game." Here are the opening lines:

> The crowd at the ball game
> is moved uniformly
>
> by a spirit of uselessness
> which delights them—
>
> all the exciting detail
> of the chase
>
> and the escape, the error
> the flash of genius—

The words are not particularly visual but the format of the couplet at once isolates and disrupts the flow of the poem. This leaves the reader with a feeling that each couplet has been visually constructed. Williams's couplet is not a rhythmic unit as much as it is a visual unit. "Here," it says, "the poem is divided into units for the sake of units." Together, these units have a herky-jerky quality—why, for instance, put a line space after "uniformly"? Williams is portraying a fairly frenzied, mass gathering. He wants to capture the uniformity of the scene—everyone cheers at certain junctures—and he wants the intensity of feeling to come through. The abrupt, small-scale stanzas keep socking the reader with feelings and observations. The transitions from stanza to stanza aren't especially smooth; it's more like people getting up and then sitting down, a compact but hardly graceful movement. Williams did write poems in the spatial couplet form such as the well-known "The Red Wheelbarrow" where he rejoiced forthrightly in the couplet's ability to freeze and frame images. "At the Ball Game," however, feels more cinematic: Action is occurring but Williams is framing the action for his own expressive purposes.

There are many more adroit instances of the couplet in modern American poetry than we can cite in this book. One example that is of special interest is Donald Justice's "Psalm and Lament." Justice uses the same form as Williams for very different ends. We quote the first four stanzas:

> The clocks are sorry, the clocks are very sad.
> One stops, one goes on striking the wrong hours.
>
> And the grass burns terribly in the sun,
> The grass turns yellow secretly at the roots.
>
> Now suddenly the yard chairs look empty, the sky looks empty.
> The sky looks vast and empty.
>
> Out on Red Road the traffic continues; everything continues.
> Nor does memory sleep; it goes on.

Whereas Williams's stanzas seem almost distracted as he fragments a sentence into couplets, Justice's couplets are all end-stopped and possessed of a deep gravity. Each couplet is individually a meditation. Here the spaces between the couplets highlight the daunting isolation of the occasion, the pain of trying to make sense of death. There is an awful finality in the couplets; they do not recognize one another the way Williams's run into each other. The feeling one gets from reading them is weariness: Things do not run forward—they halt. The feeling is at once strong and tentative as the effort to come to terms with grief is powerfully realized.

One further instance of this popular form is Mark Doty's elegy for the jazzman Chet Baker, "Almost Blue." We quote some stanzas that are part of a long sentence:

> two weeks before the end, Chet,
> and you're playing like anything,
>
> singing *stay little valentine*
> *stay*
>
> and taking so long there are worlds sinking
> between the notes, this exhalation
>
> no longer a voice but a rush of air,
> brutal, from the tunnels under the river ...

Although there is variety among the couplets, for example that one-word line, the calm grace of the couplets resides in their uniform framing of the narrative. The couplets are a steady pulse of form which in Doty's hands structures his salute to an often wayward, self-destructive life. Since there is a relatively high proportion of space to text in the spatial couplet form, the couplets may emphasize the precariousness and fragility of the poem's words: worlds sink between the stanzas. The emptiness following the lonely, imploring "*stay*" is particularly expressive. The poise of Doty's narrative is all the more poignant as it moves steadily forward in what is a two-page long sentence. The couplet, as it highlights each observation, says in effect that "this matters and this matters and this matters.... " The challenge for the poet is to make the words equal to the scrutiny the brief stanzas invite. (3)

Beyond the couplet there are recognized stanza forms of up to eight lines. The three-line, unrhymed stanza (the "tristich") and the quatrain are the most commonly used contemporary stanzas. Compared to the hallowed quatrain whose origins go back in English to the Middle Ages, the tristich is a much more recent form. As a rhymed form it is the favorite of the African-American blues:

Got a letter this morning, what do you reckon it read?

Oh got a letter this morning, what do you reckon it read?

It said "Come home, come home" 'cause the one you love is dead.

The way the tristich allows for repetition before concluding allows the blues singer to set the listener up and then deliver a clinching line. The listener is made to fully feel the situation before further explanation is given. The taut insistence of the repetitive lines is matched by the clarification of the final line. Emotionally it is a deeply satisfying equation.

Typically the blues tristich rhymed but the unrhymed form has been popular with many poets. Wallace Stevens and William Carlos Williams, to choose two of many, made sophisticated use of it. Although the way they handled the stanza varied a great deal from one another, both poets appreciated the self-effacing, modest quality of the tristich as it stood between the self-aware minimalism of the couplet and the formal, historical overtones of the quatrain. The tristich works very well as a stanza that signifies form without imposing any special set of limitations and preconceptions. It can be firm and fluid at the same time, able to incorporate more matter than the couplet without raising the issues of balance and structure the way the quatrain does. For Stevens, in a long poem such as "Notes Toward a Supreme Fiction," the tristich signifies the sheer strength of form. The first section of the poem, "It Must Be Abstract," begins with an end-stopped stanza:

Begin, ephebe, by perceiving the idea

Of this invention, this invented world,

The inconceivable idea of the sun.

The second section, "It Must Give Pleasure," begins with run-on stanzas:

To sing jubilas at exact, accustomed times,

To be crested and wear the mane of a multitude

And so, as part, to exult with its great throat

To speak of joy and to sing of it, borne on
The shoulder of joyous men, to feel the heart
That is the common, the bravest fundament ...

Stevens emphasizes proposition and definition in the first instance and ebullient, physical energy in the second, but the form is hospitable to both aspects as Stevens writes consistent pentameter lines that give his tristichs a very orderly aspect: "So many lines and a space, so many lines and a space." The spaces between the stanzas are at once a rest and a leap from one unit to another, a leap that for all its predictability retains a quiet electricity. As in architecture where there are walls and spaces, the spaces in the poem are as integral as the masses of the stanzas. The spaces are emptiness and presentiment: More is to come but what is said is apportioned and we must pause ever so slightly before we move on. Against the forthright articulation that is a poem, the spaces between stanzas are counterweights of silence. As with architecture the mass defines the entity but space softens it. Stevens could have run his lines all together in one block; he chose not to. Instead he decided to offer many occasions where the poem halts fully or marginally and then continues on according to a logic that is purely poetic. Stevens's tristichs are not as near-existential as the couplet form of varying line lengths (recall Doty's one-word line); rather, they are calmly assertive as they halt and resume, halt and resume or rush forward like squadrons intent on an objective.

Williams also favored the tristich but he used it very differently. Particularly in his later poems he chose to break sentences into three units according to three margins on the page: left, center, and right. Typically Williams, while creating a tripartite form, does not separate the tristichs but runs them together. He cherishes the presence of a strictly notional form while maintaining a headlong momentum. It is a delicious balance, as in "The Pink Locust":

I'm persistent as the pink locust,
      once admitted
           to the garden,

you will not easily get rid of it.

      Tear it from the ground,

           if one hair-thin rootlet

remain

      it will come again.

      It is

flattering to think of myself

      so. It is also

           laughable.

It is a sort of subjugated stanza, not able to exist on its own (and be defined as a stanza) but a very distinct presence in the poem. The effects Williams achieves within this form are noteworthy. He imparts a great sense of forward movement as the lines honor their margin positions while the sentences flow on. The proportions among the lines vary so that the reader is always alert to the duration of each line. Williams's unpredictable enjambments heighten this feeling. To read the poem aloud is to honor the placement of the lines while preserving the sense of the sentences. It is very dance-like, as movement exists within a notion of precision that is whimsical and rigorous at the same time.

Many poets have pursued the tristich as an expressive form in its own right. Sue Payne's poem "Mother May I" typifies much contemporary practice:

Mother, may I take four baby steps? I ask, placing one foot in front
of the other to show how little ground I'd cover.
No, you may not, says Mother, who is my little brother.

Patty's turn. The girl-next-door sucks up:
Mother, may I please, please, please take two giant steps
with a running start? He's sure to say Yes, you may.

Tommy gets jazzed and shouts Umbrella Steps are best,
then helps himself to six. Mother leans back
out of reach. We screech: You forgot to say Mother may I!

The sun burns up the Road to Mother, melts my Keds
on the driveway while I invent another step to tempt
my brother into letting me get closer to Mother.

Mother may I please take five Rabbit steps? I inquire.
He eyes my furry coat, my twitchy feet and nose, reluctant
to grant anyone one of those.

No, you may not, Mother declares. He never lets me win!
Stops me before I get within his shadow, holds up one hand
like a crossing-guard's paddle, imitates a stern face.

I watch what steps he allows the neighbor kids to take.
See how he orchestrates the finish line, making certain
that the role of Mother will never be mine.

Permission sits on his tongue like a lemon drop. He rolls it
into the pocket of his cheek and grins.
My mouth waters, our Mother calls, another game begins.

The stanzas structure a narrative according to the particular balance
of the tristich. Generally Payne end-stops the stanzas, thus miming
the game where one can go only so far and then must stop. She is able
to include varying degrees of the narrative within each stanza: some
hold a couple of events, others dwell on one issue. Part of the pleasure
of her poem resides in how she apportions her material to her approximately uniform stanzas: each stanza is a chapter of sorts and has a distinct life of its own. As readers we move from discrete step to discrete
step within the stanzas and from stanza to stanza. The narrator's frustration—that she doesn't move all the way to the goal—is mocked
gently by the deliberate pace of the stanzas. The poem reaches its
stanzaic end only to announce ironically that "another game begins."
The tristich holds all feelings and observations even-handedly. (4)
The stanza form acknowledges what the poem imparts: there are rules
to the game and they must be observed. There is room within the rules
but what happens depends on who is in charge. Not the least of the ad-

vantages of writing poems is that one can revenge oneself artfully for the slights of childhood.

The quatrain (a four-line stanza) has had a long and distinguished career of embracing polarities, opposites, and contrasts. As it offers more possibilities for rhyme, the quatrain is more strongly rooted in rhyme than the couplet and tercet (a rhymed three-line stanza such as the blues stanza). The editors of *Strong Measures: Contemporary American Poetry in Traditional Forms* distinguish among seven sorts of quatrains, to say nothing of the ballad and eight-line forms ("octaves") that are in effect double quatrains. The most common rhyme schemes are *abab*, *aabb*, and *abba*. What the poet gains from the rhymed quatrain is a blend of discursiveness and pointedness. The frame of the quatrain is ampler than the couplet or tercet and allows for more material to be incorporated. On the other hand, the rhyme scheme keeps creating associations as various end words rhyme. Al Young's poem "Lester Leaps In" about the great saxophonist Lester Young is included in the *Strong Measures* anthology. Here is the final quatrain:

> Here lived a man so hard and softspoken
> he had to be cool enough to hold his horn
> at angles as sharp as he was heartbroken
> in order to blow what it's like being born.

Young makes strong use of the quatrain's ability to construct and hammer home definitions. The stanza is an epitaph as it concisely presents the sum of an artist's life. The quatrain's rhyme scheme of *abab* is a powerful reinforcer as the rhyming words highlight the poem's themes. Within one quatrain and one sentence Young makes a poetically irrefutable statement. With its balances and antitheses the quatrain is a species of logic.

Contemporary masters of the quatrain such as Richard Wilbur and X. J. Kennedy deploy all the standard rhyme schemes and come up with their own variations. In "B Negative" Kennedy writes a quatrain that rhymes *aaba*:

> I used to purchase in the Automat
> A cup of soup and fan it with my hat
>   Until a stern voice from the change booth crashed
> Like nickels: *Gentlemen do not do that.*

Wilbur contracts a line in "The Walgh-Vogel":

> More pleasurable to look than feed upon
> Hence unconserved in dodo-runs, the round,
> Unfeathered, melancholy, more than fifty pound
> Dodo is gone …

Just as a baseball pitcher is said to take something off a pitch so that it is not the standard speed, so Wilbur takes something off the quatrain. Our expectations are met and not met: The quatrain with its rhyming logic remains but the short fourth line is disconcerting. Its awkward brevity mimics the dodo's fate.

Just as the couplet and tercet have been used without rhymes so has the quatrain. What the reader is likely to feel is the ghost of the rhyme, the pull of a force that is no longer present. Here is the beginning of "Stone and Flower" by Kenneth Rexroth, a poem dedicated to the English poet, Kathleen Raine:

> Here in America
> By the other ocean—
> Your book, two years delayed—
> In the spring evening.
>
> I look from my window
> Over a steep city,
> From a hilltop higher
> Than most of your England.
>
> West of the dark mountains,
> Over the white ocean,
> That female planet burns,
> Twisting in the green sky.

The quatrains are crisp and measured but the rhyme has vanished. Rexroth is able to bring two worlds together as he maintains a casual diction that calls no special attention to itself while evoking the determined form of the quatrain. He does not want the chiming aspect of rhyme, but he esteems the careful space of the form as he moves from observation to observation in quatrain to quatrain. The poem is more meditative than declarative; the zinging, clinching energy of rhyme is not wanted, but the architecture of the quatrain that allows him to purposefully structure an experience is.

Similarly, Robert Hayden's " 'Lear is Gay' " evokes the skeletal strength of the quatrain while eschewing end-rhyme:

> That gaiety oh
> that gaiety I love
> has white hair
> or thinning or none,
>
> has limbs askew
> often as not,
> has dimming sight.
> Can manage, can
>
> in fevers, rags,
> decrepitude.
> And oh can laugh
> sometimes
>
> at time as at
> a scarecrow whose
> hobo shoulders are
> a-twitch with crows.

Hayden's brief quatrains have a sprightly effect that is a comment in its own right about the deranged, Shakespearean king. Again the spark of form mingles with the notion of form. Hayden sticks to his quatrains as precisely as Rexroth does. End-rhyme would be too arch and forceful for Hayden's purposes. To pun a bit on Shakespeare,

"Lightness is all" here. The quatrain is just enough of form as it echoes ballads and songs, for the poem is an evocative echo of a state of mind. Hayden's ear for rhythm makes the poem sing without rhyme. The stanzas seem to formalize what would otherwise blow away in the wind of feeling. (5)

Thus far the stanzas we have examined are similar in that they all are isomorphic: Each stanza in the poem is the same length. There are many poems written in stanzas that are not like this, where the stanza lengths vary. The stanzas in such poems are akin to what is referred to as a "verse paragraph" because, as with the prose paragraph the stanza's length is not set beforehand. The verse paragraph originates from the handling of blank verse (an unrhymed poem consisting of five weak/strong units to the line), as in Milton where indentations at the beginning of the line indicate a new stanza—except that Milton wrote the likes of *Paradise Lost* out as one, long, solid, stanza-less mass. The term "verse paragraph" honors the logic and flow of narrative and is applicable to contemporary poetry in that way. Poets who write blank verse poems and who indent sections still use the verse paragraph in its strict sense.

In certain forms, such as the ode (e.g., Wordsworth's "Ode: Intimations of Immortality from Recollections of Early Childhood") the stanza lengths vary but there is a general sense of the shape of the form. There are longer and shorter stanzas according to Wordsworth's expressive intentions. The first two stanzas, for instance, are relatively brief (nine lines each) as Wordsworth is concerned with succinctly imparting a strong sense of the actuality of childhood impressions. More philosophical and expository stanzas take up more lines. (6)

Likewise, in recent American poetry, free-verse poems, in particular, rely on various stanza lengths as they move from perception to perception. Such a poem is open-ended in the sense that the exposition is indeterminate; the poet is finding her or his way through the poem. By varying the lengths of the stanzas, the poet gives the poem a contingent, spontaneous quality. The poem's emotional pulse contracts and expands, as in Timothy McCall's poem "Beatle Boots (Milwaukee, Wisconsin, 1964)":

I sailed past Vicky Shuffton's desk
So cool
'cause I got 'em
Black pointy toes
No laces
No zippers
Just elastic
at the ankle

Dad drove me
to a bad neighborhood
two weeks ago
to buy them

$8.99

Now bent nails
gnaw at my heels
chew craters through my socks

I still wear 'em though
Every day

I'm not even supposed to like the Beatles
Girls like the Beatles
And I hate girls
Especially Vicky Shuffton

McCall's brief stanzas of various lengths demonstrate the quick, quirky tempo of an adolescent's emotions as the narrator jumps from feeling to feeling and fact to fact. "$8.99," for instance, is very much a stanza in its own right despite its brevity. Stanzas of identical length would routinize the poem and suppress the poem's bouncy freshness: Expressing feelings and making choices is glorious, however much the boots hurt. (7)

Variable length stanzas in narrative, free-verse poems tend toward an approximation of prose paragraphs as they carefully construct scenes and moments. Rosa M. Arenas's "What I Can't Tell You" is a moving example of how the variable stanza does its work:

> When I was 7 and you were 14,
> I recited "The Raven" to you,
> and you said "Good but try putting more
> expression in your voice,"
> as if you knew Edgar Allan Poe, personally.
>
> You liked the Kinks and the Ventures and played
> "Walk, Don't Run" all the time, the electric guitar
> insistent and teasing, a tongue circling lips.
>
> You made sure we tuned in when
> the Beatles first appeared on the Ed Sullivan show.
> In their black suits they were formal, yet distracted.
> We watched, surprising the fluttering screams from the set
> like streamers curling loose at a party.
>
> When Simon and Garfunkel sang "The Sounds of Silence"
> you nudged me, saying it was a good song,
> so I listened to the words escaping from the radio,
> a bleak picture in studied harmonies.
>
> For a while you came to me in dreams
> telling me why you went to Vietnam,
> showing me photographs of twining vines and helicopters,
> while a voice said you committed suicide by enlisting.
>
> I dreamt you in army fatigues, beneath the
> green shadow of cavernous barracks.
> On a narrow cot, not having room to turn around,
> a cry came from your sleep.

On the night you became memory,
Mother woke me with a winding sob,
standing at the foot of my bed in her nightgown,
her grey hair disarranged, her face contorted,
saying she heard you calling
through a yellow tunnel and that you needed her.

I am now nearly twice the age you always are
saying goodbye in the airport,
not having time to turn around, but looking back
smiling as if you are going on vacation.

And now that you are nowhere in particular
I try putting expression in my voice and
listen for the good songs, since something
in me wants the heart beat, common
time, insistent and familiar.

The slight variations in stanza-length allow Arenas to subtly register the natural shape of the narrative. The poem has a great gravity that the verse paragraphs give expression to. One feels the poet piecing together her feelings as she tells the story. The stanzas, which are the freedom of space, give her the room to do this. The poem traverses a lot of time. Its stanzas point to a norm (there are four quatrains in the poem), the way months and years point to a norm. The way we experience time, however, cannot be objectified in terms of any norm. The architecture of Arenas's poem is attuned to this subjective actuality. (8)

The architecture of stanzas tends to be strictly vertical as the page shows block being laid upon block as if a chimney were being built. Such a chimney is a poetry structure, however, in that the top block begins rather than finishes the structure. Sometimes poets consciously play upon this sense of the poem as a way of building. Thus, Elizabeth Bishop's poem "Jerónimo's House" is literally a work of architecture that mimes the structure of a building: The poem is composed of two stanzaic columns of double quatrains. The poem's title acts as a lintel of sorts. Here is Bishop's poem:

My house, my fairy
        palace, is
of perishable
        clapboards with
three rooms in all,
        my gray wasp's nest
of chewed-up paper
        glued with spit.

My home, my love-nest,
        is endowed
with a veranda
        of wooden lace,
adorned with ferns
        planted in sponges,
and the front room
        with red and green

left-over Christmas
        decorations
looped from the corners
        to the middle
above my little
        center table
of woven wicker
        painted blue,

and four blue chairs
        and an affair
for the smallest baby
        with a tray
with ten big beads.
        Then on the walls
two palm-leaf fans
        and a calendar

and on the table
        one fried fish
spattered with burning
        scarlet sauce,
a little dish
        of hominy grits
and four pink tissue-
        paper roses.

Also I have
        hung on a hook,
an old French horn
        repainted with
aluminum paint.
        I play each year
in the parade
        for José Marti.

At night you'd think
        my house abandoned.
Come closer. You
        can see and hear
the writing-paper
        lines of light
and the voices of
        my radio

singing flamencos
        in between
the lottery numbers.
        When I move
I take these things,
        not much more, from
my shelter from
        the hurricane.

One aspect that always has fascinated us about this poem is that Bishop creates a tangibly columnar structure on the page, yet she chooses to indent every other line. One can read this choice in various ways but for us the rickety nature of the house is mimicked in the precarious nature of the columns. The columns waver steadily; the "shelter" is skeletal yet a house. The care with which all the possessions are noted is poignant. Before the awful power of "the hurricane," dignity will have its way. Form, Bishop implies, is both strong and weak, brave and tenuous.

Poems that challenge stanzaic structure may project all sorts of feelings: free-floating declamation, for instance, or emotional edginess, or sprawling indecision, or deftly unpremeditated movement. Consider the opening of the first of Robert Duncan's "A Set of Romantic Hymns":

> Sweet tone! Vibrant wing!
> Towards-melody-shimmering lure
>   I'd leap once more
>
>   to catch
>
> barb, pang and outpouring
>
>   spasm of air
> that in the sheen of fish-scale's seen,
>
>   hummingbird's sheath
>   dazzling
>   above the pungent horn
> or where the flashing thing's
>   sensed in Tiffany's glass; of fire
> and golden life workt to endure,
>
>   to be endured,
>   in pure Beauty.

Duncan's expansiveness is robust and delicate as he opens the stanza up to what feels like air and light. The words on the page have a firm liveliness as Duncan places them according to his sense of articulate movement. The largely enjambed lines have great momentum yet they have a lingering quality as Duncan allows for so much space to be present within the poem. In conventional stanzas, the line is uniform and self-effacing as it builds the stanza, but in Duncan's poem the line has its own strength and may at any moment go it alone. When in his poem the lines are together in a regular stanzaic mode, it feels as if Duncan has made a definite aesthetic decision, that he is proposing a balance for the time being between the mass of the stanza and the energy of the individual line. With its uplifted, exuberant tone—beginning as it does with exclamations—Duncan's "Hymn" is a paean to the freedom of form. (9) It shows that architecture can dance. (10)

ARCHITECTURE
In the Classroom

1. Find a poem written as one long stanza (over ten lines). Why is it written as one unit rather than broken up into separate stanzas?

2. Trace the origins of the word "stanza" in detail.

3. Write a poem in the spatial couplet form. Try to explain how the form relates to the subject matter of your poem. Find several poems that use the spatial couplet form and explain why you think the authors use that form.

4. Read a few more poems that use the tristich form. (Don't forget blues poems.) Write a poem using the tristich form.

5. Read several rhymed and unrhymed poems that use the quatrain. Based on your reading, write your own poem using rhymed or unrhymed quatrains.

6. Read several odes from different eras. What do they have in common? How do they differ from one another?

7. The variable stanza allows for spontaneity in recounting a sequence of events. Having read Timothy McCall's poem, write a poem of your own that recalls a specific sequence of events that affected you. Use various stanza and line lengths. Also use images to tell your story.

8. Examine the stanzas in Rosa M. Arenas's poem. How do the stanzas affect the rhythm of the poem? What happens to the poem if stanzas are combined?

9. Robert Duncan's poem is an example of "projective verse," as it emphasizes the kinetic energy of words on the page. Take one of the poems you have written in stanzaic form and re-line it according to the notion of projective verse. What happens to your poem? Find more examples of poems written according to the concept of projective verse.

10. Based on your experience in reading and writing stanzas, write an opinion piece examining which stanzaic form you prefer and why.

ARCHITECTURE
Five-Day Lesson Plan

Day 1   The teacher brings in poems that consist of one stanza but are of different lengths. Have students read the shortest poem. What advantages or disadvantages does the single unit present in the poem? What was it like having read the poem as one unit? Repeat this process with the other single stanza poems, moving toward the longest one.

Days 2 & 3

Show students different stanza forms (couplet, tristich, quatrain, longer stanza, and variable stanza) from a sampling of poems from different eras. Have students do a comparison of these different forms based on "What if ... " questions. For example, what if the couplet poem became a quatrain poem? Ask student what difference the change makes. Proceed through a series of "what if ... " questions with various stanza forms. Remember that any change in stanza is a change of the poem's expression.

Day 4   Ask students to take a poem that they have written from their poetry notebook and rewrite it by changing its architecture but not its words. Ask students to answer the following questions: How does this exercise change the poem? Which stanzaic form do you prefer for the poem?

Day 5   Have students present their two versions of the poem from Day 4 and speak to the architectural differences.

Beyond the Week

Students write in their poetry notebook examples of various stanzaic poems based on reading outside the classroom.

ARCHITECTURE
Bibliography

Poems

"At the Ball Game" by William Carlos Williams from *Selected Poems*, New Directions, 1969; "Psalm and Lament" by Donald Justice from *The Sunset Maker*, Alfred A. Knopf, 1987; "Almost Blue" by Mark Doty from *My Alexandria*, University of Illinois Press, 1993; "Notes Toward a Supreme Fiction" by Wallace Stevens from *The Palm at the End of the Mind*, Alfred A. Knopf, 1971; "The Pink Locust" by William Carlos Williams from *Pictures from Brueghel and other poems*, New Directions, 1962; "Lester Leaps In" by Al Young from *Heaven: Collected Poems 1956–1990*, Creative Arts Book Company, 1992; "B Negative" by X. J. Kennedy from *Nude Descending a Staircase*, Carnegie Mellon University Press, 1994; "The Walgh-Vogel" by Richard Wilbur from *New and Collected Poems*, Harcourt Brace, 1988; "Stone and Flower" by Kenneth Rexroth from *The Collected Shorter Poems*, New Directions, 1966; " 'Lear is Gay' " by Robert Hayden from *Collected Poems*, Liveright Publishing, 1985; "Jerónimo's House" by Elizabeth Bishop from *Collected Poems*, Farrar Straus Giroux, 1983; "A Set of Romantic Hymns" by Robert Duncan from *Roots and Branches*, New Directions, 1964.

Strong Measures: Contemporary American Poetry in Traditional Forms, edited by Philip Dacey and David Jauss, Harper & Row, 1986.

Prose

"The Way to Say Pleasure" by Donald Hall in *Poetry and Ambition*, University of Michigan Press, 1988. For a discussion of the verse paragraph consult the redoubtable *Historical Manual of English Prosody* by George Saintsbury, first published in 1910.

11

Form
(Sonnets, Sestinas, etc.)

Summary

A poetic form is an ordained pattern. It can be very modest: There are numerous poems consisting of one couplet. It can be quite formidable: The chant royal, a French form, is sixty lines long and turns on a mere five rhymes. Form, for the poet, is a further exaction beyond the exactions of syntax, rhythm, sound, grammar, and word choice. The precision of form fascinates and that no doubt is part of the reason why poets continue to write sonnets and villanelles and sestinas and odes and ballades. A form is explicitly a bequest from the past and to write in form is to acknowledge a tie with countless others who gladly have accepted the rules that define how a certain sort of poem must be constructed. To put one's own imprint on a form is a great challenge. The goad of form may elicit imaginings on the poet's part that otherwise never would have occurred.

A meter is a rhythmic pattern; a stanza is a unit (sometimes rhymed) of a particular number of lines. Both are instances of form in the sense that the poem that incorporates meter and stanza is shaped according to some specific dictates. Many poems are written in form in a more overall sense: The poem as a whole has a specific pattern. Human ingenuity knows no bounds as to poetic form: English-language poetry possesses, for instance, forms that are (among other lengths) five lines long, fourteen lines, nineteen lines, thirty lines; forms that repeat end words; forms that repeat whole lines; forms that

181

count accents or syllables; forms that interlock rhymed stanzas. The list goes on and on.... (See the bibliography at the end of this chapter for some books about form.) (1)

Before detailing some representative forms, it seems wise to ask the question, Why would anyone do this? Why—to choose the Petrarchan sonnet—would someone write a fourteen-line poem of five weak/strong units to the line that rhymes in a specified fashion? What advantage is to be gained in subjecting oneself to such tight rules? What if the poem seems to want to be fifteen or thirteen lines long? Is it any less of a poem? Why bother in the first place?

Prior to the twentieth century, poetry (excepting the likes of Walt Whitman) was considered to be synonymous with form. Poems were ballads and sonnets and odes and songs and blank verse narratives among other forms. Form was esteemed because form forces the poet to try to make something shapely, carefully put together, and ordained by custom. To work within a pattern is at once reassuring—one has seen it before—and a challenge—what new wrinkle will the poet bring to it? Writing in form is hard work; sonnets don't tend to write themselves before breakfast. As the scholar Mark Richardson notes in reference to Robert Frost and William Shakespeare: " ... the control over fortune extravagantly promised on behalf of poetry in the sonnets [Shakespeare's] is of course impossible. In Frost's view this is no disgrace: the forms of poetry almost always outlast anyone's ability to master them." At the least, an acquaintance with form is humbling.

Indeed, the poet who uses form discovers that there is a lot of resistance on the part of the form: it is what it is. It is precisely this resistance that poets who write in form cherish. The form makes them look for words to fit the form and it makes them try to adapt the form to their particular expressive ends. This is difficult but often exhilarating work, as the poet is responding to the various demands the form imposes. It needs to be said, however, that writing in form is not a virtue in and of itself. There are countless mediocre sonnets where the poet has fulfilled the requirements of the form and said, "Done." How much sense the sonnet makes or how trite its sentiments may be is beside the point for such a poet. In such cases the form rather than the poet has won the struggle.

The complaints against form that the twentieth century has made over and over again are perfectly valid ones. Forms that were set hundreds of years ago may seem to have outlived their aesthetic lives: What could be done with them has been done. Forms easily become tiresome as they force poems into preset grooves. As far as modernism has been concerned, art that doesn't set itself new tasks isn't art. The avatars of twentieth-century English-language poetry—T. S. Eliot, Ezra Pound, William Carlos Williams—were all questioners of established forms. By the end of the century, much American poetry, in particular, favored a free verse that was notable for its line-by-line, improvisatory openness and its indifference to set forms. (2)

Certainly, forms are not for every occasion or even for most. Each form tends to enforce a certain logic: A sonnet, for instance, is good for making or arguing a point. It may not be the right choice for casually relating the various things that happened in school yesterday. A great deal of contemporary poetry wishes to attest to the emotional resonance of feelings and events; it has no interest in arguing points but seeks to let moments and images and places speak for themselves. Form, as it is tightly woven, promotes memorableness, but it may do so at the cost of undervaluing and undermining what the poet is writing about. Hence the prevalent, modern-day distrust of form. It is important, however, to remember that form was never intended to be a steamroller or straitjacket. Form is more like a stimulating game; its artifice is meant to encourage spontaneity—not to discourage it. (3)

The sonnet (to choose the best-known example of overall form) has a long pedigree that has been traced to Sicily in the thirteenth century. English poets eagerly took up the sonnet (*sonet* in old Provencal, a song or air) in the sixteenth century. It's easy to see why; for a society that valued the expressiveness of rhetoric the sonnet was bliss. The poet could enumerate or analyze or plead his or her feelings in a consistently imperative manner. The sonnet was a little stage: poets had fourteen lines to make their points and then their time was up. The rhetoric that every schoolboy learned taught persuasion: how to write appropriately, forcefully, and clearly. The sonnet reveled in persuasion. The very structure of the Petrarchan sonnet (named for Francesco Petrarch, 1304–1374) lent itself to such persuading: in the first eight lines (the octave) the poet stated a dilemma and in the concluding six lines (the sestet) the poet solved it. Argument and poetry could both be satisfied.

Sir Philip Sidney was a well-known Elizabethan sonneteer and his "Sonnet #72" from *Astrophel and Stella* indicates how well the sonnet was suited to the purposes of rhetoric:

> Desire, though thou my old companion art,
> And oft so clings to my pure love that I
> One from the other scarcely can descry,
> While each doth blow the fire of my heart,
> Now from thy fellowship I needs must part;
> Venus is taught with Dian's wings to fly;
> I must no more in thy sweet passions lie;
> Virtue's gold must head my Cupid's dart.
> Service and honor, wonder with delight,
> Fear to offend, will worthy to appear,
> Care shining in mine eyes, faith in my sprite—
> These things are left me by my only dear.
> > But thou, desire, because thou wouldst have all,
> > Now banished art; but yet, alas, how shall?

The notion of using a sonnet to address a feeling may seem somewhat forced but it is hard to argue with the admirable structure it provides Sidney. He is able to lay out the rather tricky situation in which he finds himself, then to make a resolution (sonnet writers were wild about making resolutions) buttressed by examples of how he should behave, and finally to end with a disturbing yet delicious doubt. Is desire this easily gotten rid of? Don't, as we say over four hundred years later, bet the farm on it. The sonnet form was made for "but" and "yet," as the poet considers one side of an issue only to be immediately assailed by the other side. Since a lot of our feelings tend to be mixed, one can understand the long life the sonnet has had.

Sidney's sonnet is Petrarchan but Shakespeare wrote sonnets that consisted of three quatrains and a concluding couplet. Shakespeare's "Sonnet #75" is not a peak of his art but it is a very representative hill.

The form of the poem has come to be called the Shakespearean or English sonnet:

> So are you to my thoughts as food to life,
> Or as sweet-seasoned showers are to the ground;
> And for the peace of you I hold such strife
> As 'twixt a miser and his wealth is found;
> Now proud as an enjoyer, and anon
> Doubting the filching age will steal his treasure;
> Now counting best to be with you alone,
> Then bettered that the world may see my pleasure;
> Sometime all full with feasting on your sight,
> And by and by clean starved for a look;
> Possessing or pursuing no delight
> Save what is had or must from you be took.
>> Thus do I pine and surfeit day by day,
>> Or gluttoning on all, or all away.

The very first word of the sonnet speaks to the mainspring of the poem's logic. It initiates a structure of comparisons that carries the reader to a thorough understanding of the impossibility of the lover's position. The rhetorical signposts—"Now," "Now, " "Sometime"—move the poem along briskly. The concluding couplet begins with one of the most conclusive connectives, "Thus," the work of the sonnet being, after all, to argue and prove a case. The rhymes and meter contribute to the pace while assonance (the "ou" sound, for instance) and repetition ("all") create a web of sound. Shakespeare's sonnet is representative as it consciously values articulation—elaboration, comparison, vivid description—as a good in itself. It is a spirited example of how poetry can reason and feel at the same time. (4)

Over centuries the sonnet has prospered and waned according to what sort of art poets were looking for. The eighteenth century, relishing as it did the concise power of the couplet, did not especially favor the sonnet. The Romantic poets of the early nineteenth century, however, eagerly took up the sonnet, at once to further tradition by declaring their link to the likes of Shakespeare and to make their own distinctive claims upon the form. John Keats, who was never a poet to shirk a challenge, sought in "Bright Star" to meet Shakespeare on his own ground:

> Bright star, would I were steadfast as thou art—
>   Not in lone splendour hung aloft the night
> And watching, with eternal lids apart,
>   Like nature's patient, sleepless Eremite,
> The moving waters at their priestlike task
>   Of pure ablution round earth's human shores,
> Or gazing on the new soft fallen mask
>   Of snow upon the mountains and the moors—
> No—yet still steadfast, still unchangeable,
>   Pillow'd upon my fair love's ripening breast,
> To feel for ever its soft fall and swell,
>   Awake for ever in a sweet unrest,
> Still, still to hear her tender-taken breath,
> And so live ever—or else swoon to death.

Keats follows a common rhetorical path in the first part of the poem. He makes a conditional statement in the first line and then offers an extensive negative definition—in this case, describing a star. He reiterates at the beginning of the ninth line that he is not that star in the sky yet possesses star-like qualities. The shift in the tenth line makes the reader appreciate the long description that was the first part of the poem, for the contrast could not be more emphatic between the "lone," distant, detached star and the poet and his love. The poet stays with the personal definition of steadfastness only to snap it with the dramatic caesura in the final line. That break is not Shakespearean; it is Romantic in the sense we commonly use the word—the affirmation of feeling for the sake of feeling. Shakespeare's conclusion in "Sonnet #75" fulfills the terms of the argument—this or that or that—but Keats chooses to make a nakedly emotional point. Within the logic of the sonnet (in this case a sort of debate—"would I," "Not," "No," "or else") Keats treasures personal avowal. He reprises the sonnet tradition—the Shakespearean sonnet pivots precisely at the beginning of the third quatrain which corresponds to the beginning of the sestet in the Petrarchan form—but adapts it to his own ends. The echo of the poem's last words is strong: The sonnet was known in the nineteenth century as "The Last Sonnet" for its having been written and revised late in Keats's brief life. (5)

Keats created a fairly elaborate poem from the single sensation of laying his head on his beloved's breast. Another Romantic poet, Percy Bysshe Shelley, used the sonnet for very different purposes: hortatory, political ones. Here is Shelley's "Sonnet: England in 1819":

An old, mad, blind, despised, and dying king,—
Princes, the dregs of their dull race, who flow
Through public scorn,—mud from a muddy spring,—
Rulers who neither see, nor feel, nor know,
But leech-like to their fainting country cling,
Till they drop, blind in blood, without a blow,—
A people starved and stabbed in the untilled field,—
An army, which liberticide and prey
Makes as a two-edged sword to all who wield—
Golden and sanguine laws which tempt and slay;
Religion Christless, Godless—a book sealed;
A Senate,—Time's worst statute unrepealed,—
Are graves from which a glorious Phantom may
Burst, to illumine our tempestuous day.

Shelley exults in the power of the sonnet to structure a description. He builds and builds and the reader wonders, "To what end? Where is the verb?" The fact that the verb turns out to be the modest "Are" at the beginning of the thirteenth line is part of the poem's genius, for it throws "graves" (an accented syllable unlike "Are") into very sharp relief. Similarly, Shelley's liberties with the rhyme scheme—*ababbacdcdccdd*—reverse the Petrarchan form so that the sestet comes before the octave. Again, this throws the reader a bit off balance as Shelley seeks to make his traditional form query its presuppositions. The clamor of the dashes is tempestuous in its own right: One imagines an orator flinging an emphatic arm out at the end of many lines. Like Keats, Shelley relishes the drama inherent in the sonnet form; as he elaborates nouns but withholds a verb, Shelley creates suspense. The concluding couplet is an ultimate one as it defines the preceding twelve lines. The rhetorical impulse of the sonnet has been harnessed to radical purposes. There is nothing awkward in the fit; rhetoric is indifferent to parties. The poem was deemed much too strong to be published in his lifetime. (6)

Shelley's radical overview makes an important point about the nature of form. It would be a mistake to think that somehow writing in form is tantamount to conservatism of any stripe. Tradition is malleable; if it isn't, it dies. Ideally, the presence of formal dictates acts as a spur to the imagination, not a clog. The concision of form can hone all manner of sentiments. The poet Marilyn Hacker—to cite a contemporary poet—has imbued the sonnet with a chatty, almost finger-popping verve:

> Friend (this is an imaginary letter
> to someone I don't know), out of the hewn-
> rock mountains, with the muddy morning rain
> raising steam on spring pools (but a scatter
> of snow fields on the peaks), the train descends
> to prairies looking shabby under storm
> blankets. I am eating bread and cheese
> to stretch two dollars out over three days.
> (Vancouver was extravagant.) I'm warm
> jackknifed under my fur. The train's growl blends
> with night sounds of old men, babies, a plains-
> woman's beery laugh. Legs cramped, I go
> to sleep, rocked by a Cree kid's radio
> wailing blues' soul solace on the night train.

Hacker deploys a different rhyme scheme but the taut scope of the sonnet remains. The rhythm is the basic, weak/strong line that works firmly yet unobtrusively, as one observation steadily yields to another.

Parentheses, constant enjambment, end words split between lines ("hewn-rock," "plains-woman's"), variety of sentence lengths: all go to make the sonnet a more informal place where the author and other people live without calling rhetorical attention to themselves. Hacker's sonnet has the feeling of a snapshot, a vignette, a journal entry. It is a testimony to her art that she breathes so much down-to-earth life in a centuries-old form. By re-imagining what could be done with the form, she rebuts any strictures about the sonnet being hopelessly out-of-date. (7)

Just as the English language has assimilated so many words from other languages, so English-language poetry has adapted a remarkable variety of forms to its practice. A look at a volume such as Lewis Turco's *The Book of Forms* reveals forms from the French, Arabic, Welsh, Irish, Malayan, Greek, Spanish, Italian, Portuguese, and Japanese. Some are astonishingly complex; others, such as the cinquain, an unrhymed, syllabic, five-line form, are quite simple. How the poet adapts her or his emotional motivation to a particular form is in many ways a mystery. Sometimes the poet knows at the outset that the poem wants to be in a certain form; at other times, the formal intent emerges during the writing process. In any case the characteristics of various forms are identifiable. The French villanelle, for instance, has nineteen lines divided into five triplets and one quatrain. Two rhymes are used throughout the nineteen lines and certain lines are repeated in their entirety: thus line one, for instance, reappears as lines six, twelve, and eighteen. The villanelle, as it sticks to two rhymes and keeps repeating lines, is well-suited to conveying obsessions. Whether the obsessive quality is light or dark in tone depends, of course, on the poet. (8) A number of late-nineteenth-century English poets were fond of the villanelle as a playful token of infatuation. Here is Ernest Dowson's "Villanelle of His Lady's Treasures":

> I took her dainty eyes, as well
>   As silken tendrils of her hair:
> And so I made a Villanelle!

I took her voice, a silver bell,
　As clear as song, as soft as prayer;
I took her dainty eyes as well.

It may be, said I, who can tell,
　These things shall be my less despair?
And so I made a Villanelle!

I took her whiteness virginal
　And from her cheek two roses rare:
I took her dainty eyes as well.

I said: "It may be possible
　Her image from my heart to tear!"
And so I made a Villanelle.

I stole her laugh, most musical;
　I wrought it in with artful care;
I took her dainty eyes as well;
And so I made a Villanelle.

A contemporary poet, Baron Wormser, has used the same form to very different ends. For Wormser the obsessive quality of the villanelle is a way of making the reader experience an obsessive behavior that ends in suicide. "A Later Death" tells the story of a woman who becomes obsessed with the horror of the Holocaust. Just as the Holocaust will not leave her consciousness, so the villanelle returns and returns:

She'd been depressed, is what the papers said.
In her photo she gazes out, pretty and pert.
It's hard to imagine her being dead,
Much less her killing herself. One who'd been bred
For other things, there seemed in her no home for hurt.
She'd been depressed, is what the papers said.
Her mother believed it came from what she'd read
About the Jews. She'd become strangely alert—

It's hard to imagine her being dead—
To the slightest things. Those Jews and their deaths spread
A net over her, their torment was her shirt.
She'd been depressed, is what the papers said:
She wished to lie down in the Jews' ruined bed,
She wished to touch their flesh that had turned to dirt.
It's hard to imagine her being dead
Who for so long had been a stranger to dread
And care. Like history she grew pale and curt.
She'd been depressed, is what the papers said.
It's hard to imagine her being dead.

For sheer intricacy the sestina form seems to have taken pride of place in contemporary poetry. Also a French form, the sestina consists of six sestets and a triplet, which is called the envoi. The enormous challenge the sestina poses to the poet is that the six end-words of the first stanza are reused in a particular order as end-words of the other stanzas. In the concluding triplet, one end-word is embedded in each line while another end-word concludes each line. The sestina thus makes a great, recurrent to-do about a handful of words. The effect of a sestina is something like that of a Ferris wheel: One moves in a circuit and keeps seeing the same sights from slightly different vantage points. Sustaining this movement requires a good deal of artfulness. Here is Christopher Jane Corkery's sestina entitled "The Song":

Late one night they make a baby.
It's fall and nobody cares about birth.
The men with briefcases on the train
read about trenches as they go rocking.
Yet nobody really mentions death,
and the night is far too wet for flame.

It never takes an obvious flame
to make the seed that becomes a baby.
And babies don't give a hoot about death.
They can't even say the word for birth.

All they want is sucking and rocking,
a breast, or a lap, or a choo-choo train.

No matter how hard, you can't stop the train
that hurtles out of the tunnel where flame
and blind desire are the start of that rocking,
those long dark lunges that push out the baby
to lights and the grinning faces of birth.
But the baby can't tell it a bit from death.

No one goes through that fast dark death,
that slamming, tunneling, slippery train,
with any intention, no knowledge of birthday cakes or snappers or pink candle flame.
All that lights up the mind of the baby
is dreams of the dark where water was rocking.

Soon baby in mother's arms goes rocking,
forgets every little thing about death.
And she sings to it, *Lullaby little baby,*
I'll get you a bright blue wooden train
and a white little sheep, and the candle flame
on your cake will show, each year, that your birth

was the grandest, most magnificent birth!
And on your sixth we'll give you a rocking-
horse with a saddle the color of flame.
And there won't be any time for death,
and later there'll be an electric train
(which would be too much for a little baby).

So love's hard flame is the only death
she sings, and it's just like birth, the rocking,
the shoot's green train, the blossom, the baby.

The sestina as it insists on certain words creates a world unto itself. This suits Corkery's enterprise perfectly, for the new baby is a world unto itself. The child is also born into a world beyond "birth" and "baby," where all sorts of things exist—some quite practical such as "train," some elemental such as "flame" and "death." There are also actions in that world, for instance, "rocking." The words define the baby's world but they do so in a kaleidoscopic fashion. The words literally keep moving. Almost more than any other form, a sestina, as it embodies changes, resists summary. To make the narrative line of a sestina intelligible and compelling rather than obscure and arbitrary takes great resourcefulness on the part of the poet. A sestina invites tangents—what do these words have to do with one another?—while it must resist going off on tangents that have little to do with the poem's concerns. One way of keeping a sestina focused yet fresh is to use the end-words in different senses. Corkery thus uses "rocking" as a simple noun, a compound noun, and a verb. The reader cannot assume how the final words will be used and this degree of uncertainty is part of a sestina's pleasure: The words will be there but how they are used is pure poetic prestidigitation.

Form need not be quite so exacting. The limerick, for instance, is a five-line form, that can be improvised on the spot. It is a determinedly inelegant form as it insists on a rollicking rhythm, groan-eliciting puns, and doggerel rhymes. It is thus well-adapted to mirth about sexual issues. For some people the mere mention of the word brings a knowing smile to their limerick-spouting lips (9):

> Two lovers worked up their nerve
> While learning irregular verbs.
>   Is it "lie" or "lay?"
>   Who cares any way
> As long as you do it with verve.

The limerick, of course, does not have to be about sex. A look on the Internet reveals limerick competitions about everything from extra-terrestrials to dieting. The joy of the limerick lies in its ability to concisely and wittily present any issue:

The question we ask every night
As we stare at the vast starry light:
    Are there other beings
    Who go in for seeing
Or are we the only with sight?

Although determinedly inelegant, the limerick is, nonetheless, very much a form. The qualities of form—fidelity, concentration, respect for tradition—apply as much to the limerick as to the sestina and sonnet. Form insists on the creation of a world unto itself. Given its remarkable accomplishments over centuries, it would be unwise to throw that insistence away.

FORM
In the Classroom

1. After you familiarize yourself with different forms (from a book such as Turco's), look at poems by writers from the seventeenth, eighteenth, and nineteenth centuries and see how many specific forms you can identify.

2. Read about the origins of modernism (see chapter bibliography). To what degree do you sympathize with modernism's attitudes? Why?

3. Although established forms have taken something of a back seat in twentieth-century poetry, one of the greatest of formalists is very much a twentieth-century poet—W. H. Auden. Auden loved the challenges that different forms presented. Choose one poem by him in a recognizable form and decide for yourself how well he meets the form's requirements.

4. The Elizabethan era was sonnet-crazy. Read sonnets by some Elizabethan poets other than Shakespeare, such as Philip Sidney, Edmund Spenser, and Samuel Daniel. What individual differences do you note among the poets or do the sonnets—even though various poets wrote them—seem the same to you?

5. Keats reprised other forms such as the ode. Read about the ode as a form, then read some of Keats's odes. What qualities distinguish them? What words would you use to characterize the ode form?

6. Shelley was another Romantic master of form. He made particular use of the Italian terza rima form as in his "Ode to the West Wind." Read about this form and then describe the effect that the interlocking form of Shelley's poem has on you. Again, what sorts of words would you use to describe the form?

7. Recent decades have seen an interest in writing in forms, as attested to by the anthology *Rebel Angels* (see chapter bibliography) that focuses on neo-formalist poets. Find a poem in that book that you enjoy and explain to what degree form is a factor in the poem.

8. The repetitive quality of the villanelle can hit a broad emotional range of unrelenting notes. Find examples of contemporary villanelles and compare their subjects and tones.

9. Writing in forms is an earnest undertaking but the limerick is not. Write a limerick of your own. When you try a more advanced form such as a sonnet or villanelle, give yourself time to write a number of drafts. Whether you finish the poem to your satisfaction or not, the experience of working at a form is bound to be an engaging one. As regards form, there is nothing like a direct encounter.

FORM
Five-Day Lesson Plan

Days 1 to 5

Have students choose a poetic form such as the villanelle, sonnet, sestina. Use the entire week for students to:
• Research the history of their form;
• Find examples of the form;
• Begin drafting a poem in this form.

Students can pool their research on various poetic forms to create display visuals for the classroom such as a time-line of forms and posters displaying examples of these forms.

Beyond the Week

Have the students report to the class about the form and present their favorite example to the class.

FORM
Bibliography

Poems

XIV of "Separations" by Marilyn Hacker from *Selected Poems 1965–1990*, W. W. Norton, 1994; "A Later Death" by Baron Wormser from *The White Words*, Houghton Mifflin, 1983; "The Song" by Christopher Jane Corkery from *Blessing*, Princeton University Press, 1985. For a deft collection of limericks by a talented poet see Conrad Aiken's *A Seizure of Limericks*, Henry Holt, 1964. *Rebel Angels: 25 Poets of the New Formalism*, edited by Mark Jarman and David Mason, Story Line Press, 1996, and *A Formal Feeling Comes: Poems in Form by 60 Contemporary Women Poets*, edited by Annie Finch, Story Line Press, 1994.

Prose

The New Book of Forms by Lewis Turco, University Press of New England, 1986; *The Teachers and Writers Handbook of Poetic Forms*, edited by Ron Padgett, Teachers & Writers Collaborative, 1987; *Patterns of Poetry* by Miller Williams, Louisiana State University Press, 1986. *The Ordeal of Robert Frost* by Mark Richardson, University of Illinois Press, 1997.

Three On the Tower: The Lives and Works of Ezra Pound, T. S. Eliot, and William Carlos Williams by Louis Simpson, William Morrow, 1975; *A History of Modern Poetry: Modernism and After* by David Perkins, Belknap Press of Harvard University Press, 1987.

12

Tone and Lyric

Summary

Tone is the emotional fingerprint of a poem. Because it is every-where in the poem, we cannot say that one aspect or another defines the tone. Tone is the result of all the artistic choices about words, sounds, rhythm, syntax, and line, plus the emotional point of view of the poem. How close the poet is to her or his subject (or how ambivalent or anxious or distant) dictates a great deal about what the poem's tone will be like. The lyric tone is unfettered feeling, the soul's outpouring, be it of desire or ardor or regret. It is a pure tone; although life being what it is, the lyric inclination is often alloyed with complicating and conflicting feelings. The course of love, for instance, may not run true. When we make a judgment about tone, we are making a judgment about truthfulness: Is the poet at one with her or his material or is there some disjunction that makes the poem less than convincing?

Many of us may remember from childhood when we said something sassy or sarcastic to a parent and were told that our parent did not like our tone. That word "tone" was usually not a word heard often. Life went by—we played, pouted, exclaimed, ate, babbled—and did not think much about the tone of our experiences. When we look back, however, it is not hard to note that different feelings and experiences had distinctly different tones. Going to Susie Gilbert's birthday party where Mrs. Gilbert asked you every 4 minutes if you were having a good time was not the same thing as going to Sally Mosher's birthday party where Mrs. Mosher put out more food and soda than possibly could be consumed and then said she had to go shopping for a couple of hours and to have a good time. Those two parties had very different tones.

Just like those parties or those confrontations with a parent, poems can be characterized by their tones. Many factors create tone—word choices, rhythm, the occasion that calls the poem into being—but the most crucial factor is a very hard one to define: the degree of feeling the poem demonstrates. Why tone matters and why we are pursuing it in this chapter is that tone is the emotional fingerprint of a poem and how compelling we feel that tone is has a lot to do with whether we read a poem or not. What compels is communicated feeling. The range of feelings in poems is close to infinite but if the tone feels false or flat or merely clever, the poem is not going to compel us.

Tone may be a matter of one pure note or it may be a medley of notes. Some occasions, after all, are very focused; others are decidedly mixed. Poems in which one feeling dominates tend to be poems with definite tasks. They mourn or celebrate or try to cajole or console. Section 50 from Alfred, Lord Tennyson's *In Memoriam* is such a poem as Tennyson addresses the spirit of his dead friend, Arthur Hallam:

> Be near me when my light is low,
>> When the blood creeps, and the nerves prick
>> And tingle; and the heart is sick,
> And all the wheels of Being slow.
>
> Be near me when the sensuous frame
>> Is rack'd with pangs that conquer trust;
>> And Time, a maniac scattering dust,
> And Life, a Fury slinging flame.
>
> Be near me when my faith is dry,
>> And men the flies of latter spring,
>> That lay their eggs, and sting and sing
> And weave their pretty cells and die.

Be near me when I fade away,
　　To point the term of human strife,
　　And on the low dark verge of life
The twilight of eternal day.

The poem pleads for help and pursues its goal unswervingly. Repetition enforces the poet's sense of need as he returns to his supplication at the beginning of each stanza. Tennyson knows he requires the help of Hallam's spirit for he faces terrible obstacles: the drying up of his faith, fear of mortality, the oblivion of time. The fierceness of the language—"a maniac scattering dust"—convinces us of the ordeals Tennyson must deal with. It is an affecting poem because its tone is so direct and honest. It confesses vulnerability without shame; Tennyson feels the loss of his friend to the core of his being and the tone of the poem—humble yet emphatic—testifies to that feeling. (1)

Tennyson's poem makes public a private loss. As a book-length poem *In Memoriam* registers an extraordinary range of tones as it moves from dazed grief to doubt to religious acceptance. Different tasks dictate different tones yet the poem's emotional foundation does not waver. Hayden Carruth's *The Sleeping Beauty* is a contemporary, book-length poem that is comparable to Tennyson's in many ways. It too comprises a series of poems that vary one form: Carruth writes variously rhyming, fifteen-line poems whereas Tennyson wrote poems of different lengths in the same quatrain form of *abba*. Similarly, Carruth's poem also registers many dominant tones. *The Sleeping Beauty* tells the story of Rose in the Thorn, the Sleeping Beauty, who is a woman named Rose Marie Dorn who lived in the real world ("alive exactly when the Red Army came / To that crook of the Oder where she was born") and who is the spirit of femininity. Here are two sections, numbers 17 and 23:

Oaks and dark pines, remote, the northern forest.
What does the woman's face in the water mean?
Traces of snow. This the oldest, the purest,
Naiad alive in the stream,
Ophelia drowned in eternity. She nearest

And most distant, coldest, stillest, dearest.
Crystals gleam in the brown leaves
Without sunlight. Mythological lives
Exist in dreams. Leaves twist and turn in the current,
Drift over the face and on.
Passage and change obscuring the eternal moment.
The feminine in a face of stone
Unchanged, there in cold water, the face of sleep.
Wind in the pines. Dream sound. Snow. Alone.
Woman. Forever. Water. Watching. Deep.

"Good-bye," they always whisper, "oh God," clinging—
And he walks down the steps in early lilac light
And she drives off in her Volkswagen
Into the snow-curtained street
And he turns and raises his hand by the elevator
And she clings sobbing and desperate at the stone gate
And he looks back in the autumn haze
From a distance under the yellow trees
And she finds his dear stinking pipe left on the bookcase
And he writes a letter
Ten pages long and tears it up and mails a postcard
And "Good-bye."
                    "Good-bye."
                              "Good-bye."
                                        Never
Shall they meet again.
                    Good-bye whispered, murmured,
                                                  furled
In the creative wind,
                    incredible cosmic command
                                        to sever,
Disjoin, separate, break—
                    death in the world.

How does Carruth create two such distinct tones? In the first canto (i.e., a principal division of a long poem) we have cited, he uses phrases and eschews verbs. This creates a literal stillness as not much occurs: The poem is focused on the mystery of the woman's face in the water. There is a halting quality to the poem as regards lineation. A number of lines run on and stop in the middle of the following line. This creates an almost lurching, ruminating tone that the final two lines with their many one-word sentences epitomize. There is no give in the poem: It feels cold and clear. In its facing a conundrum, it is precise and careful.

The other canto is also all-of-a-piece tonally but it registers a very different tone. Lovers fall out of love and the poem conjures up the reality of what that means. Here Carruth uses a long, run-on sentence to register a sense of how many variations there are on the theme of separation. Whereas the tone of the first canto is downright witchy, the second may be called truly melancholy. The anguish of the last lines is unmistakable as Carruth uses four verbs to make his emotional point. The repetition of the good-byes and the italicized echo of fairy tale language makes the terribly sad tone of the poem's ending credible. Both cantos especially use syntax and rhythm to register pure, strong feeling. (2)

In terms of tone, the topic of love presents the poet with perhaps the greatest range of possibilities. So many things can happen in love—falling in (and out) of love, unrequited love, jealousy, infatuation, ecstasy, longing—and love is as much a verbal field as it is an emotional and physical one. We speak our loves, we seek to persuade, and we insist. Again, the undiluted, single-minded tone matches a definite task. Robert Browning's "Meeting at Night" is a proclamation of love that is rendered not through declaration but descriptions:

> The grey sea and the long black land;
> And the yellow half-moon large and low;
> And the startled little waves that leap
> In fiery ringlets from their sleep,
> As I gain the cove with pushing prow,
> And quench its speed i' the slushy sand.

Then a mile of warm sea-scented beach;

Three fields to cross till a farm appears;

A tap at the pane, the quick sharp scratch

And blue spurt of a lighted match,

And a voice less loud, through its joys and fears,

Than the two hearts beating each to each!

The exclamation mark at the poem's end speaks for a world of feeling. The breathless tone of the poem works perfectly as we read eagerly along to learn what will happen (note how few punctuated caesuras there are and how the poem consists of only two sentences). The great vibrancy of the description, as it makes us see and hear, lets us experience what it takes ("a mile," "three fields to cross") to bring these lovers together. When the words "joys and fears" appear in the next-to-last line, they resound strongly because the poem has created such a vivid context. (3)

Although Browning's poem tells a story in its way and is thus a narrative, its tone—as that exclamation mark indicates—is lyric. It is the product of strong feeling and it gives off strong feelings. A lyric poem (derived from the Greek word for the lyre) is a short poem that especially manifests the pressure of emotion. The lyric tone is intense; even as it engages thought and action it never lets go of feeling. The lyric mode seeks to compel—not because it has a grand truth to impart or epic story to tell but because the poet has been moved and wants to communicate that. Tennyson, Carruth, and Browning illustrate how diverse lyrics can be in regards to language, yet similar as they register a tone of direct feeling. The lyric tone goes back to the ancient Greeks and Romans who in the eloquent words of W. R. Johnson (see chapter bibliography) created poetry "that made visible the invisible forms and rhythms of personality, that incarnated and affirmed the misery and beauty of the individual's existence in a world that delighted and terrified him [sic], that confessed the greatness of the soul's becoming under the sign of being."

The Elizabethans took up this lyric tone (which in many ways had slumbered during the Middle Ages) with great enthusiasm and set many lyrics to music as the Greeks once did. Even today at the dawn of a new century, if you ask anyone who has read more than a smattering of English poetry what typifies that poetry, a common response is the Elizabethan lyric that declares someone's love. The first stanza of John Dowland's "To His Love" is representative:

> Come away, come sweet Love,
> The golden morning breakes:
> All the earth, all the ayre,
> Of love and pleasure speakes.
> Teach thine armes then to embrace,
> And sweet Rosie lips to kisse:
> And mix our soules in mutuall blisse.
> Eyes were made for beauties grace,
> Viewing, ruing Loves long paine:
> Procur'd by beauties rude disdaine.

The import of the song is a very old one but the pleasure of the language remains considerable. As a lyric, its tone is unabashed and uncomplicated. Although simple in language and structure, it is quite a challenge to write such a lyric. Among other difficulties, poets often have reflected on how few words are available that rhyme with "love." One can only do so much with "glove" and "above." Finding language as fresh as our feelings is never easy. (4)

In a lyric one person is speaking to another as, for instance, a lover speaks to his or her lover. There is, as Johnson puts it, a "dialectic of I and You." The tone of the poem is anchored in the poem's sense of purpose and audience. (Recall that Carruth's poem is addressed to the Sleeping Beauty and Tennyson's is addressed to his deceased friend.) In the course of time, which is to say especially over the past 200 years, the tone of purposefulness has changed. What poets have had to face in the modern, industrialized, mass-society world is that the occasions for lyric are not as simple as they once seemed. The lyric tone is based on the humanist assumption that feelings are worth artfully declaring. The great Romantic poets such as Wordsworth and Keats passionately affirmed that worth but doubt crept in during the nineteenth century as human beings felt more and more dwarfed by their own creations. The twentieth century with its radical inhumanity of concentration camps, unbelievably destructive weapons, and genocides has turned that doubt, in some cases, into despair and self-mockery.

A poet from the nineteenth century, Matthew Arnold, and a poet from the twentieth, Sylvia Plath, may stand as examples of the fate of the lyric. Both were lyric poets in the pure sense that they were able to register feelings and perceptions with great sensitivity and vividness. Consider Arnold's well-known poem, "Dover Beach":

> The sea is calm to-night.
> The tide is full, the moon lies fair
> Upon the straits;—on the French coast the light
> Gleams and is gone; the cliffs of England stand;
> Glimmering and vast, out in the tranquil bay.
> Come to the window, sweet is the night-air!
> Only, from the long line of spray
> Where the sea meets the moon-blanched land,
> Listen! You hear the grating roar
> Of pebbles which the waves draw back, and fling,
> At their return, up the high strand,
> Begin, and cease, and then again begin,
> With tremulous cadence slow, and bring
> The eternal note of sadness in.
>
> Sophocles long ago
> Heard it on the Aegean, and it brought
> Into his mind the turbid ebb and flow
> Of human misery; we
> Find also in the sound a thought,
> Hearing it by this distant northern sea.

The Sea of Faith
Was once, too, at the full, and round earth's shore
Lay like the folds of a bright girdle furled.
But now I only hear
Its melancholy, long, withdrawing roar,
Retreating, to the breath
Of the night-wind, down the vast edges drear
And naked shingles of the world.

Ah, love, let us be true
To one another! For the world, which seems
To lie before us like a land of dreams,
So various, so beautiful, so new,
Hath really neither joy, nor love, nor light,
Nor certitude, nor peace, nor help for pain;
And we are here as on a darkling plain
Swept with confused alarms of struggle and flight,
Where ignorant armies clash by night.

This lyric is meditative in a particular way. At first the reader may think the poem is going to be a straightforward evocation of the beauty of nature. The exclamation mark at the end of the first stanza speaks to the rapturous tone of the descriptions. The lovely second stanza with its powerful descriptive and rhythmic presence—"Begin, and cease, and then again begin"—ends not with an exclamatory affirmation but an evocation of "The eternal note of sadness." Beyond the sheer feeling for the actuality of the scene, there is "in the sound a thought." That thought is a troubling, unhappy one of a world without faith that is abandoned to the "turbid ebb and flow / Of human misery."

From rapture Arnold has moved to pensiveness and melancholy. In the poem's final stanza he tries to rally his feelings as he begins with an exclamation. Still, the reader may wonder who this "love" is Arnold evokes. Certainly it is not a love of the sort Dowland was addressing.

Here the "love" seems more like a rabbit pulled out of a hat, for although Arnold has used the language of address—"Come" and "Listen"—the reader knows nothing of the one who is being addressed. The typical occasion of the lyric—someone addressing someone else—here feels more like Arnold talking to himself but trying to evoke another person so he doesn't feel so terribly isolated. We can sympathize with his intentions but feel that mere human sympathy and feeling are overwhelmed by the cosmic darkness of the poem's ending, which moves beyond sadness to real bleakness about human life. One wonders how many soldiers who fought in World War I had Arnold's final line in their heads. In any case, the poem, as it mixes tones, is "turbid" in its own way. This is Arnold's prerogative as an artist; "Dover Beach" is a memorable poem. For Arnold, who as a prime cultural figure of his epoch is a representative figure, the simple purposefulness and self-sufficiency of the lyric tone paled. "Dover Beach" explains why it paled. Lyric occasions did not die: People were still falling in love and grieving and relishing the first flowers of spring. The faith in the efficacy of lyric, however, was not what it once was. (5)

In Sylvia Plath's poetry, written approximately 100 years later, the tone of ruefulness and desolation has become harshly electrified. Whereas Arnold offered the hope of being "true / To one another" (however sketchily he imagined the person to whom he was speaking), Plath actively disparages others, as in the scarifying "Daddy," which trades on the horrors of Nazism to present her loathing. The hellishness Arnold evokes is still picturesque and poetic; the hellishness Plath evokes is truly hellish. People destroy one another and they destroy themselves. The awful history of the twentieth century is in her bones. She is willing to fling open unbearable doors. Her tone is fiercely pure:

> And the language obscene
>
> An engine, an engine
> Chuffing me off like a Jew.

Over the years many of our students have protested when we read Plath in class. What they say is very similar to what our mothers said when we were children: "I don't like her tone." Of course, Plath didn't write to be liked. For her, poetry is not about getting along in the world and honoring life's personal occasions; rather, it is about honesty. Plath mocks the modern world unrelentingly (see "The Applicant," for instance, which begins "First are you our sort of a person?") and she mocks herself. Humanist confidence in the validity and sanctity of the individual life is no match for a poem like "Lady Lazarus" where Plath revels in the annals of self-destruction and the hideous voyeurism of the spectacle-loving crowd, where "Dying / is an art, like everything else." (6) Perhaps what haunts the most about Plath is how, for all the violence, the gently lyric tone never leaves her. A poem such as "Sheep in Fog" ends with these lines:

> My bones hold a stillness, the far
> Fields melt my heart.
> They threaten
> To let me through to a heaven
> Starless and fatherless, a dark water.

The plight of the abandoned lyricist who feels beauty yet is too anguished to be helped has rarely been more strikingly evoked. The tone is heart-felt in the true sense of the word. To ask the question of a poem's tone is to ask the question of the poet's emotional engagement as it works into the poet's art. As readers, it is a question we should never be afraid to ask. It is our right to ask the poet, "Why this tone?" To ask less of poems is to sell short the achievement of a poet such as Plath who risked and accomplished so much. (7)

TONE & LYRIC
In the Classroom

1. *In Memoriam* bears comparison to *Birthday Letters* by Ted Hughes. Both books focus on a person who was close to the poet (Arthur Hallam and Sylvia Plath, respectively) and whose short life haunts the poet. Read some sections of Tennyson's poem and some poems in Hughes's book. How do the poems differ? Are there points of similarity? What tones do you feel are present in the poems?

2. Carruth's long poem is an astonishing feat of writing, as Carruth moves through so many tones within the single form of a fifteen-line poem. Choose several cantos from *The Sleeping Beauty* and note how Carruth constructs each one in terms of lines and rhymes. How in terms of construction do they differ from one another? Do the various constructions affect tone or are other factors more important? What are those factors and what distinct tones do you detect?

3. Robert Browning was one of the great communicators of strong feelings. He was especially fond of creating personae that narrate the poems. Read some of Browning's personae poems such as "My Last Duchess" and "Porphyria's Lover." Are the speakers convincing to you? How? Write a persona poem in which someone is talking about an "ex"—ex-husband, ex-wife, ex-boyfriend, or an ex-girlfriend.

4. Listen to some recordings of Elizabethan airs and madrigals; then listen to some recordings of lyricists such as Lorenz Hart and Cole Porter. They are all writing about love: What differences are there in tone between the Elizabethan and the modern approach to that topic? Do the modern lyricists use rhyme to the degree the Elizabethans do?

5. Beneath the cheerful aura of progress, the nineteenth century has many other tones. Read, for instance, some of the sonnets of the American poet, Frederick Goddard Tuckerman. What tone characterizes them?

6. The impact of Plath's last book, *Ariel*, has been enormous. Read that book and write a response about why you think the poems have had so much impact on so many people. Cite particular po-

ems and speak to the tones that are in Plath's work. What are her predominant tones? Are they convincing? Why?

7. Read some contemporary poems and consider their tones. Is there a distinct tone to each poem? Do the poems compel you? Again, why (or why not)?

TONE & LYRIC
Five-Day Lesson Plan

Days 1 to 3

Feelings are tones. Show students a range of love poems that display various feelings about love. Ask students what words in each poem help to define the poem's tone. Are there other factors at work in the poem that help to define its tone, such as syntax, rhythm, sound, and grammar?

The teacher should model an example of this process with the entire class, then break the class into groups to work on the same poem. Groups then report their findings to the class. Finally, students work individually on the remaining poems.

Days 4 & 5

Students begin drafting a love poem. (Remember to remind students that they do not have to write about themselves; they can write about someone else.) Ask students to think about what sort of tone they want to take toward love. It may be quite lyrical or it may reflect that pithy sentiment once voiced by the J. Geils Band—"Love Stinks."

Beyond the Week

Examine poems about other important feelings such as grief, loss, and friendship. Find at least three poems that show different tones about the same feeling.

TONE & LYRIC
Bibliography

Poems

The Sleeping Beauty by Hayden Carruth, Copper Canyon Press, 1990; "Daddy," "The Applicant," "Lady Lazarus," "Sheep in Fog" from *The Collected Poems* by Sylvia Plath, Harper & Row, 1981. *Birthday Letters* by Ted Hughes, Farrar Straus Giroux, 1998; *Complete Poems* by Frederick Goddard Tuckerman, Oxford University Press, 1965; *Ariel* by Sylvia Plath, Harper & Row, 1965.

Prose

The Idea of Lyric: Lyric Modes in Ancient and Modern Poetry by W. R. Johnson, University of California Press, 1982.

13

Repetition

Summary

Repetition is insistence: One time is not enough to achieve the effect the poet desires. What is beguiling about repetition is how many varieties such a straightforward action comes in. For instance, repetition may use whole stanzas, thereby drumming a refrain into the reader's or listener's mind. It may simply insist on a word and say it over and over. It may create a chant-like effect as the initial word or group of words in a line is repeated while the other words in the lines change. More subtly, repetition can be varied so that words appear and reappear in different combinations. Repetition mesmerizes; the challenge to the poet is to use it so it engages rather than dulls, entices rather than restates the obvious.

We repeat words for many reasons. Perhaps the simplest is sheer emphasis: "I want it, I want it, I want it" means that the person really wants it. Such emphasis speaks to how important something is to someone; it registers an emotional pulse. It is meant to compel by getting attention. The degree of repetition can move a statement from something unremarkable to something mesmerizing. The refrains that many ballads and blues feature have this mesmerizing quality. After each of the nineteen stanzas of "Greensleeves," a well-known ballad from the mid-sixteenth century, there is a refrain:

> Greensleeves was all my joy,
>> Greensleeves was my delight;

>Greensleeves was my heart of gold,
>>And who but Lady Greensleeves.

The refrain comforts, steadies, lulls, echoes, endures. It posits a degree of stillness as it insists on the unchanging nature of some words. The instrumental music that intertwines with the words removes any tedium from the repetition, for we do not tire of a good melody. Reading a refrain 19 times is a chore, whereas listening to the sung ballad is a pleasure. (1)

The refrain functions as a totality, a unit that is repeated over and over. Poems on the page use repetition in ways that are highly effective in their insistences but not so massive. Perhaps the best-known form of poetic repetition is anaphora. Whereas the Greek root of "metaphor" is "carrying over," the Greek root of "anaphora" is "carrying up and back." Anaphora thus repeats a word or words at the beginning of lines. Walt Whitman is celebrated for his passion for anaphora. On one hand, Whitman used anaphora in a poem such as "Song of Myself" as a sort of testifying glue. He was the man who was there and he anchors his perceptions in that fact:

>I hear bravuras of birds, bustle of growing wheat, gossip of
>>flames, clack of sticks cooking my meals,
>I hear the sound I love, the sound of the human voice,
>I hear all sounds running together, combined, fused or
>>following ...

On the other hand, Whitman reveled in what might be termed the uniformity of variety: many aspects of life that hearken to a simple, anaphoric construction. It may be as simple a repetition as "the" as in the same section (26) of "Song of Myself":

>The angry base of disjointed friendship, the faint tones of
>>the sick,
>The judge with hands tight to the desk, his pallid lips
>>pronouncing a death-sentence,
>The heave'e'yo of stevedores unloading ships by the wharves,
>>the refrain of the anchor-lifters,

The ring of alarm-bells, the cry of fire, the whirr of swiftly
    streaking engines and hose-carts with premonitory
    tinkles and color'd lights ...

Whitman loved making lists that spoke to the sheer volume and amplitude of being. The geography of the United States intoxicated him:

Chants of the prairies,
Chants of the long-running Mississippi, and down to the
    Mexican sea,
Chants of Ohio, Indiana, Illinois, Iowa, Wisconsin and
    Minnesota,
Chants going forth from the centre from Kansas ...

Amid the variety of the place names, the anaphora provides a steady-
ing effect. The lines do not spin out into that vast American space;
rather, they return to a subject. Anaphora unites. (2)

    We think of Whitman as a poet of expansiveness, and given the
look of his work—long, accumulating lines—and his feeling for the
open road, that is understandable. What shouldn't be forgotten and
what anaphora makes plain is how much Whitman is a poet of recur-
rence. He needs solid ground under his tramping feet and anaphora is
part of that ground. "When Lilacs Last in the Dooryard Bloom'd" explicitly evokes in its opening lines the fact that "I mourn'd, and yet
shall mourn with ever-returning spring." The implacable rootedness
of the seasons, of plants and birds and animals is a solace. Within the
poem anaphora sometimes works unabashedly to call attention to
feeling as in the second section:

O powerful western fallen star!
O shades of night—O moody, tearful night!
O great star disappear'd—O the black mask that hides the star!
O cruel hands that hold me powerless—O helpless soul of me!
O harsh surrounding cloud that will not free my soul.

At many other moments Whitman uses prepositions to firmly situate
the poem in a physical context:

> With many a pointed blossom rising delicate, with the
>   perfume strong I love,
> With every leaf a miracle ...

Or

> In the close of the day with its light and the fields of spring,
>   and the farmers preparing their crops,
> In the large unconscious scenery of my land with its lakes
>   and forests,
> In the heavenly aerial beauty ...

Whitman's huge imagination spoke to democratic actuality and democratic spirituality. America was not a utopian fantasy; it existed. Anaphora was a way for Whitman to insist upon that actuality. It moored his urgent, declaiming voice that shared his fellow Americans' love of oratory. What better way to proclaim the variety of America than by focusing through the repeated lens of the self, that "I" that is the same and yet changes constantly? The first-person, singular pronoun is the anaphora of each life: Whitman saluted it.

Whitman embodied anaphora; in many ways it was his poetic signature. For other poets anaphora has not been so much a way of life as a helpful device when the poet wants to make an unmistakable point. Langston Hughes does this in his poem about a young, African-American doctor, "Interne at Provident":

> White coats
> White aprons
> White dresses
> White shoes
> Pain and a learning
> To take away to Alabama.
> Practice on a State Street cancer,
> Practice on a stockyards rupture,
> Practice on the small appendix
> Of 26-girl at the corner ...

There is no avoiding the adjective and all it connotes at the outset of Hughes's poem. Its flat, unpunctuated relentlessness sets the scene for the doctor's trials. Actuality and cool irony mingle in the emphasis on the absence of color. Hughes turns soon after to another aspect of anaphora—physical repetition, doing something over and over. "Practice ... " "practice ... " "practice ... " There is no getting away from that word and the work it spells. In its way the poem makes the reader physically experience what it is like for the doctor. Repetition can be tedious—as the young doctor comes to know. Yet it is also necessary, for without the practice there cannot be a doctor. For Hughes repetition spoke to the core of the African-American blues tradition. (3) The blues' love of repetition testified to how African-Americans refused to have their experience explained away by know-nothing whites:

> Missus in de big house,
> Mammy in de yard.
> Missus holdin' her white hands,
> Mammy workin' hard,
> Mammy workin' hard,
> Mammy workin' hard,
> Missus holdin' her white hands,
> Mammy workin' hard.

The repetitions speak to a world of unacknowledged, endless labor. They honor it as they proclaim it. If, on one hand, repetition represents hopelessness, the same work again and again with no way out, it speaks on the other hand to the satisfaction of the truth: One woman works, one woman doesn't. (4)

A contemporary African-American poet, Cornelius Eady, has raised repetition to a vibrant and fine art. Here is his poem "The Dance":

> When the world ends,
> I will be in a red dress.
> When the world ends,

I will be in a smoky bar
   on Friday night.
When the world ends,
I will be a thought-cloud.
When the world ends,
I will be steam in a tea kettle.
When the world ends
I will be a sunbeam through
   a lead window,
And will shake like the
   semis on the interstate,
And I will shake like the tree
   kissed by lightning,
And I will move; the earth will move
   too,
And I will move; the cities will move
   too,
And I will move, with the remains of
   my last paycheck in my pocket.
It will be Friday night
And I will be in a red dress,
My feet relieved of duty,
My body in free-fall,
Loose as a ballerina
   in zero gravity,
Equal at last with feathers
   and dust,
As the world faints and tumbles
   down the stairs,
The jukebox is overtaken at last,
And the cicadas, under the eaves,
   warm up their legs.

The repetitions simmer with the energy of the dance. Envisioning how the world will end is a harrowing act of imagination; Eady makes it personal and plausible by creating a powerful momentum. He moves through three sets of repetitions before reaching the definition of that Friday night that ends the poem (and the world). At the beginning of the poem the repetitions are distinct and end-stopped. It's as if the dance were beginning; one insistence after another charges the air and the room. Once the dance begins, the sentences are long and propulsive: Their motion overwhelms. "The Dance" testifies to how poetry is foremost a physical presence and how that presence can be made vivid on the page. Remarkably, the poem manages to be down-home and apocalyptic at the same time; its rhythms and repetitions do not let the reader pause until the dance is over. (5)

We have focused thus far on anaphora, but poetry exhibits many other sorts of repetitions. The simplest is the repetition of a word or phrase. Emotionally such a repetition may tend to raise the temperature of a poem as when someone says "No, no, no" rather than a plain "No." When King Lear fantasizes about revenging himself upon his sons-in-law, he shouts, "Then, kill, kill, kill, kill, kill, kill!" Lear is almost literally beside himself and his words reflect that desperation. Ratchet-like each repetition cranks up the intensity of feeling.

Repetition such as Lear's is harrowing but repetition can also soothe. A lullaby is a lulling that says goodbye to wakefulness. Jim Harrison's lovely, haunting "Lullaby for a Daughter" repeats phrases at the beginning of lines and in the middle of lines. It creates two formulas: one slightly formal—"Night is ... "—and one slightly informal—"night's a ... ." Here is the poem:

> Go to sleep. Night is a coal pit
> full of black water—
>   night's a dark cloud
> full of warm rain.

Go to sleep. Night is a flower
resting from bees—
                    night's a green sea
swollen with fish.

Go to sleep. Night is a white moon
riding her mare—
                    night's a bright sun
burned to black cinder.

Go to sleep,
night's come,
cat's day,
owl's day,
star's feast of praise,
moon to reign over
her sweet subject, dark.

When Harrison lets go of the repetitions, sleep is coming. We feel it as the poem winds down in little lines to its final word. The rhythm created by the back and forth movement between an imperative and a declarative has done its work. In contradistinction to the pain of Lear, Harrison's lines affirm that a pleasure of repetition lies in dwelling on something and indulging the richness of a feeling. To repeat a phrase may mean that we do not want to let go of it. (6)

Repetition calls attention to something unreserved and to be unreserved is sometimes to act in child-like ways. Nursery rhymes are very fond of repetition, of saying the same thing over and over for the joy of saying it. Probably everyone knows "London Bridge." Here are the first two stanzas:

London Bridge is broken down;
    Broken down, broken down,
London Bridge is broken down,
    My fair lady.

Build it up with wood and clay,
    Wood and clay, wood and clay
Build it up with wood and clay
    My fair lady.

The rhyme of course goes along with a game children play and there is an element of menace in that game. The sing-song repetition lulls but puts one slightly on edge also: The bridge may fall down on you. Indeed the rhyme hearkens in part to the gruesome superstition that a child must be entombed in a bridge to placate the river. (7)

The repetition in "London Bridge" is physical foolery. Another nursery rhyme, "See-saw, Margery Daw," is similar:

See-saw, Margery Daw,
The old hen flew over the malt house;
She counted her chickens one by one,
Still she missed the little white one,
And this is it, this is it, this is it.

Iona and Peter Opie in *The Oxford Dictionary of Nursery Rhymes* note that this is a toe rhyme. Repetition of a phrase speaks to the human body directly and simply and is the foundation of more elaborate repetitions. Shakespeare's songs play all manner of variations on repetition. (8) In *Twelfth Night* he repeats imperative phrases:

Come away, come away, death,
    And in sad cypress let me be laid;
Fly away, fly away, breath;
    I am slain by a fair cruel maid.

Later in the same play he repeats whole lines:

When that I was and a little tiny boy,
    With hey, ho, the wind and the rain;
A foolish thing is but a toy,
    For the rain it raineth every day.

But when I came to man's estate,
  With hey, ho, the wind and the rain;
'Gainst knaves and thieves men shut their gates,
  For the rain it raineth every day.

In *Measure for Measure* he echoes the ends of lines:

Take, O take those lips away,
  That so sweetly were forsworn;
And those eyes, the break of day,
  Lights that do mislead the morn:
But my kisses bring again, bring again,
Seals of love, but seal'd in vain, seal'd in vain.

And in *Macbeth* he has the witches repeat three times a formula that has become famous:

Double, double, toil and trouble
Fire burn and cauldron bubble.

Repetition is equally delightful and unnerving in its insistent energy. It took the poetic genius of T. S. Eliot to modulate repetition so that the quiver between pleasure and pain, between alert assertion and dreary, soul-numbing routine, could be communicated. Anyone who has read "Ash Wednesday" remembers its truly haunting opening lines:

Because I do not hope to turn again
Because I do not hope
Because I do not hope to turn

From the beginning of his work in "The Love Song of J. Alfred Prufrock," Eliot was attuned to how delicate repetition could be, how it could be reflective and perturbed at the same time, as the mind searches for formulas and assertions and is stymied: "'This is not it at all, / This is not what I meant, at all.'" In Eliot's hands repetition makes us feel how the mind turns something over and over, meditating, sifting, faltering, challenging. Whether in nursery rhyme, Walt Whitman, or a contemporary poem, repetition is spellbinding as it evokes a presence and dwells on it. Eliot's work pushes the spellbinding aspect very far, at once adhering to set words and changing them, settling and unsettling them. Repetition is certainty, perhaps desperate certainty, but Eliot unnerves certainty. Certainty mocks the likes of J. Alfred Prufrock.

Eliot's fondness for themes and variations came to fruition in "The Four Quartets." The title speaks to the musicality of the poem and repetition is, indeed, one way for a poet to shadow some of the effects of music. To listen to "Ash-Wednesday" being read is to feel how phrases can be plucked like notes; now diminishing, now forthright. The poem is a tissue of echoes and this suits Eliot's purposes exactly. The poem is arduous—not in the sense that it is remarkably difficult—but rather in the sense that nothing comes easily to the narrator, that any degree of revelation must be earned by patiently engaging the auspices of prayer and delusion, of articulation and loss. (9)

Repetition as it partakes of rhythm is one of the ancient veins of poetry. It looks to the world of incantations, talismans, charms, rituals, and spells. It has no use for the modern notion of linear progress, of getting from point a to point b and congratulating oneself for it. Repetition is attuned to cycles and circles; it keeps returning. Theodore Roethke's poem entitled "The Cycle" uses repetition to evoke the elemental world of earth and atmosphere. It is concerned with how repetition inheres in earthly life and refuses distraction:

> Dark water, underground,
> Beneath the rock and clay,
> Beneath the roots of trees,
> Moved into common day,
> Rose from a mossy mound
> In mist that sun could seize.

The fine rain coiled in a cloud
Turned by revolving air
Far from that colder source
Where elements cohere
Dense in the central stone.
The air grew loose and loud.

Then, with diminished force,
The full rain fell straight down,
Tunneled with lapsing sound
Under even the rock-shut ground,
Under a river's source,
Under primeval stone.

In the modern world advertising uses the insistence of repetition to instill product recognition, to make us sub-conscious slaves who cannot get a cola jingle out of our minds. As Roethke's poem illustrates, repetition in a poem has other agendas. The beginning of the poem uses repetition to summon the elements; the end of the poem uses repetition to meditatively evoke the mystery of the earth-world. In Roethke's hands repetition takes us to a reality that is very hard to get to and that feels undeniable. (10)

REPETITION
In the Classroom

1. Read some twentieth-century poems that feature refrains (such as "Song of the Beggars" by W. H. Auden). What do the refrains add to the poem?

2. Read the 1855 version of "Song of Myself" by Walt Whitman. What cumulative effects do Whitman's uses of anaphora have? Write a short "Song of Myself" that talks about who you are and what America is to you. Use anaphora in your poem.

3. Langston Hughes is a poet of great directness and subtlety. Read more of his work and copy some of the poems of his that you like in your poetry notebook. Does Hughes use anaphora commonly or does he reserve it for certain occasions?

4. The history of the blues is the history of a remarkable, African-American, art form. Listen to various blues artists from different eras. Do blues songs always feature repetitions and refrains? Write a response piece about who is your favorite blues artist and why.

5. Cornelius Eady's poem comes from a volume entitled *Victims of the Latest Dance Craze*. All the poems in the book are, in one way or another, about dance. Copy a poem of his into your poetry notebook. How does Eady use lines to give a sense of dance? Write your own poem (using anaphora) about where you might be when the world ends.

6. Write a lullaby that uses a degree of repetition. Pay careful attention to rhythm, as you want the poem to be truly lulling.

7. What was your favorite childhood nursery rhyme? What about it charmed you? Write a modern-day nursery rhyme that speaks to the world you live in.

8. How do Shakespeare's songs fit into the contexts of various plays? Consider such plays as *Twelfth Night, As You Like It,* and *Hamlet*.

9. T. S. Eliot is a master of repetition. Choose an Eliot poem that uses repetition and write a response piece about how repetition is integral to the art of the poem.

10. Write a poem that uses repetition to speak to the cycles and rhythms of the natural world.

REPETITION
Five-Day Lesson Plan

Day 1   The teacher brings in songs that feature refrains. Have students listen to the songs and write down the refrains. Show students the entire song with the refrain included. How does the refrain work in each song? What is the relationship of the refrain to the rest of the song?
- Does it summarize?
- Does it provide a crucial detail?
- Does it display an emotional attitude?
- Is it a commentary on what is happening in the song?

For homework, each student needs to bring in a song on a CD and a written version of the song. (No xeroxed copies of the song lyrics; students should write out the song.)

Day 2   Class time is spent presenting songs and discussing the relationship of the refrain to the song. At the end of class, students write a short piece about how refrains work in different songs.

Day 3   One of the strongest forms of repetition is anaphora. Show students examples from such poets as William Carlos Williams, T. S. Eliot, and some religious texts such as the King James Version of the Bible, a sutra, or a Native American chant. Students then discuss how anaphora works. Why do poets use anaphora?

Day 4   Students, as a class, brainstorm what sorts of occasions lend themselves to anaphora. List these occasions on the blackboard. (Ask students to think about the occasions of Walt Whitman's poems.) Then, have students choose an occasion and draft a poem using anaphora.

Day 5   Have a poetry reading of these drafts of anaphora poems. At the end of the reading, students can write a piece in their poetry notebook in which they explain which poem struck them the most and why. Ask them to explain to what degree anaphora was a factor in the poem.

Beyond the Week

Have students examine a poem such as T. S. Eliot's "Ash Wednesday." Have them explain how repetition plays an integral part in the poem.

REPETITION
Bibliography

Poems

"Interne at Provident" by Langston Hughes from *Selected Poems*, Random House, 1959; "The Dance" by Cornelius Eady from *Victims of the Latest Dance Craze*, Carnegie Mellon University Press, 1997; "Lullaby for a Daughter" by Jim Harrison from *Selected and New Poems 1961–1981*, Dell Publishing, 1982; *Oxford Dictionary of Nursery Rhymes* by Iona and Peter Opie, Clarendon Press, 1969; "Ash Wednesday" and "The Love Song of J. Alfred Prufrock" by T. S. Eliot from *Collected Poems 1909–1962*, Harcourt Brace, 1963; "The Cycle" by Theodore Roethke from *The Collected Poems*, Anchor Books, 1975.

14

Endings

Summary

Poems conclude in certain recognizable ways. Typically a poem ends with a statement (or a question) or an action or an image (or metaphor): "John was a basketball player" or "John threw the basketball away" or "Blue, shapeless smoke hung over the backboard." Any conclusion is the result of all the prior moves within the poem, but there is no formula that says, for instance, if a poem is constructed of declaratives it must end with a declarative. On the contrary, a satisfying ending may represent a sudden switch syntactically or the appearance of an image where none was before. Although certain endings are avoided (poets don't sum up at the end the way prose writers might do), an ending presents infinite possibilities that grow out of finite choices.

"How does it end?" we ask someone about a novel or a movie or a television program. Or we say, "Don't tell me the ending. I want it to be a surprise." The satisfaction that a good ending provides is a satisfaction not quite like any other. It is not, for instance, like winning an athletic competition or reaching a destination. Those events may be elating but a work of art offers opportunities to fashion resonances that are somehow more than the last word in series of words or the last scene in a series of scenes. Effective endings linger in our minds as they at once finish the work and elucidate it. They are more than stopping points; they are fulfillments.

The endings of poems tend to fall within a few broad categories. A poem may end with an image—an apple on a kitchen counter or a ca-

thedral in a snowfall. It may end with an action—someone walks out
of a house or runs down an empty street. It may end with a statement—"I am taller now" or "Truth is not beauty." Within these general categories the poet may choose to vary the tone. A poem may end
with a question—"Am I taller now?"—or an exclamation—"I am
tall!" Also a poet may choose to provide an ending that is less than a
full, end-of-a-sentence ending. Using ellipsis is a way of doing this: "I
am taller now, perhaps ... " (1)

Probably a statement is the most common way to end a poem. Here
is John Clare's charming poem "Insects":

> These tiny loiterers on the barley's beard,
> And happy units of a numerous herd
> Of playfellows, the laughing summer brings,
> Mocking the sunshine in their glittering wings,
> How merrily they creep, and run, and fly!
> No kin they bear to labour's drudgery,
> Smoothing the velvet of the pale hedge-rose;
> And where they fly for dinner no one knows—
> The dew-drops feed them not—they love the shine
> Of noon, whose sun may bring them golden wine.
> All day they're playing in their Sunday dress—
> Till night goes sleep, and they can do no less;
> Then, to the heath-bell's silken hood they fly,
> And like to princes in their slumbers lie,
> Secure from night, and dropping dews, and all,
> In silken beds and roomy painted hall.
> So merrily they spend their summer day,
> Now in the cornfields, now the new-mown hay,
> One almost fancies that such happy things,
> With coloured hoods and richly burnished wings,
> Are fairy folk, in splendid masquerade
> Disguised, as if of mortal folk afraid,
> Keeping their merry pranks a mystery still,
> Lest glaring day should do their secrets ill.

The final lines comprise a statement that caps Clare's observations and metaphors. The fullness of the statement seems fitting as the poem has considered at some length who insects are and what they do. Clare spins out a final and fanciful notion that provides another imaginative perspective on the creatures. "The insects are this and this and this," according to Clare, "and in summary they are almost like another thing." As it is a detailed surmise, the ending feels proportionate to the rest of the poem—neither brief nor exhaustive. That Clare's speculation moves the poem to a purely imaginative plane seems just when we consider how magical the world of insects has been in Clare's poem. (2)

Poems that consist of statements often have a rhetorical quality as the author is establishing relationships and emphases among the aspects of the topic at hand. "Yet," "but," "though," "still," are words that often crop up in such poems as they help to order and define the poet's various feelings and perceptions. The last six lines of Shakespeare's "Sonnet 44" feature three "but's":

> But, ah, thought kills me that I am not thought,
> To leap large lengths of miles when thou art gone,
> But that so much of earth and water wrought,
> I must attend time's leisure with my moan,
> > Receiving naught by elements so slow
> > But heavy tears, badges of either's woe.

The poem is based on a notion presented in the first line: "If the dull substance of my flesh were thought." For better or worse, flesh cannot be thought and such a conjecture cannot be realized. "If" is a word that has launched many a poem and "but" is a word that has brought many a poem down to earth. "But" is what cannot be avoided. (3)

Clare is poetically describing a scene and Shakespeare is juggling thoughts about thoughts, but many times poets simply are declaring their feelings. Ending such a declarative poem often calls for a degree of intensification to make the reader feel that the poem's conclusion is warranted. Wordsworth does this in his well-known sonnet "The World is Too Much With Us":

The world is too much with us; late and soon,
Getting and spending, we lay waste our powers:
Little we see in Nature that is ours;
We have given our hearts away, a sordid boon!
This Sea that bares her bosom to the moon;
The winds that will be howling at all hours,
And are up-gathered now like sleeping flowers;
For this, for every thing, we are out of tune;
It moves us not.—Great God! I'd rather be
A Pagan suckled in a creed outworn;
So might I, standing on this pleasant lea,
Have glimpses that would make me less forlorn;
Have sight of Proteus rising from the sea;
Or hear old Triton blow his wreathed horn.

The dash that precedes the exclamation is like an electric spark. Wordsworth blows up (in his nineteenth-century way) and the last six lines leave the reader with no doubt about Wordsworth's emotions. We already knew that Wordsworth felt strongly on account of the earlier exclamation. The ending raises the intensity as Wordsworth disrupts the poem with a passionate outburst and goes on to describe his feelings at length. The ending cements the poem's emotional logic: Dissatisfaction is voiced and then opposed by the strength of unfettered feeling. (4)

Molly Peacock's poem "Petting and Being a Pet" illustrates how a contemporary poem of statements proceeds (also in sonnet form though not quite as strictly rhymed):

Dogs, lambs, chickens, women—pets of all nations!
Fur or feathers under the kneading fingers
of those who long to have pets, relations
of softness to fleshiness, how a hand lingers
on a head or on the ear of a head, thus the sound
of petting and being a pet, a sounding horn:
needing met by kneading of bone which is found
through flesh. Have you ever felt forlorn

looking at a cat on someone else's lap, wishing
the cat was you? Look how an animal is passed
from lap to lap in a room, so many wishing
to hold it. We wish to be in the vast
caress, both animal and hand. Like eyes make sense
of seeing, touch makes being make sense.

From her initial exclamation Peacock moves to consideration, then a
question, then a direct address, then a statement of feeling ("We wish
... "). She ends with a form of statement much favored in poetry—a
simile. It is the only simile in the poem and it is not so much fanciful as
instructive. As a final statement, the last line and a half makes us feel
what "Petting and Being a Pet" is about. The poet has presented us
with a number of aspects; the conclusion wittily and succinctly ties
them up. (5)

Endings are only as good as the poet's imaginative instincts, but after an initial draft the poet may consider what sort of ending is appropriate. As we have stressed, poems are composed of moves: some of
this move, some of that move. The poems we have looked at thus far in
this chapter end with statements as the author declares a final perception that concludes a series of perceptions. Many poems, however, do
not end declaratively; instead, they end visually. The last word or
phrase in the poem is a verbal picture rather than a statement of feelings or an observation or a noting of a possibility or a wish or a desire.
Galway Kinnell's poem in Chapter 7 does this with its "blue milk." A
great deal of feeling is held in that image; it speaks for a world of solitude and hard living.

Kinnell's poem ends with a list but often the poet isolates the final
image. Bin Ramke does this in his poem "Why I Am Afraid to Have
Children":

A morning like others, and a father
stood there, black against the light.
The screen of the door buckled softly
in brief wind, the morning heat
already rising.

This ground never made anyone rich,
least of all his father. So his job was in town
and he didn't know how sad he was playing
with his toy farm, paying for it.

I didn't know. I was a child
as small as I would ever be. It is
only a memory, a ragged edge,
and perhaps meaningless. A spindly morning glory
glowed the only spot of color
over his shoulder.

In its quiet way the poem tells the story of a son's perception of a father's disappointment. If we follow the moves with which Ramke
constructs his poem, we see that in the first stanza he sets the scene,
in the second stanza he tells about his father, and that through most
of the third stanza he tells about himself. In the last lines of the poem
the poet returns to the actuality of the scene in the first stanza. He
prods it and what he finds is an image that speaks to the lives of the
child and the father. The morning glory that Ramke describes is an
expressive actuality. A reader can relate easily to the feelings the
image speaks to but the wonder of the image is its there-ness, its in-
vincible precision and its own stubborn life. It is not a "flower" but a
"morning glory," and a "spindly morning glory" at that. It seems un-
likely that any further statement Ramke could make would have the
effect that the image has. The image, after all, has nothing to de-
clare; it simply exists. (6)

Ramke's poem tells a story about a life but chooses to conclude with
a physical actuality. Often poems that tell stories about lives do so by
relating actions, what someone did at various times. A natural way for
such a poem to end is by describing a final action. Consider Debora
Greger's poem "The Light Passages":

A day later than he said in the letter,
still humming, half-whistling
the theme of the piece he stayed on to practice,

he leaves the car at the last road sign
and climbs the fence, taking the old shortcut
through the orchard at sunrise.
He stumbles through weeds,
sending up sleepy birds,
the only sounds their stiff wings
and ice cracking on the branches
from which they have risen,
thinking not of them but of how
Beethoven, playing a new sonata for friends,
hardly touches the keys
in the *pianissimo*,
imagining a light passage
that the others, not deaf, could not hear.

From the porch he looks back—
the orchard, still again,
is another world, a trick of the eye,
as the house in silhouette was before.
The house, still dark inside,
is still home.
Careful not to wake his family
after all the years,
he slips through the door
and surefooted as if he had never left
goes to the piano
and begins to play.

Revisiting his life, the pianist also revisits the music he has never left. The final sentence of the poem describes a series of actions. The absence of punctuation in the final four lines and the way Greger matches each action to a line gives a sense of deliberate momentum, of graceful inevitability to the ending. Like an arc, the poem traces a series of actions to the final one, the piano playing whose finality speaks to a power that triggered the poem's whole series of events. Notice that Greger does not want to end with the image of a piano; she wants her character to be playing that piano, for the poem's strength lies in its insistence in the power of doing—however lightly that happens at times, however Beethoven "hardly touched the keys." **(7)**

We do many things – play pianos, throw baseballs, mow lawns, diaper babies—but we talk a lot, too. Talking may be for the sake of talking (think of C. K. Williams's regulars in Chapter 7 chewing over life with their coffees), but it may be to a definite purpose. It may be woven with action and speak to action. Naomi Shihab Nye does this in "The Use of Fiction":

> A boy claims he saw you on a bicycle last week,
> touring his neighborhood. "West Cypress Street!" he shouts,
> as if your being there and his seeing you
> were some sort of benediction.
> To be alive, to be standing outside
> on a tender, February evening ...
> "It was a blue bicycle, ma'am, your braid was flying,
> I said hello and you laughed, remember?"
>
> You almost tell him your bicycle seat is thick with dust,
> the tires have been flat for months.
> But his face, that radiant flower, says you are his friend,
> he has told his mother your name!
> Maybe this is a clear marble
> he will hide in his sock drawer for months.
> So who now, in a world of figures,
> would deny West Cypress Street,
> throwing up clouds into this literal sky?
> "Yes, Amigo"—hand on shoulder—
> "It was I."

Fictions are words about actions. By ending her poem with a direct quotation, Nye raises words to the status of actions, for it is words that may confirm or deny actions. The fact that the narrator's bike has not been used "for months" seems irrelevant to the moment at hand. The

poem honors that moment and uses direct speech to bring it to a satisfying conclusion. Words— and especially words in poems—have to
do with definite situations. Perceptions, actions, and feelings compound those situations. The richness of the situation is presented in
the poem's final words: A lie is a fiction and an action may depend on
someone's perception of the action. Since we are much less than
all-knowing creatures, those perceptions may be flawed. Nye's ending
affirms the importance of considering the context of a perception: she
has gained a friend.

All the poems we have considered in this chapter end decisively.
Yet poems may end on other notes. Robert Morgan's poem "Passenger
Pigeons" is a question that ends with another question:

> Remembering the descriptions by Wilson
> and Bartram, and Audubon and other
> early travelers to the interior, of the sky
> clouded with the movements of winged pilgrims
> wide as the Mississippi, wide as the Gulf
> Stream, hundred-mile epics of equidistant wings
> horizon to horizon, how their droppings
> splashed the lakes and rivers, how
> where they roosted whole forests broke down
> worse than ice storms, and the woods floor
> was paved with their lime, how the settlers
> got them with ax and gun and broom
> for hogs, how when a hawk attacked
> the endless stream bulged away
> and kept the shift long after
> the raptor was gone, and having read how
> the skies of America became silent, the fletched
> oceans forgotten, how can I replace
> the hosts of the sky, the warmblooded jetstreams?
> To echo the birdstorms of those early
> sunsets, what high river of electron, cell and star?

The last thing a poem constitutes is a policy for certainty. That the great mass of description in the poem leads to questions is integral to the situation the poem addresses. How could there have been so many of these birds and now they are extinct? How could that be? It is a question that the poem answers as it pithily describes what happened and yet it remains a question, a mystery. By personalizing the whole issue—"how can I replace"—Morgan makes his questions not rhetorical ones but living and breathing ones. Faced with mystery and frustration, the poet rightly resorts to questioning. The sheer physical momentum of the long sentence that ends with the poem's first question makes the reader experience the overwhelming fact of the birds' existence. The relative brevity of the second question is terribly poignant against the mass of the first. The pigeons were taken for granted; there was no precious mystery to them. The poem makes us feel how wrong that was. (8)

In the key of uncertainty there is another frequent note besides questioning. This is the conclusion that does not quite conclude. The poet may use ellipsis of some sort or simply break off the poem in mid-sentence and thus make it a fragment. Consider James Richardson's poem "The Lake":

A heart's length above the high-water mark,
trees begin, leaning away. Clear streams
back in. There are no visible
outlets, except the sky, and this
only at sundown when the lake
chills in its socket with reflected bitterness.
Some men come here, and dream
small, throbbing, eye-sized dreams
that will not break. The fires, too,
are small, but they are superfluous.
There are no currents, though bones
spiral from the shore. The zodiac
spins in the surface red red red ...

The dream world the poet conjures up is essentially a static one. The descriptions work to convince us of its strange reality. Everything seems under control but there is a powerful undercurrent (no pun intended) of menace, of "bitterness" and "bones," of emotional duress. How in a dream world that has no clear beginning and end does one come to a conclusion? Richardson uses ellipsis as an emotional dissolve. It is a compelling move, for the repetition of the word "red" is an intensification in a poem that has been very restrained. Yet that intensification fades into the mystery of those three dots. The logic of the ending is poetic logic; it proceeds according to the emotional terrain of the poem. (9) That is why there can never be a recipe for how to conclude a poem. Sometimes a poet wants to use the full resources of meter and form and end the poem with utter finality—a door slammed shut. At other times a poet wants the poem to fade into the shadows of silence. How conclusive the ending may be has to do with how much conclusiveness the poem has entertained before the ending comes along. In any case, a good ending is like the final turn of a key that manages at once to close the poem and make a further vista possible.

ENDINGS
In the Classroom

1. In terms of how they end, consider some of the poems by various poets that you have written down in your poetry notebook. Can their endings be categorized as to action, image, and statement, or do they end in other ways?

2. Choose a poem that ends like John Clare's with a statement and write a response piece as to why the ending is satisfying. Does the statement that occurs in the final lines summarize the poem or does it add a new dimension to the poem?

3. A sonnet is not a long form. How does Shakespeare reach conclusions in the space of fourteen lines? Pay close attention to the syntax of his sonnets.

4. Wordsworth wrote other notable sonnets such as "Composed Upon Westminster Bridge, September 3, 1802" and "To Toussaint L'Ouverture." How are those sonnets structured in comparison with "The World is Too Much With Us?" Are the endings similar?

5. In certain ways the ending of Molly Peacock's poem with its careful, playful turns of phrase summons up the metaphysical poetry of the first half of the seventeenth century. In that poetry, poets constructed elaborate, often punning comparisons; sometimes so elaborate as to be called far-fetched. Read a poem such as "Loves growth" by John Donne and note the comparisons Donne makes in the poem. How does he conclude that poem?

6. Find another contemporary poem that ends with an image. How did the poet reach that ending—is there, for instance, a whole trail of images leading up to the final image? To your mind, does the final image in the poem make for a satisfactory ending? Why?

7. Debora Greger deftly traces a skein of actions. Write a poem that similarly follows the course of someone doing something. Rhythm is crucial to the pace of such a poem. Think carefully about how you lineate the poem.

8. Write a poem that poses a series of questions and that ends with a question.

9. Find another contemporary poem that ends with an ellipsis. Is the effect similar to what happens in James Richardson's poem or is it different?

ENDINGS
Five-Day Lesson Plan

Day 1   Distribute to class a week's worth of contemporary poetry as follows: three poems that end with a statement, three poems that end with an action, and three poems that end with an image or metaphor. Ask students to read all of the poems. Discuss the different sorts of endings. As a class, come to conclusions about the type of ending that each poem has.

Day 2   Hand out the following set of questions to the class.

- Thematically, why does the ending take the form that it does?
- What images, statements, or actions lead up to the final image, statement, or action?
- Endings can strike various notes. Endings can be surprises, climaxes, anti-climaxes, denouements, ironies, and utterly imaginative leaps. What note does the ending of each poem strike?

Ask students to answer these questions for each of the poems that have been distributed.

Day 3   Continue with the previous day's work.

Day 4   Panel Discussion on "Poetry Endings": For this panel, the teacher assigns one of the nine poems to a group of students and proceeds around the class until all students are in groups and each group has its own poem. Each group then must prepare a 10-minute presentation based on their findings about the poem's ending. Each student will speak in the course of the group's panel presentation. The rest of the class will take notes on each presentation so that questions can be asked afterwards.

Day 5   Panel Discussion on "Poetry Endings" continues.

Beyond the Week

Have students look at their own poems in their poetry notebook. Have them respond to the following questions: What sort of ending do you tend to favor? Why do you think that is? Students write their response in their poetry notebook.

ENDINGS
Bibliography

Poems

"Insects" by John Clare from *Selected Poems*, J. M. Dent and Sons, 1965; "Petting and Being a Pet" by Molly Peacock from *Raw Heaven*, Random House, 1984; "Why I Am Afraid to Have Children" by Bin Ramke from *White Monkeys*, University of Georgia Press, 1981; "The Light Passages" by Debora Greger from *Movable Islands*, Princeton University Press, 1980; "The Use of Fiction" by Naomi Shihab Nye from *Words Under the Words: Selected Poems*, Far Corner Books, 1995; "Passenger Pigeons" by Robert Morgan from *At the Edge of the Orchard Country*, Wesleyan University Press, 1987; "The Lake" by James Richardson from *Reservations*, Princeton University Press, 1977.

15

Narrative

Summary

Many poems tell stories. The epic poems such as *The Iliad* and *The Odyssey* and *The Aeneid* upon which a substantial amount of Western literature is based represent storytelling on a grand scale. Although poets nowadays have by no means ceased writing book-length, narrative poems, they tend to tell many of their stories in a page or two. (1) It is a remarkable ability of poetry that it can turn anything into a story, for poetry can dwell so fully on the texture of any experience that the texture becomes a story in its own right. Also, thanks to rhythm, metaphor, sound, line, and stanza, poetry can proceed in many directions at the same time. From line to line it can jump among minds, moments, eras, details, images, and geographies like an intergalactic cricket. Prose patiently assembles sentences that form a narrative; poetry creates narratives as it darts and leaps, snowballs and spirals, rambles and hurdles. Poetry can link anything to anything.

A narrative tells a story. The ways, however, that poems tell stories and the ways that prose tells stories are not identical. Typically a prose story focuses on a conflict, a misunderstanding, an illusion. Short stories and novels are deeply socialized art forms in the sense that they deal with the collisions that are inevitable when people are at cross-purposes with one another. In terms of technique, prose trowels sentence upon sentence to create a story; it is patient, laborious.

Poems are different. A poet, too, can construct a narrative out of an event, but a poet can also narrate a feeling, a mood, an intuition, a

247

sliver of perception, a memory, or an epoch or eternity. Poets can tell stories about anything. This is because the way poets tell stories is not like prose in that the poem can tell its story by moving from one image or statement or action to another. Such movement is uniquely poetic energy and it is borne by rhythm, the energy in the accents and lines. This energy has been described variously as flowing, leaping, pulsating, drumming, but in any case the confluence of narration and rhythm has been considered in many cultures for thousands of years to be the heart of poetry.

Our ancestors in the nineteenth century had a powerful sense of what a narrative was. The ballad form was a great favorite of theirs and all the ballad required was an event to set it in motion. How poems told their stories was a thrilling pleasure. Who could resist the likes of Henry Wadsworth Longfellow's "The Wreck of the Hesperus," with its emphatic opening stanza? (2):

> It was the schooner Hesperus,
>   That sailed the wintry sea;
> And the skipper had taken his little daughter,
>   To bear him company.

Off we go on the rhythmic current! The powerful mnemonic energy of meter insists that this event is memorable. In Longfellow's hands the language is equal to the rhythm. So is Samuel Taylor Coleridge's "The Rime of the Ancient Mariner," which also begins in the emphatic way ballads do:

> It is an ancient Mariner,
> And he stoppeth one of three.
> "By thy long grey beard and glittering eye,
> Now wherefore stopp'st thou me?"

Again we are implicated and caught in the pace of the rhythm. Indeed, this rhythmic force became in the hands of a nineteenth-century poet such as Edgar Allan Poe an obsession in its own right. Poe's rhythmic and sonic sense is so strong that the stories he tells seem pretexts for the intoxication and sheer power of the rhythm. "Ulalume—A Ballad" begins thus:

The skies they were ashen and sober;
        The leaves they were crisped and sere—
        The leaves they were withering and sere;
    It was night, in the lonesome October
        Of my most immemorial year ...

The mixed rhythmic units (weak/strong and weak/weak/strong) are mesmerizing. As an artist Poe reveled in the effects rhythm and sound could accomplish. He could have cared less about writing ballads to commemorate events. Poetry, in and of itself, was the main event for him and the self-consciousness of his work points the way to the poetry of the twentieth century.

In the twentieth century the reasons waned for narrating an event for the sake of the event. There were new means of narration, most notably moving pictures, that dwarfed a mere poem. Poets continued to write ballads but they were playful and rueful and self-aware about what they were doing. W. H. Auden's "James Honeyman," for example, tells the story of a genius chemist who develops a deadly gas that winds up killing his own family. The tone of the poem mingles lyric, comic, narrative, descriptive, and dramatic notes while maintaining the imperative pace of the ballad. In addition, Auden conjures up a wealth of detail that is as crucial to the ballad as the story he tells. He knows that the ballad is somewhat absurd in its galloping way, but he enjoys the challenge of, at once, tweaking and indulging its inevitability. The grim, riveting determination of Longfellow's poem is no longer narrative's emblem. Indeed, what happens to the ballad in twentieth-century poetry indicates what happens generally to narrative, namely that it expands beyond the confines of a memorable event to tell all sorts of personal stories. Modern poetry is notable for the sheer proliferation of topics and aspects of life that find their ways into poetry for the first time. As far as narrative is concerned, there is no such thing as "unpoetic."

Though most twentieth-century poets tended to eschew the thumping beat of the ballad, they certainly did not discard rhythm as a component of narrative. Joe-Anne McLaughlin's poem "Complicated" tells a compelling story not of a shipwreck or a battle but of a woman working in a nursing home:

Like at the rest home, this old vegetable
farmer name of Yank Burns, calling me by his dead wife's
name, calling sweet Alice this, sweet Alice that,
and then steady refusing to eat except on

my shift, meaning of course I couldn't quit
if I wanted to, and Christ—who didn't?
What with the shit wages and urine smell
so cruel somedays it'd like to blister the skin

off your eyeballs. And if you could hack that,
there was the dayroom all the time rigged out
like a funeral parlor. No kidding. Grave baskets
and whatnot, wake flowers (you've seen them)

long-stemmed fancy arrangements
in cheap baskets, sashed like Miss America
contestants, only instead of a Miss
Nevada or Jersey or Texas or Kansas

you'd get REST IN PEACE, over and over.
Now you talk about creeps; and those old timers,
sitting there, joints sealing, stiffer
by the minute, fat good it did them—good

riddance maybe. But does anybody listen?
So finally one night my car skids sideways
into a tree—you see this scar? Three weeks
I'm on leave and sure enough they had

Old Yank packed off to the VA inside
the second week. Force feeding him,
I betcha. Gone, anyway. So I quit—
five years ago this May, and you know

what? Call it fate, which it ain't. Or call it
psychology, which it probably ain't either,
but I haven't held a steady job since.

What particularly compels is the poem's voice, the frankly human
quality of someone talking. The rhythmic fascination is not with the
pattern of accents but the tangible, tells-it-like-it-is voice. The very
first word of the poem is a stressed syllable and that accent kicks the
poem into gear: This narrator has something to say. When poets talk
about "voice" (and it is a word many of them use), they often mean the
tone that makes a narrative credible. The narrator is *someone*—not an
omniscient, detached perspective—but a definite person who is fully
implicated, who has feelings of regret, exasperation, and anger,
among others. In many ways the narrative resides in the texture of
those feelings. How the story is told, the emotional pressure that influences word choices and syntax, is as critical as the story's events.
As far as the poem is concerned, those events exist because someone
cared to tell about them. Although McLaughlin wrote the poem, it is
unwise to assume the narrator of the poem is the same person as the
poet. Poetry is not journalism; it lives according to imaginative truth
and that is not the same thing as factual truth. (3)

One thing that is fascinating about narration is how wide or narrow
its scope can be. Whereas McLaughlin's poem focuses on a personal
episode, Louis Simpson's poem "The Western World" tells in three
stanzas about the European discovery and settling of America. Richmond Lattimore's poem "The Crabs" is about boiling some crabs:

To the Western World

A siren sang, and Europe turned away
From the high castle and the shepherd's crook.
Three caravels went sailing to Cathay
On the strange ocean, and the captains shook
Their banners out across the Mexique Bay.

And in our early days we did the same.
Remembering our fathers in their wreck
We crossed the sea from Palos where they came
And saw, enormous to the little deck,
A shore in silence waiting for a name.

The treasures of Cathay were never found.
In this America, this wilderness
Where the axe echoes with a lonely sound,
The generations labor to possess
And grave by grave we civilize the ground.

The Crabs

There was a bucket full of them. They spilled,
crawled, climbed, clawed; slowly tossed
and fell: precision made: cold iodine color of their own
world of sand and occasional brown weed, round stone
chilled clean in the chopping waters of their coast.
One fell out. The marine thing on the grass
tried to trundle off, barbarian and immaculate and to be killed
with his kin. We lit water: dumped the living mass
in: contemplated tomatoes and corn: and with the good
cheer of civilized man,
cigarettes, that is, and cold beer, and chatter,
waited out and lived down the ten-foot-away clatter
of crabs as they died for us inside their boiling can.

The poems are virtually the same length yet their narrative intents are very different. For the purposes of his narration, Simpson personifies a whole continent as he creates a full yet taut perspective. Centuries are telescoped into three stanzas. Rhyme and meter lend a feeling of conclusiveness to what was (as Simpson indicates) a confused enterprise. The poem's ending speaks to the continuing difficulty of the endeavor: The inescapable past influences the present. In terms of how a poem can cover a great deal of time in a very short space, Simpson's poem is exemplary. Its compression is its energy; each word bears the weight of history. (4)

Simpson's poem is self-consciously momentous; its story is real yet mythic. Yet who would say that Lattimore's poem about cooking some crabs at a party is any less substantial than Simpson's poem about the New World? As with Simpson, Lattimore skillfully constructs a story out of details that move forward in time. Whereas Simpson summarizes events in images—"A shore in silence waiting for a name"—, Lattimore portrays the moment-by-moment demise of some living creatures. The focused narrative is relentless and the punctuation reinforces this quality as Lattimore piles colon upon colon. The feeling one gets from such punctuation is that when people want something, they do what they have to do to get it. The echoing rhymes reinforce the sense of linkage as human activity moves purposefully ahead even as a crab seeks to move away from its imminent demise. The scene is not historical but it speaks as a narrative to some habits regarding life and death that are worth pondering; indeed that underlie some of the events to which Simpson alludes in his narrative about civilizing. Some of those habits have to do with language (as represented by such phrases as "The marine thing," "the living mass") and its ability to put dire realities at a seemingly comfortable distance.

Narrative thrives on connections, what one thing has to do with another. This is a deep human predilection that we attend to each day as we tell stories about our lives. Each of us has a sense of a self who does things and to whom things are done. Each of us has notions of an identity that is the result of innumerable circumstances. The ways narrative poets can braid the moments and days of human lives into poems are inexhaustible. Consider Christianne Balk's poem "Dusk Choir":

> We slipped under the split-rail fence,
> Maggie and I. Our bodies left wings in the snow.
> The new powder rose up around our feet
> and we ran to get away from Father.
> Stopped at George Duncan's. Twenty-four dogs
> chained up in his front yard. Howling, filling

our ears with sound. They were pure
sound. Their mouths. Feet. Legs. Their bones.
The clink of tin buckets. George Duncan ladled
ground horse meat and corn meal, slopping one ladle
on each pine slab, one ladle for each dog
except the one who had not pulled the sled hard
enough. He said she was not worth the cost
of corn. Then they were quiet, lapping.
We could smell the cereal and blood.
The one dog shook as she watched
the others eat. We listened to the lapping,
wet tongues on wood. Beyond the trees, Fountain Lake
moved against the shore, blue and cold, its ice skin
split by straps of light. If we crawled under
the lake ice, Maggie and I, the water would fill
our ears. Pure water. When we crawled out
we'd stand on top of the ridge
with the hickories and burr oaks looking
east at Father's barns. Our farmhouse would look
small, smaller than a doghouse. The dog looked
at us. She had one blue eye and one gold eye.

Two girls leave their house and watch some dogs eat: such is the poem.
Yet the "choir" of elements from which Balk makes her poem is remarkable. There are the girls, their father, George Duncan, his dogs, a landscape, a time of year, a dog who is not fed, a lake. There is also
imagination, the whole flight of mind that is initiated by the little word
"If." Of course how a poet assembles a narration is a profound act of
imagining in itself, for a good narrative makes us aware of how much is
present in every moment in this world and how much one thing bears
on another. Our minds are jumbles of intuitions, feelings, perceptions.
What the narrative poet does is to link some of that jumble together in
meaningful ways. One thing that is notable about poetry is how indifferent it is to distinctions between what is outside of us and what is inside. Balk's poem moves effortlessly from the dogs to the lake to the

imagining of being underwater and finally back to the image of the dog's eyes. What do these things have to do with one another? They are all part of a current of feeling: The talent of the poet is to make that current convincing by honoring all that is there. One can look at the poem and say among other things that it is about not fitting—how the girls flee and the one dog is left out and how humans cannot stay under a lake and even how a dog's two eyes do not quite go together. These are reasonable statements but the mystery of what one thing has to do with another remains intact. All it takes is one little action, two girls slipping under a fence, and the sense of narrative begins. (5)

Balk's poem focuses very carefully on a particular scene. Her "choir" is dense with feelings and perceptions that go along with that scene. The weave of a narrative, however, may be looser while the poem retains a strong narrative sense. David Keller's "The Man Who Knew the Words to *Louie, Louie*" is a good example of this:

Impossible, the way one black walnut, fallen
from the tree at the top of the street rolled
some forty feet down the hill where in ten years
the tree across the street from my house grew,
and so on, slowly, slowly across the country
like a cousin who moved to Idaho you could stay with
if you were passing that way:
some place not completely unfamiliar.

At the theater, the movie'd been on half an hour,
so I bought an ice cream cone, disappointed,
and drove home slowly to the radio, summer
ending, the full moon only a week off,
and me lonely for something I couldn't name.

They played *One Summer Night*, from the 50's and *The Stroll*
by the Diamonds. I never knew it was their song;
I used to be crazy for them the year my family
was in Germany, a boys' school for me, and I felt far away.
And then *I Haven't Got Time for the Pain*, Carly Simon,

and something by Elvis I knew too well to want to hear,
and *Louie, Louie,* and I thought how I never understood
the words to it.

The heat-lightning flickered like regret
against the trees and lawns, the years spent
living inside the music, afraid of being alone.
How little I've learned, the songs tell me.

I hate saying this, formal as the trees
or else with no better words than those songs,
the first language we learned to feel in.
The music's demeanor is unconscious, cheerful
as the adopted Vietnamese child's, with the tape
of songs and messages from the other orphans.
So she will not forget her old life.

Put away with the clothes she arrived in,
within weeks the tape speaks a language
less and less recognizable to her. Soon
she's learned English and no longer
seems frightened. How pleased her new parents are.

The narrative here is episodic for the story is not so much chronological as associative: how one feeling connects various incidents. It is a story of adaptive instincts that range from a walnut becoming a tree to an adopted child learning a new language. The poem is also a meditation (the very first word in the poem—"Impossible"—sets the stage), and thus not a direct telling as in "Dusk Choir" or "The Crabs." It strings together perceptions and scenes about the familiar and the unfamiliar. The logic of the narrative is thematic as the speaker ponders, "How little I've learned.... " If one were to draw a figure that represents the shape of the narrative, an arc might be an appropriate one as the poem begins with "one black walnut," proceeds through memories and songs and finally lodges in the story of a Vietnamese child's new life. It is a startling progression yet a perfectly sensible one and it shows how a poem can assemble bits and pieces that may seem at first glance to have nothing to do with one another. Often enough a scene will present itself to a poet's imagination as all-of-a-piece but not always. As poems can rely on such a rich variety of aspects to tell stories—images, rhythm, statements, metaphors, details—they can cover remarkable distances. The final statement of Keller's poem resonates with wonder and a sad joy: Gains do not exactly cancel out losses. (6)

The exactitude of particulars, the pace of the narrative, the degree of conclusiveness with which a narrative ends—all are in the service of imaginative coherence, for the stories poems tell are inevitably stories of the intuitive imagination. At its furthest reach, poetic narrative can go so far as to bring to life an inanimate object. John Keats's "Ode on a Grecian Urn" is perhaps the most famous example in the English language of a poet making vivid a work of art by imagining actions and feelings. Poets remain deeply engaged in the pursuit of words that will actualize what is nonverbal. Chitra Banerjee Divakaruni's "Cutting the Sun, After Francesco Clemente's *Indian Miniature #16*" is a poem of pursuit and discovery:

> The sun-face looms over me, gigantic-hot, smelling
> of iron. Its rays striated,
> rasp-red and muscled as the tongues
> of iguanas. But I
> am not afraid. I hold in my hands
> (where did I get them)
> enormous blue scissors that are
> just the color of sky. I bring
> the blades together, like
> a song. The rays fall around me
> curling a bit, like dried carrot peel. A far sound
> in the air—fire
> or rain? And when I've cut
> all the way to the center of the sun
> I see
> flowers, flowers, flowers.

The work of art elicits a series of actions and the reader comes to feel how alive that work of art is. The poet particularly emphasizes lineation in the form of many enjambments, rich sensory evocations—not only the visual but smell, sound, and touch—and a narrative of her feelings that is both forthright and metaphorical. We feel what the miniature looks like but not through simple representational description. Poems, after all, don't simply describe—they imagine—and the poem's ending is a sort of imaginative explosion, a glow of feeling and actuality. (7)

Narrative enables the poet to go somewhere that is not on any map, but then neither is *Paradise Lost* or "The Lotos-Eaters" or *The Waste Land*. The narrative journeys in poems mime our life journeys as they testify to coherences and identities, but poems go well beyond notions of beginnings and ends. Poems can expand any moment or perception or even an object into a story. Even within the confines of the ballad, this knack cannot be rationalized; it is a mythic inclination. As in Keats's great ode, it is a way at once to step inside and outside of time.

NARRATIVE
In the Classroom

1. Poets very much continue to write book-length narratives. Read one of them (see chapter bibliography) and write a response piece as to how the way the poet tells the story differs from how a prose writer would tell it. Focus on such aspects of poetry as rhythm, image, sound, and line.

2. Read some of the ballads in the Library of America volumes devoted to nineteenth-century American poetry (see chapter bibliography). How do they differ from one another? What elements do they have in common? How do they compare with twentieth-century ballads such as Auden's "As I Walked Out One Evening" or James Merrill's "The Summer People?"

3. The title of a narrative poem typically refers to a salient aspect of the poem, such as the name of the poem's main character. How does "Complicated" refer to the events McLaughlin relates? How does the title affect your reading of the poem?

4. Read some poems that are similar to Louis Simpson's in that the poet is telling about a historical epoch. Philip Larkin's "MCMXIV" would be one example of such a poem. How does the inevitable condensing that the poet must do feel to you in terms of capturing an era's emotional reality? How much does the poet's view of an era correspond to your own?

5. Write a poem that narrates an incident from your life. Use Christianne Balk's poem as a model to help you think about how to include all that needs to be said in telling your story. Pay attention to syntax so that you don't keep using the same sentence constructions over and over as you narrate the event.

6. David Keller's narration is typical of much contemporary poetry in that he moves among an array of incidents—some personal, some not. Read another contemporary poem (such as "Money" by William Matthews) that tells a story in this way and write a response piece as to how well the poet succeeds in telling the story. What makes the narrative cohere?

7. Write a poem about a work of art that constructs, as Chitra Banerjee Divakaruni does, a metaphorical narrative of your responses. Use all your senses in your writing to make the work of art and your responses as vivid as possible. As in Divakaruni's poem, pay especial attention to image, metaphor, and lineation.

NARRATIVE
Five-Day Lesson Plan

A discussion of different forms of narrative should precede the work for this week.

Day 1   Have students write a poem no more than twenty lines long capturing an incident that has happened to them recently. Students need to consider which "moves" are crucial to telling their story: image, metaphor, dialogue, statements, descriptions, point of view, and how a poem ends.

Day 2   Divide class into pairs. Have students exchange their short narrative poems with their partner. Then, have students respond to the draft according to the following guidelines.
   • Do you understand what is going on in the poem? If you don't, what don't you understand?
   • Does each line in the poem contribute to the narrative? Are there lines that are superfluous? If so, why?
   • What "moves" contribute most effectively to the telling of the story? Explain how.
   • Is the ending satisfying? Why or why not?

Day 3   This day is devoted to the redrafting the narrative poem and conferencing about the new draft.

Day 4   Narrative depends upon scope: how big or small the slice of time that the narrative relates. Have students write a longer narrative poem (at least thirty lines) in which they narrate an incident from their childhood. Have students think about the following issues as they draft the poem.
   • You're looking back at an incident. How did you feel about it then? How do you feel about it now?
   • What details have remained in your memory?
   • What is the connection between the past "you" and the current "you"? How can that connection be captured in the narrative?
   • What is the point of view of the narrator?

Day 5   Have students finish a draft of their longer narrative and then conference with their partner, using the questions from Day 2 to structure the conference.

Beyond the Week

Students finish both of their narrative poems and print out at least four copies of their poem. Divide the class into four groups, asking them to work as group of editors. Each group will edit a book of the class's narrative poems. This means that students in each group need to agree on how to sequence the poems, whether the book should be in sections, and what its title should be.

Invite in some English teachers and have each group present to those teachers their editorial decisions. Have the English teachers choose which book will be published. Then have the winning group use a desktop publishing program to actually publish the book.

NARRATIVE
Bibliography

Poems

"Complicated" by Joe-Anne McLaughlin from *The Banshee Diaries*, Exile Editions, 1998; "To the Western World" by Louis Simpson from *A Dream of Governors*, Wesleyan University Press, 1959; "The Crabs" by Richmond Lattimore from *Poems from Three Decades*, Charles Scribner's Sons, 1972; "Dusk Choir" by Christianne Balk from *Desiring Flight*, Purdue University Press, 1995; "The Man Who Knew the Words to *Louie, Louie*" by David Keller from *Sweet Nothings: An Anthology of Rock and Roll in American Poetry*, edited by Jim Elledge, Indiana University Press, 1994; "Cutting the Sun, After Francesco Clemente's *Indian Miniature #16*" by Chitra Banerjee Divakaruni from *Leaving Yuba City*, Anchor Books, 1997.

American Poetry: The Nineteenth Century, edited by John Hollander, Library of America, 1993.

Time and Money by William Matthews, Houghton Mifflin, 1995.

Some recent book-length narrative poems are *The Sleeping Beauty* by Hayden Carruth, Copper Canyon Press, 1990; *Iris* by Mark Jarman, Story Line Press, 1992; *After the Lost War: A Narrative* by Andrew Hudgins, Houghton Mifflin, 1989; *Omeros* by Derek Walcott, Farrar Straus Giroux, 1990; *Dead Reckoning* by Brooks Haxton, Story Line Press, 1989.

16

The Didactic Poem
(How Poems Instruct)

Summary

Over millennia there have been poems that have taught every-thing from the origins of life on earth to how to tune a six-cylinder engine. Traditional societies have passed on rites and legends in the form of poems: rhythmic tellings that traced stories everyone in the society was expected to know. Some sorts of knowledge are firmly anchored in groups, but there is an enormous amount of fact and intuition that depends on the individual's perspective and for which the didactic poem has been a natural outlet. Such poems inform, satirize, lecture, or persuade, as they see fit. In all cases, they have something instructional to impart, whether it be down-to-earth or esoteric. What the didactic poet has to think about is how a poem, as opposed to an instruction booklet, can be the best way to impart some knowledge.

A didactic poem is one that teaches. What is taught and how it is taught vary from culture to culture. Since we are accustomed to read-ing instruction booklets and how-to books, the notion of imparting information in a poem may seem odd. But if we think about some of poetry's assets—concision, memorability, rhythmic force—the di-dactic impulse in poetry may not seem quite so strange.

One way traditional societies have cohered over centuries is by consciously passing on the lore of the society. This lore forms a wis-dom tradition and all sorts of material may be included: stories about gods, the origins of the particular society, cosmology, proverbs, rites, supplications, knowledge concerning material things, history, ta-boos. Native Americans, for instance, possess a rich wisdom litera-ture of instructive poems and songs such as these lines from an Inuit tribe about how the raven came to be black:

> Long ago, when animals were people,
> Raven and Loon were partners.
> They agreed to tattoo each other.
> "Me first," said Raven.
> (He was white at the beginning.)
> So Raven took lamp soot
> and drew little fire sparks
> on his partner's feathers.
> That was how Loon
> got the pattern on his feathers.
>
> But Raven tired of painting.
> He grabbed some soot and ashes
> and tossed them over Loon's back.
> That's why it's grey now.
>
> Loon was angry.
> He scooped soot from a pot
> and threw it at Raven.
>
> Raven had been white.
> Now he's black.
> He stayed that way.
> There's no more to this story.

The blunt assurance of the final line indicates in its way how the story was a part of a heritage and how no one should muck around with that heritage by adding on commentaries or opinions (or creating his or her own stories). The didactic impulse is conservative in the sense of trying to maintain something: It seeks to pass on what is esteemed by a community so that lore will not be lost. (1)

As far as the Western literary tradition is concerned, the didactic impulse goes hand-in-hand with Greek culture. Any reader of *The Iliad* or *The Odyssey* (9th C. BCE) knows how much information is packed into those two epics. A century later Hesiod shows that the intentionally didactic writer need not be a dull writer. In his long poem *Works and Days* Hesiod chose to focus on agricultural life. The narrator in this poem is giving advice to his brother Perses who is—in the narrator's eyes at least—a slacker. His basic advice (or admonition) is "*Work*, you fool Perses." Having laid down the law to his brother the narrator goes on to write about eminently practical matters:

> As for your oxen, get yourself a pair of bulls
> Nine years old—their strength won't be spent yet
> And they'll be in their prime, at the best age for work.

The poem, however, is far from being a compendium of livestock knowledge. For one, Hesiod is addicted to proverbs and is always eager to bring in a relevant saw:

> Plan harm for another and harm yourself most,
> The evil we hatch always comes home to roost.

We shake our heads in agreement. In fact, Hesiod has advice to offer about everything. Among other things he does not trust his brother to have the sense to come in out of the rain: "On your head / Wear a good felt cap, so your ears won't get wet." And for good measure he tosses into the miscellany of his poem "A List of Don'ts to Avoid the Gods' Anger" such as "Don't beget children after coming home / From a burial. Wait until after a feast of the gods." Hesiod is very much a unique and irrepressible writer. *Works and Days* is his poem and though his didactic purposes wander from topic to topic (including seafaring), the tenor of the poem is steady: He, Hesiod, is there to tell you the score. He is a purveyor of any lore he can get his hands on. One can imagine Hesiod seated at the counter of some diner or luncheonette and over a couple cups of coffee talking to anyone who will listen about everything under the sun, including the gods' Olympian and distinctly less-than-Olympian love lives. The lessons that gossip imparts never seem to go out of style. (2)

It has been said that no one ever learned to farm from reading the likes of Hesiod. That is probably true but you certainly could pick up some intriguing pointers. The Roman poet Virgil continued this mellow, mildly practical tradition in his *Georgics*. These poems discourse upon trees, vines, livestock, weather lore, and beekeeping. Virgil can impart quite detailed information in a poem:

> The best-formed cow looks fierce, her head is coarse,
> Her neck is large, her dewlaps hang down loose
> From throat to shank; flanks rangy as you wish,
> And largeness through the limbs, including feet,
> Are preferable, and look for shaggy ears
> Below the crooked horns.

Such lines may reinforce the feeling that a solid meter can sustain any sort of language (as long as it is not forced language). Virgil has, however, more up his sleeve than cowfacts. He too is fond of mixing proverbs with practical instructions:

> So, while the herd rejoices in its youth,
> Release the males and breed the cattle early,
> Supply one generation from another.
> For mortal kind, the best day passes first:
> Disease and sad old age come on, and work;
> The ruthless grasp of death ensnares us all.

In such a passage one sees what has come to be thought of as an integral aspect of didactic poetry—that there be a moral to the story. Virgil's moral about the transience of life did not seem out of place to his readers. The habit of drawing general, decisive conclusions from the great hodgepodge of human endeavors seems a basic one. Indeed as Aesop's fables (and Virgil) indicate, the endeavors need not even be human. (3) Some ages favor this moralistic habit (as the eighteenth century); some have mixed feelings about it (the nineteenth); and some have, by and large, little use for it (the twentieth).

It would be a mistake to think that all the didactic poetry of the classical world bequeathed us were some tips on cattle dealing. The incomparable Roman poet Ovid (in full, Publius Ovidius Naso) wrote *The Art of Love*, a verse manual full of lore for both sexes about the ways of love. Ovid tells men the best places to find women; he tells women about how they should wear their hair, what clothes are most becoming, about cosmetics, even about shaving their legs. He has opinions about everything amatory, plus savvy tips such as telling men that the way to a noble lady is through her handmaid. It may be that no one became a cattle dealer from reading Virgil, but one suspects that many people learned some very particular information from reading Ovid. Certainly before the flood of pornography in the late twentieth century, Ovid was considered spicy stuff, both forthright—"Haste side by side to the goal: then is pleasure full, when man and woman lie vanquished together"—and opinionated—"I hate her who gives because she must, and who, herself unmoved, is thinking of her wool. Pleasure given as a duty has no charms for me...." (4)

The didactic impulse ebbs and flows in Western literature. As we noted, the eighteenth century is definitely a high tide. In part this has to do with that era's view of poetry as more of a social rather than a personal expression. There were strong feelings that poems should be instructive. Talking about oneself for the sake of talking about oneself in a poem was not considered beneficial to anyone. Many Augustan poets admired Roman poets; such hallmarks of the age as Samuel Johnson's "On the Vanity of Human Wishes" and Jonathan Swift's "Baucis and Philemon" and "Horace, Lib.2, Sat.6" are based directly on poems of Juvenal, Ovid, and Horace.

One didactic mode the Augustans particularly favored was the satire. As it mocks people and behaviors, the satire may teach us what constitutes proper behavior. The couplet form lent itself to tart observations such as Johnson's "Wealth heaped on wealth, nor truth nor safety buys, / The dangers gather as the treasures rise" and the wry opening of Swift's imitation of Horace: "I often wished that I had clear / For life, six hundred pounds a year...." The satirist was a feared figure; only a fool would cross the likes of an Alexander Pope. Since neither human folly nor what Pope termed "the diabolical power of stupidity" ever goes into abeyance, the opportunities for satire have not diminished a whit. Indeed in the 1980s the art critic and historian Robert Hughes used Alexander Pope's *The Dunciad* (written in the 1720s) as a model for "The SoHoiad," a poem in rhymed couplets that lampooned the downtown New York art world. (5)

In modern times the didactic poem has assumed numerous artistic masks as it has both criticized and reinvented itself. The didactic impulse has been at odds with much of the modernist agenda. After all, what the didactic poem sets out to do is to tell rather than show, to make all manner of statements and assertions. One person's proverb may be another person's boring, sententious palaver. Particularly as it proffers advice, the didactic poem may be on tenuous footing: Who are you to tell me about anything? Did I ask for your advice? Are you an expert? Did Virgil go to an agricultural school? Did Ovid study the psychology and technique of sex? As moderns have been aware of how desperately contingent and perplexing life is, the confident lucidity of didacticism may seem suspect. Also societies that question many things and are tied to technological innovations for their identity are not thinking about what information to pass on to the next generation. The next generation in all likelihood will be different; lines of continuity are increasingly hard to draw.

In his poem "Manifesto: The Mad Farmer Liberation Front" Wendell Berry creates a persona, the Mad Farmer, who does not let the twentieth century stop him from being didactic. At first, however, the advice is really more like anti-advice; it is the patter of money: "Love the quick profit, the annual raise, / vacation with pay." The Mad Farmer sees a world where "When they want you / to die for profit they will let you know." To this sardonic advice he soon opposes words of a very different sort, for example: "Put your faith in the two inches of humus / that will build under trees / every thousand years." Such lines constitute the real advice of the poem and it is urgent advice as Berry enjambs most lines and begins sentences with imperative verbs—"love," "denounce," "say," "ask." The mellow horticulturist of Virgil and Horace has turned into a farmer whose values are no longer the currency of the society and who is pained by his marginality. Part of the farmer's being "mad" (a pun as it draws on both craziness and anger) is his didacticism. He is not interested in proposing fictions; he emphatically wants the reader's attention and he wants the reader to heed every word he has to say about how to live life. To the question, "Who are you to give advice?", the farmer in all likelihood would reply, "Because I am the steward of human sustenance." Berry's Mad Farmer is not humorless; he is combative. The fierce, wily streak of didactic satire is alive in such a poem that addresses a society's clichés and proposes alternative visions. (6)

Berry has not been the only American poet who has chosen the didactic vein. Denise Levertov has written a poem forthrightly entitled "Didactic Poem":

> The blood we give the dead to drink
> is deeds we do at the will of the dead spirits in us,
> not our own live will.
> The dead who thirst to speak
> had no good of words or deeds when they lived,
> or not enough, and were left in longing.
> Their longing to speak, their thirst
> for the blood of their deeds done by us,
> would leave no time, place, force,
> for our own deeds, our own
> imagination of speech.
> Refuse them!
> If we too miss out, don't create our lives,
> > invent our deeds, do them, dance
> > a tune with our own feet,
> we shall thirst in Hades
> in the blood of our children.

The structure of the poem could not be simpler: a series of propositions; a climactic, imperative outburst to the propositions; and a prophetic explanation of the outburst. It is a didactic poem as it has a teaching to impart, but it is also a dramatic poem. A contest is going on between life and death, and Levertov is harried by an almost vampire vision of the dead ruining the living. The exclamation is powerful because the scene is one of great danger. The poet cries out words of advice. The echo in the poem is that of Greek tragedy where the chorus offers advice, counsel, warnings. There is nothing far-fetched about Levertov referring to "Hades," or "the blood of your children." The poem's didactic depth lies in the perennial nature of the struggle Levertov addresses.

Berry's and Levertov's poems are poems of advice more than poems of information. The didactic poem that imparts quite definite information is, however, just as prevalent in contemporary American poetry. Thomas Lux's poem "River Blindness (Onchocerciosis)" is an excellent example. In this poem Lux describes the progress of a terrible disease. He is determinedly clinical as he discusses "Treatment," "Prognosis," and "Prevention," and as he enumerates the results of the disease: "rash, wheals, gross / lichenification, atrophy (known as 'lizard skin'), / enlarged lymph glands / leading to pockets of loose flesh.... " At the same time as he is presenting the facts, he is commenting on the effectiveness of facts and descriptions as when he writes "Some twenty to forty million (hard to be exact!) people infected." The numbers are ghastly but so, in its way, is the half-exasperated, half-doing-the-best-we-can, parenthetical exclamation. Lux not only lays out the suffering the disease entails but also the attitudes toward the disease—"Avoid Third World communities." "I'm safe," the reader in North America thinks, but then there are those "Some twenty to forty million." They are not safe, as the final allusive lines of the poem make plain: "baby flies dying, dying / in their eyes, / blinding them." The poem teaches about the disease in a way only a poem can do, for it brings a whole range of human feelings—empathy, disgust, distraction—to its subject. To the cliché of "Isn't that awful?" Lux opposes the detailed viciousness of actuality and the glib, casual ease of commentary. A number of questions are posed by Lux's poem such as "What is information?" and "What does one need to know about something to understand it?" The knowledge a textbook provides about a disease and the knowledge Lux's poem provides are very different. The knowledge we get in the poem is feeling-knowledge; it is the knowledge only art can provide. The poem can at once challenge and incorporate attitudes—including the attitude of scientific objectivity.

When poets write poems that instruct the reader how to do something, they are free to mix practical information and metaphor in whatever degrees they see fit. Furthermore, the poet as an investigator into the nature of reality asks questions about what practicality is and whether metaphor is impractical. Two poems about food illustrate these issues. Gary Snyder's poem "How to Make Stew in the Pinacate Desert Recipe for Locke & Drum" eschews metaphor entirely. Though not overly detailed ("mix the dumpling mix aside, some water in some / bisquick"), the reader feels that if one happened to be in the desert, one could cook this dish. What's wonderful about Snyder's poem is how he constructs a narrative about the whole process of making the stew that includes the shopping, building a fire, cookware, even the waiting for the dish to be done ("sit and wait or drink budweiser"). The texture of the entire experience—"stir it while it fries hot, / lots of ash and sizzle—singe your brow—" *is* the poem. The act of consuming the food that constitutes the final line of the poem is unadorned—"Dish it up and eat it with a spoon, sitting on a poncho in the dark." The poem is a lot more than a recipe: It is about cooking outside in a certain landscape at a certain time of night. The reader is made to experience the earthiness of this cooking quite literally. (7)

In the words of Nancy Willard from her poem "How to Stuff a Pepper," "Cooking takes time," and time is a grace note of didacticism: however long it takes to impart something can't be predetermined. In the poem a cook is teaching someone "how to stuff a pepper with rice," and the body of the poem consists of an extended rhapsody about peppers. Before anything happens, the peppers must be appreciated for who they are. Among other things the cook compares the pepper to "a temple built to the worship / of morning light." The cook not only composes metaphors but describes the texture of her experiences in swooning detail: "I have taken the pepper in hand, / smooth and blind, a runt in the rich / evolution of roses and ferns." The actual lesson gets no further than cutting open the pepper. Plainly, the teaching here is not so much about stuffing a pepper as about appreciating the pepper. In contrast to Gary Snyder's matter-of-factness, Nancy Willard makes a wonderful, poetic fuss. Without feeling for the ingredients there is no inspired cooking. Her poem is inspirational precisely as it makes us revisit the glory of the pepper's form and texture. As teachings go, Nancy Willard's poem is a witty yet profound lesson, for it makes the reader feel how precious and remarkable a mere pepper is.

If one reason to read poems is to expand our range and depth of feeling, then the didactic poem, as it seeks to teach us what otherwise would go unremarked, is an important sort of poem. Poems such as Philip Booth's "How to See Deer" and May Swenson's "How to Be Old" take the practical tenor of the instructional poem and apply it to concerns that are not easily taught. (8)

For his part, Booth uses the unswerving emphasis of the imperative mode—"forget," "go," "stay"—to make the reader experience what it takes to get close to deer. He talks the reader through the experience until the reader reaches a point where "You've learned by now / to wait without waiting.... " The poem is reminiscent of spirit experiences imparted over generations by traditional peoples, for it explicitly is concerned with vision. The reader who wishes to learn to see deer must go through a number of steps that are hard for the average, distracted, impatient human being. To have the vision, one must heed advice that is at once precise—"Instructed by heron, / drink the pure silence"—and that allows for the intuitive—"See / what you see." Booth's poem refutes the glib notion that poems make nothing happen. Any reader who actually follows Booth's advice is likely to experience a distinct change as to how she or he walks through woods and fields. The reverence accorded deer in many cultures as particularly spiritual creatures is encompassed by Booth's poem.

The audacity of poets is boundless; there is no experience poets will not try to enter into and bring to the reader's attention. May Swenson's poem "How to Be Old" offers rare and pithy advice: "One must work a magic to mix with time / in order to become old." Through the image of a doll she considers youth—"One must put it away / like a doll in a closet"—and age in terms of that doll:

> In time, one's life will be accomplished,
> And in time, in time, the doll—
> like new, though ancient—may be found.

As advice this is measured yet affirming. The delicacy of the verb "may" is especially notable as it indicates at once degrees of certainty and uncertainty: something will happen; something possibly will happen. The notion of the didactic poem as some overwhelming uncle who dispenses loud, unwanted advice is very far from Swenson's artful, surprising lesson. The deep murmur of poetry—"in time, in time"—affirms perspectives and attitudes that are thousands of years old and that knit one generation to another. There are certain instructions that only poems can give. (9)

THE DIDACTIC POEM
In the Classroom

1. Find some poems from other societies that pass on lore of the society. Native American literature is rich in this tradition. Copy your favorites into your poetry notebook. Explain why you chose the poems. What did the poems teach you? Did you find any cosmogonies—stories about how the world came to be? How do the details vary in such stories?

2. Write a poem based on someone you know who likes to tell people what to do, how life works, or what the score is. Think about Hesiod when you do this and read some more of Hesiod in the Stanley Lombardo translation from which we have quoted (see chapter bibliography). What makes Hesiod a credible person to be giving advice?

3. Many cultures tell animal stories that have a lot to say about human behavior. Read a sampling of Native American tales, some fables by La Fontaine, and Aesop's fables to observe how animal behavior speaks to human behavior. What similarities and differences do you notice among the three?

4. Read some of Ovid's *The Art of Love* (see chapter bibliography). How does sexuality in his time compare with present-day concepts of sexuality? Write a poem in which Ovid appears on a TV talk show. Would he be giving similar advice in our world?

5. Read some satirical poems of the eighteenth century. What sorts of behaviors are being made fun of? How are they being made fun of? What specific elements does poetry offer that makes satire effective? Based on your reading, write a poem that satirizes someone's behavior.

6. Wendell Berry's poem is entitled a "Manifesto." What exactly is a manifesto? Write a manifesto of your own about something that bothers you and about which you want to give some advice.

7. Everyone has recipes. Write a recipe poem that not only tells how to prepare a food dish but also tells about the setting where the dish has been made and who has made it and what feelings go along with it. Is it your kitchen or your grandmother's or a campfire or a dormitory?

8. Write your own "how to" poem, blending detailed information with advice. Don't be long winded; instead try to get at the heart of what the experience is about and how to do it.

9. Write a poem of advice in which a member of one generation passes on advice to a member of a younger generation.

THE DIDACTIC POEM
Five-Day Lesson Plan

Day 1   Read Philip Booth's "How to See Deer." Have students write the poem in their poetry notebook. Discuss the "moves" Booth uses to teach us how to see deer. Based on Booth's poem, have students write a poem of their own about how to see something.

Day 2   Divide students into pairs and ask them to respond to each other's poem by specifically noting what the poem has taught them. Students write these responses in their poetry notebooks and share them with their partner. Students then revise their poem according to input from their partner.

Day 3   Read Gary Snyder's poem, "How to make Stew ... " aloud and have students write the poem into their poetry journal. Based on Snyder's poem have students write a poem of practical advice on how to do something.

Day 4   Break students into pairs and have them work on these drafts according to the guidelines for Day 2.

Day 5   Have students write an "anaphora" poem that begins with, "What I have learned about ——————— is that ... " Have students read poems aloud and then discuss the points and issues that their poems raise.

Beyond the Week

Didactic poetry can instruct us on how to behave. Have students write a poem instructing someone in a particular occupation (e.g., a police officer, a school principal, a politician, a religious leader, etc.) on how to behave. Be as realistic or as idealistic as you want.

THE DIDACTIC POEM
Bibliography

Poems

"How Raven Became Black" by Tom Lowenstein from *Ancient Land: Sacred Whale*, Farrar Straus Giroux, 1993; *Works and Days* by Hesiod, translated by Stanley Lombardo from *Works and Days and Theogony*, Hackett Publishing, 1993; *Virgil's Georgics*, translated by Smith Palmer Bovie, University of Chicago Press, 1956; *Ovid: The Art of Love and Other Poems*, translated by J. H. Mozley, William Heinemann, 1929; "The SoHoiad" by Robert Hughes from *Nothing If Not Critical*, Alfred A. Knopf, 1990; "Manifesto: The Mad Farmer Liberation Front" by Wendell Berry from *Collected Poems 1957–1982*, North Point Press, 1985; "Didactic Poem" by Denise Levertov from *The Sorrow Dance*, New Directions, 1967; "River Blindness (Onchocerciosis)" by Thomas Lux from *Split Horizon*, Houghton Mifflin, 1994; "How to Make Stew in the Pincate Desert Recipe for Locke & Drum" by Gary Snyder from *The Back Country*, New Directions, 1968; "How to Stuff a Pepper" by Nancy Willard from *Swimming Lessons: New and Selected Poems*, Alfred A. Knopf, 1996; "How to See Deer" by Philip Booth from *Lifelines: Selected Poems 1950–1999*, Viking, 1999; "How to Be Old" by May Swenson from *New and Selected Things Taking Place*, Little Brown, 1978.

The Art of Love by Ovid, translated by Rolf Humphries, Indiana University Press, 1957; *The Erotic Poems* by Ovid, Penguin, 1983.

17

Place and Politics

Summary

Each one of us comes from somewhere on earth—a village, a town, a city, a suburb, a settlement—and that "somewhere" defines us profoundly. A lot happened in that place before we came into this world—not only historically but also geologically and ecologically. When a poet talks about the ground beneath her or his feet, that ground speaks both to realities that go far back in time and ones that exist in the present, palpitating moment. An integral part of that matrix of realities is the political heritage attached to a place. America, as it revels in the new and improved, would seem to banish such a heritage, but politics, like place, never goes away. Poems inescapably reflect the fact that we create geography and politics and are created by them.

Poems don't begin in poets' heads. They begin with the earth upon which poets live. Nothing exists without that sustaining ground and poets are not ones to forget that. Indeed, poets revel in earthliness and earthiness: Their task, in many ways, is to take the full measure of what it is to live on earth. They seek to take nothing for granted and to touch the particular vibrancy of any patch of that ground—or asphalt or floor—beneath their feet. Any place in this world is rich in actualities—geographical, environmental, historical, personal, and political. Poets summon up the welter of feelings that adhere to places.

That ground beneath the feet holds all sorts of surprises, however well we think we know it. Gary Snyder's "Thin Ice" confronts one small but resonant moment:

Walking in February
A warm day after a long freeze
On an old logging road
Below Sumas Mountain
Cut a walking stick of alder,
Looked down through clouds
On wet fields of the Nooksack—
And stepped on the ice
Of a frozen pool across the road.
It creaked
The white air under
Sprang away, long cracks
Shot out in the black,
My cleated mountain boots
Slipped on the hard slick
—like thin ice—the sudden
Feel of an old phrase made real—
Instant of frozen leaf,
Icewater, and staff in hand.
"Like walking on thin ice—"
I yelled back to a friend,
It broke and I dropped
Eight inches in

Snyder locates a number of things very carefully: where he is, the time of year, the weather, what he is doing. The poem is a paean to actuality and Snyder relishes each fact. The cliché of walking on thin ice, a notion evoked in contexts far removed from a February day, is no longer a cliché. The test the poet faces is how to convey the feeling of the experience. Snyder, who is a very disciplined writer, doesn't overdo his descriptions. He never loses the sense of ice-ness as he follows the experience from moment to moment. We feel those moments as Snyder moves from perception to perception and ends with an exact—"eight inches"—plummet and no punctuation. Poetry asks of every experience and moment and word—what is that? What is walking on thin ice? Cliché is language that has become dead; our senses barely connect a living experience with the words. (1) Snyder invigorates our senses and our sense of language as he walks "On an old logging road / Below Sumas Mountain."

Snyder's poem is active: he walks and drops. Faye Kicknosway's "Linoleum" is a poem of immediacy but it is a poem of memory as someone recalls the feel of linoleum:

> The floor
> has been done up with linoleum,
> but it was so scuffed
> she tacked a rug
> down
> over it
> to hide it,
>
> and the rug bunched up
> and she had to straighten it
> each time
> she moved a chair.
>
> He remembered
> the linoleum, how slick
> and cool it was, the pattern
> worn off, made slippery
> and silvery
> as freshets and streams
> in sunlight.
>
> He would slide
> his bare toes along the marks
> and grooves
> in the linoleum, thinking
> he would surely
> scoop out tiny fish, at least
> a panful.

With the pressure
of his toes
he'd work at closing off
a stream,
diverting it
to pass under a chair
where he imagined
it would be shady

and cool
and lazier fish
would fatten.
He could feel

the linoleum
under the rug, but did not like
to, for the rug was always
caught up in ridges
when she vacuumed it,
and it was bumpy

under his bare feet, and its texture
was dry
and coarse.

Our everyday minds barely think about a floor; we have so many thoughts in our heads and we are on the way to somewhere. Poetry, however, lingers and ponders. There is no hurry. As far as poetry is concerned actuality is never apprehended in a hurry. One beauty of "Linoleum" is that while it evokes an actuality it pays homage to imagination: The protagonist conjures a world of water and fish from a humble piece of floor covering. Kicknosway ends the poem with the more recent actuality—a rug has covered the covering and that rug has a very different feeling to it. The truth.to which poetry addresses itself is that every little thing, be it a rug or piece of linoleum or carpet or some boards, is something. Who can tell how many such feelings we have subconsciously in the course of a day in response to the world around us (and below us)? Poetry can touch, present, and, to a degree, sort out these feelings—not as abstractions but as responses to the myriad textures of places. (2)

"Thin Ice" and "Linoleum" present the ground beneath our feet as a very physical actuality. Linda Hogan's "Map" is also powerfully physical but the scale of reference is much vaster. The issue of the ground beneath people's feet remains, but the ground in her poem is a whole continent. She delves into a decisive and sometimes bitter truth about place: How a place is spoken of depends upon who is doing the talking. Here is "Map":

> This is the world
> so vast and lonely
> without end, with mountains
> named for men
> who brought hunger
> from other lands,
> and fear
> of the thick, dark forest of trees
> that held each other up,
> knowing fire dreamed of swallowing them
> and spoke an older tongue,
> and the tongue of the nation of wolves
> was the wind around them.
> Even ice was not silent.
> It cried its broken self
> back to warmth.
> But they called it
> ice, wolf, forest of sticks,
> as if words would make it something
> they could hold in gloved hands,
> open, plot a way
> and follow.

This is the map of the forsaken world.

This is the world without end

where forests have been cut away from their trees.

These are the lines wolf could not pass over.

This is what I know from science:

that a grain of dust dwells at the center

of every flake of snow,

that ice can have its way with land,

that wolves live inside a circle

of their own beginning.

This is what I know from blood:

the first language is not our own.

There are names each thing has for itself,

and beneath us the other order already moves.

It is burning.

It is dreaming.

It is waking up.

Hogan is careful not to particularize place too much; she doesn't want her reader to get lost in the recriminations of history. Everything, after all, depends on point of view, and for those who lived in North America for centuries before Europeans came, the land was a place that spoke for itself. People did not have to speak for it; the trees and wolves and ice that were part of the land had their own tongues. To truly apprehend place is to apprehend a web of actualities and feelings, and Hogan deftly weaves that web when she notes that "the tongue of the nation of wolves / was the wind around them." The tragedy is that one group's reality may be another group's opportunity. So, for the Europeans, the trees were merely a "forest of sticks." Maps, as they represent places, subdue them to grids and locations just as words seem to the Europeans to "make it something / they could hold in gloved hands." Purpose (as in "plot a way") may ruin feeling and create loneliness, "hunger," and "fear," to say nothing of the mass deaths visited upon Native Americans. Hogan, however, has the courage and insight to acknowledge how deep the life of place runs.

As she notes at the end of the poem, "the first language is not our own. / There are names each thing has for itself." All the subduing that the Europeans perpetrated was, for all its success, fundamentally unreal. The energies of place are the "other order"; people can be attuned to those energies but they cannot own them. "Blood" and "science" both speak to that otherness that does not care about the boasts of human purpose. Place, even as it is gutted and forsaken, abides. (3)

The burden of history is political and, as it intersects with place, never—as long as memory can speak—goes away. We may take it for granted or ignore it or wish it were otherwise; we may fanatically endorse it, but in any case the responsibility is each of ours and, in part, defines our humanity. At certain moments the history of place is so tangible as to be dramatic. Howard Levy's poem about two white college students and a black woman registering voters in Jackson, Mississippi in 1966 is such a poem. It is entitled "Jackson, MS, 1966":

When she suddenly said "jump," holding on
to the old woman's hand, not letting go at all
though the old woman was anxious to get away
from us, the trouble we brought, the mixing up
of settled things, the warm February air
of Mississippi seemed to me to collaborate,
to sustain our white college boy
arms and heads higher and longer than possible.

Mrs. Carolyn Williams, two hundred pounds if a one,
just back to her native Jackson
after the poison of Chicago, grown huge
with her appetite for change, knew
this one would never register to vote,
70, a retarded daughter in tow, scared
even by a knock at her door,
one Negro woman, two white men,
since white folks on her dirt street only meant pain,
or viciousness, the bill collectors or the police,

but still deserved a treat, a gift of a moment in the future
and a joke on the rotted past.

And so when the old woman asked which of the two white men
was in charge, Mrs. Williams just turned to us
and ordered "Jump" and we jumped:
the Red Sea didn't part, the Confederate
flag didn't come down from the gold-domed Capital
and what changed was just enough in the woman's eyes
and Mrs. Williams released her.

Too often we think "political" means taking sides, as in admonishing one's opponents and asserting the correctness of one's own views. This is simplistic. However light the hand of democracy may feel, it is a hand and a weight. Sometimes that weight is very explicit and sometimes it is covert. Levy faces the experience squarely as he uses details to convince the reader of the authenticity of the experience. It is a "dirt street"; the old woman has a retarded daughter; Mrs. Williams is a big woman. He doesn't, however, overplay his hand; he notes that "the Red Sea didn't part." Politics is about human beings and, for all the abstractions and oratory involved, the decisions are made by individuals. Levy doesn't lose track of those individuals and he doesn't load the poem with attitudes about right and wrong. He knows that politics isn't some lummox who barges into the subtle world of art and starts spewing slogans. Politics is as physical and ineluctable as gravity; the great issue, as in Hogan's poem, is whose gravity is being imposed on whom. To his credit, Levy doesn't sidestep the question; on the contrary, he makes it palpable. (4)

Levy's poem explicitly presents a politically charged moment. Most moments are not that charged. The history of a place typically feels more like a weave, a fabric of national, regional, local, and personal history. A pleasure of poetry is its ability to consider how dense or loose that weave may be. As it speaks to place, poetry can manipulate time so the poem can crisscross eras and moments. And as it maintains a personal point of view, a poem can color large and small events with the persuasive touch of individual experience. Joe Bolton's poem

"Speaking of the South: 1961" evokes time and place as the stage
upon which a future poet noisily appears:

> John F. Kennedy is alive and loved, and the moon remains
> Somewhat of a mystery, and suburbs and shopping malls
>
> Are mainly somebody's bad ideas, and you can still
> Speak of the South in a voice not wholly laden with loss.
>
> In Cadiz, Kentucky, my father pastors a Baptist church;
> My mother types up his sermons, visits the town's sick.
>
> Later, he'll leave the ministry to sell stocks and bonds,
> And she'll leave him for a journalist from Birmingham.
>
> Kennedy will be shot. People will yawn at the conquered moon.
> The South will sprout suburbs and shopping malls like tubercles.
>
> But for now, say it's December in Cadiz, Kentucky.
> Tinsel for Christmas drapes Main Street, flickering
>
> As dusk comes on cold with a blue wind off Lake Barkley.
> The poolroom and diner fill with smoke and the low voices
>
> Of men who carry inside them the stillness of the fields
> They hope to work for at least another twenty-five years.
>
> A boy kisses his girl goodbye and follows his visible breath
> Home, dreaming of her creamy thighs and a red Chevrolet.
>
> In the Wishy-Washy, the divorcee folds her stained whites.
> And in a yellow room of the Trigg County Hospital,
>
> I am born—not yet named, nor equipped with the facility
> Of language, but squalling even then to make myself heard.

To those large-scale questions we sometimes ask—such as "What is the South?"—Bolton provides one answer. John F. Kennedy, lunar exploration, suburban sprawl mingle with specific lives, a time of the year, and a geography to give a strong sense of Cadiz, Kentucky, 1961. Bolton deftly moves from scene to scene, event to event. He takes pleasure in poetry's ability to pick and choose, pick and choose. He looks backward and forward in time as he balances the poem on the fulcrum of the final event. We all are intrigued by our origins; Bolton in a quiet but firm way celebrates his. (5)

The places poets write about usually are inhabited (though there are plenty of poems about the wilderness). In one sense a place is the sum of its inhabitants. "Who was there?" is always an interesting question. Tim Dlugos answers this question quite literally in his poem that is a list, "East Longmeadow." Here are the first dozen lines:

> Endicott Peabody was the governor.
> Dick Hickey, Jerry Pellegrini and Frederick Wheeler were the
> selectmen.
> Richard Clark was the town clerk.
> Father John Wolohan was the parish priest.
> Clyde Walb was the scoutmaster.
> Donald Emerson (blond, crewcut) was the sixth-grade teacher.
> Officer Craven was the police sergeant.
> Miss Eseldra Glynn was the other sixth-grade teacher.
> Mr. Francis was the only Negro teacher.
> James Latourelle was the plumber and Little League manager.
> John Quinn was the doctor.
> James Brown was the dentist.

The marvel of Dlugos's poem is that it goes on for three pages serenely noting one person after another. Vocations along with personal attributes and histories are given without any ado. Everyone's complete name is given; no one is considered more or less important than anyone else. The poem is exhaustive and yet the reader realizes that there were plenty of other people in the town. The feeling of so many distinct lives is consoling and unnerving at the same time, as is language's ability to summarize so pithily. Everyone is identified in some social sense and that sense is, to an extent, who the person is. (6)

But only to an extent. The deeper note of place is what it means to an individual, how it speaks to a specific person. Places are mute in the sense that they do not talk, but they do speak to us in a thousand nonverbal ways. The sight of a house or a pond or a tree or a sidewalk may say a great deal to someone who has lived in that house or walked beside that pond or climbed that tree or played on that sidewalk. Our lives consecrate places, sometimes intentionally, sometimes haphazardly. What a place is, is quite definable in some ways but quite mysterious in others. W. S. Merwin's "Lackawanna" engages the mystery of place:

Where you begin
in me
I have never seen
but I believe it now
rising dark
but clear

later when I lived where
you went past
already you were black
moving under gases by
red windows
obedient child
I shrank from you

on girders of your bridges
I ran
told to be afraid
obedient
the arches never touched you the running
shadow never
looked
the iron

and black ice never
stopped ringing under foot

terror
a truth
lived alone in the stained buildings
in the streets a smoke
an eyelid a clock
a black winter all year
like a dust
melting and freezing in silence

you flowed from under
and through the night the dead drifted down you
all the dead
what was found later no one
could recognize
told to be afraid
I wake black to the knees
so it has happened
I have set foot in you
both feet
Jordan
too long I was ashamed
at a distance

The river is very much an actual river but it is also the myth of a river—cold, dark, deathly. We may fear places—not just old, vacant houses—but places whose otherness is unsettling. The narrator of the poem was "obedient" but the river had no interest in his obedience. It was up to him to come to terms with the river and its figurative depths. The shifting, quavering, unpunctuated style of the poem perfectly registers the narrator's plight. Often poetry takes courage, for the poet must acknowledge something that the conscious, trying-to-get-from-one-day-to-another mind would rather not acknowledge.

In writing "Lackawanna" one feels Merwin exorcising his fear. He is able to name it without flinching—not to prove himself or show off, but to honor his feelings and the river that spoke to him so powerfully.

Poetry honors mystery, and our time in this vast world that was here so long before us is mysterious. The mingling of earth and sky that we witness each day speaks to our most basic sense of being alive. At some moments when we focus on the extent of the mystery, place is limitless and yet precise. Jane Gentry's poem "Exercise in the Cemetery" captures this feeling. (7) It is the bass note of place and returns us to the observation that poems begin with the ground beneath our feet:

> At dusk I walk up and down
> among the rows of the dead.
> What do the thoughts I think
> have to do with another living being?
> In the eastern sky, blue-green as a bird's egg,
> a cloud with a neck like a goose
> swims achingly toward the zenith.

PLACE AND POLITICS
In the Classroom

1. Write down some other clichés similar to "on thin ice." Then find new language to make the experience of being hot or cold or lonely or happy come to life. "I was happy as"—what?

2. Faye Kicknosway's poem captures the details and the dreaminess of a childhood experience in which one small space is a whole world unto itself. Think back to your own childhood and write a poem about a room or a yard or a field or a sidewalk or a porch and what you did there and how you felt about being in that place.

3. Read some other poems by Native Americans that speak to a sense of place (see chapter bibliography). After you've chosen a favorite poem, write a response piece about how a sense of place figures in the poem. Is there a political dimension to the poem?

4. The anthology *Letters to America* (see chapter bibliography) is devoted to poems about race. As an especially charged topic, race presents a challenge to any poet to create a poem that is both artful and powerful. Choose a poem that moves you and write a response piece about how the artistic elements of the poem—such as image, tone, syntax—reinforce what the poem says.

5. Write a poem based on a time and a place but in your parents' lives rather than your life. Narrow the poem so it looks at a year and a specific place. Think about to what degree national and world events might enter into your poem.

6. A poem that lists a number of people doesn't seem difficult, but the art of the poem lies in who is put into the poem and how much is said about each person. Write your own list poem that lists people in a certain community or neighborhood or school. Keep the poem to two pages in length so you have to do some real choosing.

7. Jane Gentry uses image to evoke place. Write a brief, imagistic poem (no more than 20 lines) that gives a sense of a person being out of doors in a certain place at a certain time of day or night.

PLACE AND POLITICS
Five-Day Lesson Plan

Day 1   Have students listen to Bruce Springsteen's "My Home-town." Distribute the lyrics to the song. Have students discuss this song. What does Springsteen tell them about his hometown? Is it convincing? Why or why not? Have the students write a poem about their hometown. Students need to consider the following points: What details stand out about your hometown? Think about the actualities of place: buildings, streets, parks, and geography. In what direction is your hometown headed? Do you want to leave your hometown?

Day 2   Students work on their draft of their place poem.

Day 3   Students write a response to the prompt, "What political realities have affected your hometown?" Ask students to discuss these realities and how they affect people in the town. Then, have students write a poem about someone in the town (not yourself) who is affected by those realities.

Day 4   Students work on the draft of this new poem.

Day 5   Students write a response piece to a pair of poems by a classmate. The response will focus on how well each poem accomplishes its task.

Beyond the Week

Students create a dramatic presentation based on their poems about their hometown. To help them stage their performance, students can view videos of productions such as Thornton Wilder's *Our Town* and Dylan Thomas's *Under Milkwood*.

PLACE AND POLITICS
Bibliography

Poems

"Thin Ice" by Gary Snyder from *Riprap and Cold Mountain Poems*, North Point Press, 1990; "Linoleum" by Faye Kicknosway from *Who Shall Know Them?*, Viking, 1985; "Map" by Linda Hogan from *The Book of Medicines*, Coffee House Press, 1993; "Speaking of the South" by Joe Bolton from *Days of Summer Gone*, The Galileo Press, 1990; "East Longmeadow" by Tim Dlugos from *Powerless: Selected Poems 1973–1990*, High Risk Books, 1996; "Lackawanna" by W. S. Merwin from *Selected Poems*, Atheneum, 1988; "Exercise in the Cemetery" by Jane Gentry from *A Garden in Kentucky*, Louisiana State University Press, 1995.

Letters to America: Contemporary American Poetry on Race, edited by Jim Daniels, Wayne State University Press, 1995.

For an anthology of Native American literature see *The Remembered Earth*, edited by Geary Hobson, University of New Mexico Press, 1981. An anthology that focuses straightforwardly on politics and oppression is *Poetry Like Bread*, edited by Martín Espada, Curbstone Press, 1994.

18

Occasions
(The Social Contexts
of Poems)

Summary

When someone dies or a couple marries or someone graduates or
gains an honor, it is natural to want to write a poem to register
the significance of the occasion. Poetry, after all, can go to the
heart of the matter without any apologies or fears; it can look
grief and joy in the face. Poems that stem from occasions tend to
be social acts because as humans we share occasions. Even the
solitude of loss may be bridged by the act of writing a poem others
will read and hear. When there are no notable occasions on the
calendar, poetry is always glad to celebrate the most basic of occasions—the amazing fact of being. That something or someone
simply exists is, as far as poetry is concerned, an occasion not to
be taken for granted.

Poems mark occasions. The first occasion each poem marks is its inspiration. At a certain moment on a certain day a person was moved to
write a poem. What moved the person—a dream, a thought, a memory, a word, a story, the sight of a dog or car or photograph or plate of
spaghetti, another poem—may be subsumed in the course of refining
the poem. It is, after all, not uncommon for a poet to put a poem
through dozens of drafts. It is also not uncommon for the impulse behind the poem to move in unforeseen directions: An aunt may wind
up living in Houston rather than Cleveland, a Buick may become a

Mazda. It all depends on what's happening with the direction of the poem as it exists on paper. Still, the poem testifies to its inception. Without that evanescent spark there is no poem. It is a truism that a poem cannot be willed. (1)

Although inspiration always represents a personal occasion, poems mark a myriad of social occasions. Among other things they praise, celebrate, lament, commemorate, narrate, instruct, elegize, satirize, complain, plead, exclaim, wish, take leave, regret, grieve, commiserate, confess, meditate, pray, and protest. These verbs mirror events. Over the years we have learned that to the question, "Have you ever written a poem?" most people respond in the affirmative, perhaps bashfully but nonetheless acknowledging their authorship. Typically, this writing stems from a desire to celebrate or commemorate or mourn another person. It is writing that comes from an occasion—a death, a birthday, an anniversary—and the writer has a powerful feeling that only a poem will do that sort of job, that only a poem speaks essentially to the spirit, not in a hocus-pocus way, but directly, without embarrassment. The accurate, vibrant, and unsentimental expression of feeling is literally priceless because it has nothing to do with money values that dominate so many of our exchanges. A poem is unique; there are no mass-produced poems. A greeting card saves time and has an understandable social function, but it is no equivalent to a poem one person writes for another person.

The most searching human occasion is death and to speak one's feelings about the dead is one of poetry's primary tasks. People recite poems at gravesides, at wakes, at services and remembrances. A poem that laments and sorrows and remembers, properly called an "elegy," knits the human generations together. Such a poem seeks not to dull the pain of loss but to recognize what the loss is. Ben Jonson's poem "On My First Son" (dated 1616) is surely one of the most focused and forceful expressions of grief and consolation in our language:

> Farewell, thou child of my right hand, and joy;
> My sin was too much hope of thee, loved boy.
> Seven years thou wert lent to me, and I thee pay,
> Exacted by thy fate, on the just day.
> O, could I lose all father now. For why

Will man lament the state he should envy?
To have so soon 'scaped world's, and flesh's, rage,
And if no other misery, yet age?
Rest in soft peace, and asked, say here doth lie
Ben Jonson, his best piece of poetry.
For whose sake, henceforth, all his vows be such,
As what he loves may never like too much.

To wring something articulate from the wilderness of loss is a great achievement. Jonson's poem is particularly remarkable in that he says so much within such a short space. He moves from aspect to aspect of the death—from a farewell that tells about his son and about Jonson's feelings to a wish ("O, could I ... ") to questions about death and salvation to a further address to the child ("Rest in soft peace") to a candid admission of his own sense of loss. Jonson uses poetry's resources—syntax, metaphor, concision—as a stay against raving grief. The poem is not a way out of grief; it is a way through it.

The very title of Donald Justice's villanelle "In Memory of the Unknown Poet, Robert Boardman Vaughn" addresses the main intent of the elegiac poem: to memorialize a person in words. Such poetry acts in opposition to the oblivion of forgetting; it speaks "In Memory of.... " That Boardman was "Unknown" gives the poem a further urgency; the memory of fame and recognition, however fleeting, is not a factor here:

> But the essential advantage for a poet is
> not, to have a beautiful world with which
> to deal: it is to be able to see beneath both
> beauty and ugliness; to see the boredom,
> and the horror, and the glory.
>
> T. S. Eliot

It was his story. It would always be his story,
It followed him; it overtook him finally—
The boredom, and the horror, and the glory.

Probably at the end he was not yet sorry,
Even as the boots were brutalizing him in the alley.
It was his story. It would always be his story,

Blown on a blue horn, full of sound and fury,
But signifying, O signifying magnificently
The boredom, and the horror, and the glory.

I picture the snow as falling without hurry
To cover the cobbles and the toppled ashcans completely.
It was his story. It would always be his story.

Lately he had wandered between St. Mark's Place and the Bowery,
Already half a spirit, mumbling and muttering sadly.
O the boredom, and the horror, and the glory!

All done now. But I remember the fiery
Hypnotic eye and the raised voice blazing with poetry.
It was his story and would always be his story—
The boredom, and the horror, and the glory.

The villanelle form is insistent and that is the note Justice treasures as he evokes the death and life of one of his mentors. There is no shying away from the squalor of the poet's circumstances but there is no backing away from his grandeur, either. The refrains enforce the factuality of identity, the imprisoning yet proud sense of how "It would always be his story," while the terse "All done now" honors the finality of the poet's death. To the question "Who was this person?" Justice conjures a sense of Vaughn's very being, his anguished essence. After one reads the poem, the poignancy of "Unknown" resonates even more. In its way the poem has made the unknown known. (2)

It is to the mystery of a human being and the elucidation of that mystery that many poems honoring the dead attend. Reuben Jackson's "Thelonious" is about the great jazz composer and pianist, Thelonious Monk:

bizarre?

mysterioso?

i say no.

for he swung like branches in march wind,

reached down
into the warm pocket of tenderness.

"little rootie tootie"
makes me dance a fat soft-shoe,

"monk's mood"
makes me sail.

but no bizarre,
no mysterioso.

he tilled song
like it was earth,

and he
a gardener
hell bent
on raising

any beauty
waiting
on the other
side.

As a famous jazzman Monk was a public person, but he was resolutely a private person at the same time. People inevitably have had all sorts of ideas about Monk, most of them about what an utterly eccentric soul he was. We are known, in part, through language, and Jackson questions some of the stereotypes about the man. Through metaphor

(a natural route in talking about a nonverbal form such as music)
Jackson presents his perceptions as to what Monk did and who he was.
Monk once told an interviewer who was questioning him about his
music, "I lay it down. You got to pick it up." Similarly, Jackson shows
us "his Monk"; it's up to us to respond. (3)

In Robert Lowell's poem "Alfred Corning Clark [1916–1961]" the
person whom the poem commemorates is not a public figure. He is an
old schoolmate of Lowell's. Whereas Jackson writes himself out of the
poem at the end, Lowell focuses throughout the poem on his relationship with Clark:

> You read the *New York Times*
> every day at recess,
> but in its dry
> obituary, a list
> of your wives, nothing is news,
> except the ninety-five
> thousand dollar engagement ring
> you gave the sixth.
> Poor rich boy,
> you were unreasonably adult
> at taking your time,
> and died at forty-five.
> Poor Al Clark,
> behind your enlarged,
> hardly recognizable photograph,
> I feel the pain.
> You were alive. You are dead.
> You wore bow-ties and dark
> blue coats, and sucked
> wintergreen or cinnamon lifesavers
> to sweeten your breath.
> There must be something—
> some one to praise
> your triumphant diffidence,

your refusal of exertion,

the intelligence

that pulsed in the sensitive,

pale concavities of your forehead.

You never worked,

and were third in the form.

I owe you something—

I was befogged,

and you were too bored,

quick and cool to laugh.

You are dear to me, Alfred;

our reluctant souls united

in our unconventional

illegal games of chess

on the St. Mark's quadrangle.

You usually won—

motionless

as a lizard in the sun.

Who Clark was—"Poor rich boy"—comes through very clearly, yet Lowell pauses at points—"There must be something—," "I owe you something—". A degree of mystery lingers. Lowell chooses to end the poem with the image of an animal (as he does in "Skunk Hour"). There is no explaining a lizard, just as there is no explaining the remembered adolescent who grew into this man who "died at forty-five." The second-person pronoun is literally halfway between the first and third: We are not in the narrator's "I"-consciousness totally nor do we see Clark as an independent person, a "he." Accordingly, the poem is more of a confrontation than a review; the bond Lowell discovers at the poem's end—"our reluctant souls united"—seems genuine. Lowell doesn't try to make Clark a large figure in his life and that is part of the poem's strength. How many people do each of us spend some time with and then lose track of? Then we hear about them or read about them. Lowell speaks to the integrity of Clark's being. The judgments made about a millionaire who had a number of wives tend to tell us more about people's feelings about wealth than about the actual millionaire. Lowell rescues the person, the abrupt "you." (4)

Death has inspired countless poems but all manner of other occasions also have inspired poems. Poems are great celebrators—of marriages, honors, triumphs, births, accomplishments. In some ways joy seems harder to express than sadness; its surface, so to speak, is smoother, there are not so many wrinkles to fasten upon. We talk about our troubles but we exclaim our joys. One poet who had the gift of articulating joy was Dylan Thomas. "Poem in October" is one many people have by heart. Here is the second stanza:

> My birthday began with the water-
> Birds and the birds of the winged trees flying my name
> Above the farms and the white horses
> And I rose
> In rainy autumn
> And walked abroad in a shower of all my days.
> High tide and the heron dived when I took the road
> Over the border
> And the gates
> Of the town closed as the town awoke.

Thomas could summon the amplitude, zest, verve, and zip of the physical world in image after image. In his hands language feels kinetic; all of life is a verb. Statelier but equally full of feeling is Edmund Spenser's poem celebrating a marriage in the late sixteenth century. (5) Here are some lines from "Epithalamion" that evoke the sounds of celebration:

> Harke how the Minstrels gin to shrill aloud
> Their merry Musick that resounds from far,
> The pipe, the tabor, and the trembling Croud,
> That well agree withouten breach or jar.
> But most of all the Damzels doe delite,
> When they their tymbrels smyte,

And thereunto doe daunce and carrol sweet,

That all the sences they doe ravish quite,

The whyles the boyes run up and downe the street,

Crying aloud with strong confused noyce,

As if it were one voyce.

While Thomas and Spenser speak *about* occasions, many poets have spoken *to* occasions. One way or another, these poets seek to influence a course of events. How much a poem influences actions has been debated for thousands of years, but that debate has not stopped anyone from writing love poems that seek to sway the beloved. Such poems will not influence the course of history but they may convince another person of the sincerity and intensity of the writer's feelings. To that end, there are love poems that praise the loved one, that expound upon the writer's affections, that lament the indifference of the loved one, that describe what will happen if the writer's affection is not reciprocated, and on and on. One of the wittiest poems in the language concerns a man who is trying to persuade a woman to enjoy the fruits of love. Here is Andrew Marvell's "To His Coy Mistress":

Had we but world enough, and time,

This coyness, Lady, were no crime.

We would sit down, and think which way

To walk, and pass our long love's day.

Thou by the Indian Ganges' side

Should'st rubies find: I by the tide

Of Humber would complain. I would

Love you ten years before the Flood:

And you should, if you please, refuse

Till the Conversion of the Jews.

My vegetable love should grow

Vaster than empires, and more slow.

An hundred years should go to praise

Thine eyes, and on thy forehead gaze;

Two hundred to adore each breast;

But thirty thousand to the rest:
An age at least to every part,
And the last age should show your heart.
For, Lady, you deserve this state;
Nor would I love at lower rate.

    But at my back I always hear
Time's winged chariot hurrying near;
And yonder all before us lie
Deserts of vast eternity.
Thy beauty shall no more be found,
Nor, in thy marble vault, shall sound
My echoing song: then worms shall try
That long preserved virginity:
And your quaint honor turn to dust,
And into ashes all my lust.
The grave's a fine and private place,
But none I think do there embrace.

    Now therefore while the youthful hue
Sits on thy skin like morning dew,
And while thy willing soul transpires
At every pore with instant fires,
Now let us sport us while we may;
And now, like am'rous birds of prey,
Rather at once our time devour,
Than languish in his slow-chapt power.
Let us roll all our strength, and all
Our sweetness, up into one ball,
And tear our pleasures with rough strife,
Thorough the iron gates of life.
Thus, though we cannot make our sun
Stand still, yet we will make him run.

If there is any question in the reader's mind as to what Marvell is getting at, an etymological look at the word "quaint," as in "And your quaint honor turn to dust," reveals that it is an old noun for the female sex organ. The occasion Marvell addresses is biologically a perennial one but it is very much a fleeting one—seize the day or the day goes by. One delight of the poem is how Marvell tries to rationally argue about something—"lust"—that is irrational. Marvell knows this but the pleasure he takes in allusions and analogies is palpable. If words can sway a mind, Marvell's must have succeeded. (6)

Seizing the day depends on the context. Marvell's is buoyantly sexual; Kate Rushin's poem about Rosa Parks is political. When Rosa Parks refused to move to the back of the bus she was acknowledging the system of segregation and saying "no" to it. Not somewhere else in some other time but right there, right then, in that bus. Activism is about seizing the day and in "Rosa Revisited" Kate Rushin celebrates the strength of one woman's activism:

for Mrs. Rosa Parks, activist

Quietly rough
Tough quiet
A dignified riot
Quietly outrageous
Rough righteous
Up/right/us
Up/lift/us
Connect us
Quietly bless us
Rough righteous
Right time
Right now time
Think how time
Do it now time
Decidedly quiet
Correct us
Caress us
Connect us

Encourage us

In/courage/us

In/rage/us

We walked/we walked/we walked

It was our hurts

Our lives

Our minds

Our time

Who said

Who was it said

When was it ever

It was never

About

Anybody's

Aching feet

As with Marvell, Rushin's wordplay ("In/courage/us / In/rage/us") celebrates the witty sinews of language. "Rosa Revisited" is very much a poem—aware of its lineation, its puns, its syntax, its lack of punctuation—yet it speaks very directly. One of the benefits of writing about an occasion is that it gives the poet an unmistakable focus. The question that has dogged many a would-be writer—"What is this about?"—vanishes before the immediacy of the event. Rushin's poem invigorates as it commemorates. (7)

The occasions we have noted thus far all involve human relations—loves and deaths, birthdays and marriages. Plenty of occasions exist, however, that involve other relations—with the spiritual world, for instance, or with land and other creatures and weather. George Herbert's "Lent" is very firmly about an occasion on the church calendar but speaks in its last stanza directly to God:

Yet Lord instruct us to improve our fast

By starving sin and taking such repast

As may our faults control:

That ev'ry man may revel at his door,

> Not in his parlour; banquetting the poor,
>
> > And among those his soul.

For Herbert, God is an intimate, revered but still an intimate. This attitude gives Herbert's poetry an astonishing freshness as the poet pleads, examines, praises, questions, wonders. Many of Herbert's poems are about occasions on the Church calendar. Each occasion has spiritual meaning; Herbert's task is to try to fathom mysteries of his religion that in many ways seem unfathomable. The various occasions—Christmas, Lent, Whitsunday, Good Friday—provoke encounters. These encounters have a dramatic quality because Herbert's religion is not a one-way street; God responds to the poet's words. (8)

In Irene McKinney's "Phoebe, Phoebe, Phoebe" the poet addresses not God but some birds. The occasion is simply the fact of their being:

> Oh you sweet birds. I heard your voices trilling
> and I figured the day wasn't lost at all,
> although you don't even know me. That you're here,
> you've arrived, is amazing, and coming from *reptiles?*
> If that's so, then I don't know how I've lived this long
> in such darkness. Come on out, then, and make
> that sound you make, that series of sounds,
> so incomprehensible and so straight, full
> of solids and liquids and your knowledge
> of the depths of the sea, which you've translated
> into tides of air. That's another world up there,
> currents flowing, great storms, huge landscapes,
> airscapes, invisible forever to me. The way it
> is to live there I can hear through you, jays,
> sparrows, phoebes, chickadees, who passed back
> and forth all winter long like a parallel
> universe, though you sweet birds know nothing
> of me and my strange heart. It makes me
> want to listen, and keep the lines of our

worlds in tandem. I try to fly here
in these odd ways, while you are warbling
that liquid from the other sea.

McKinney's poem moves beyond the strict definition of occasion; she is not celebrating National Phoebe Day. What she is celebrating and what poetry continually celebrates is the occasion of life—birdy, human, and otherwise. If poetry did nothing else than to wake us up to how much is going on around us at any given moment in this world, that alone would be a great achievement. "That's another world up there," McKinney writes in acknowledgment of the fact that there are worlds beside the human one. These worlds may be up or down, around or beyond; they may be "like a parallel / universe" and they may not. The crucial matter is that they exist and can be celebrated for that. (9)

Occasions and poems go together naturally. Over the years we have read poems ranging from "On the Occasion of My Gerbil Molly Having Babies" to "On the Occasion of My Brother Passing His Driving Test." Sometimes a poet will delve deeper into the nature of what occasion is. Jeffrey Skinner's "Late Afternoon, Late in the Twentieth Century" addresses a small occasion, a father watching his daughters play, and an impending large one, one century turning into another:

Dusk in Creason's Park comes on slow,
darkening the folds in the children's jackets,
the fall air beer-colored, thick
as remembrance, and the climbed trees shiver
down last leaves. I try to watch both kids
at once, though they tend to drift
from one steel-and-colored-plastic
jerryrig of slides, bridges and swings,
to another, independent, drawn to separate
peers, and I have to call them back
into one field of vision. There are other
parents here, sitting on the sawhorse
picnic benches, talking or smoking, their
arms spread the table's length, their legs

straight out. One man in his fifties
sits alone, an open briefcase before him,
making notes on a legal pad; office
alfresco ... It is close to finished
this century. Soon the 1 will change
to a simple 2, like a circuit changing
its mind from yes to no, like the short
step of a wounded soldier. We have filled
the universe with blood again, to no
one's surprise. And by the river's edge
we complained of thirst, we eyed
the forests and filled them with glare.
We said this edge will fit that space
and it did—the concrete oozed through
wooden forms, a thousand blank faces
rose above us, and we were happy
as a smooth surface, as a just-shot
arrow. We ridiculed the old questions,
stabbing our fingers in their leather chests
until they'd had enough, and headed back
to the salt caverns. We found love shivering
in a bus station and took her home,
tenderly sponging off the superficial
wounds. We gave her tea before the fire.
When she grew old we sold the company
and put her back on the bus. We died,
and the others were outraged, they pounded
fists, they petitioned, they did everything
but join us. Then they joined us. We
starved language, until the bones showed
through and the head dropped off
and rolled away, laughing like an idiot ...
The dusk in Creason's Park comes on, slowly,

and the parents reel their children in
on the soft hook of their names, and they all
drift toward their cars and thoughts
of food and sleep. *Girls*, I yell, *let's*
go! and they come, breathless and glazed
from play. In them I am well pleased,
and would build a city for their future.
But I will not take credit for their failures.
Lord, they are close to me as my skin
and I snarl when the dress is torn, when
the milk spills. Hear me. I am still that lost.

Skinner's poem peers into the frailty of the whole world of occasion. Occasion occupies an immediate foreground, as in a trip to the park, but the backdrop is the immensity of time—whether we measure it in years, decades, centuries, millennia, eons. To look back at an entire century, particularly one so rich in unprecedented events, can make anyone queasy. Skinner returns to the reality before him: "*Girls*, I yell, *let's* / *go!* and they come, breathless and glazed / from play." The poet goes on to consider his willingness and unwillingness. He is the man who sometimes is an irritable father and he is the man who is unsettled by much of what the twentieth century has wrought. In face of the terrific pressure to say, "I know. I know what this is all about. I can explain it." Skinner ends with the word "lost." He resists the temptation to tie his feelings up in a neat package. He does not shrink from the century's shortcomings or from his own. He cries out. He is left at the poem's end with the mingled sum of his articulation; his poem considers and marvels and probes, all at the same time. Many poems, after all, exist in a sort of equipoise where several inclinations are held together without being reconciled. The poet's task is to make us feel the situation, to make grief and joy and doubt and confidence actual. The occasion vanishes but the poem remains.

OCCASIONS
In the Classroom

1. Look over your drafts of one particular poem. Write a response piece in which you discuss the differences among the drafts. Are you satisfied with your most recent draft? Why or why not?

2. Read some elegies from the twentieth century such as Theodore Roethke's "Elegy for Jane," Dylan Thomas's "A Refusal to Mourn the Death by Fire, of a Child in London," and Randall Jarrell's "Say Good-bye to Big Daddy." How does each poem recognize the fact of death? Does the feeling of grief make itself felt in each poem?

3. Write a poem about a well-known person who is deceased. Try to conjure up who that person really was. (You may want to read a biography to help you do this.) Was the person's real identity the same as what the world at-large thought about the person? Elvis Presley, for instance, was a great reader of spiritual, mystical books. Is that how the world perceived him?

4. The second-person pronoun can create a powerful sense of intimacy and directness. Write a poem in the second person that addresses someone who was in your life but is not any longer there.

5. Take a close look at the whole of "Poem in October" and the whole of "Epithalamion." Write a brief response piece that examines the word choices in each of the poems. What words create a specifically celebratory feeling? Does syntax play a role in the expression of joy?

6. The Latin phrase "carpe diem" means literally to seize the day. Write a poem entitled "Carpe Diem" in which you urge someone to do something because the time is right. Try to present some definite arguments in your poem as to why it is a good time to seize the day. Consider the possibility of using a form such as the sonnet for your poem.

7. Write a poem commemorating the life of an activist. How have that person's actions influenced your own life?

8. The English language is rich in poems that are specifically Christian. Read more poems by George Herbert (an Anglican) and Gerard Manley Hopkins (a Catholic). Write a response piece that investigates how each poet brings his religion to life. What similarities do you note between the two poets?

9. Irene McKinney's poem addresses some birds. One of the marvels of poetry is that birds can talk back. A poet can write a poem in anyone's voice or anything's voice, for that matter. In that way a poet is a shape-shifter who becomes others. Consider Peter Wood's poem "Voice from the Crack between Gutter and Curb" (printed below) that is spoken by none other than a dandelion. After reading the poem, write a poem of your own in which an animal or a plant or a tree or a bird—or anything that is not human—talks about its existence.

Once I set my foot
no fire or flood will move it
no curse turns me away

With all this gold
I can afford to love
the one who scalds me

It's only me
I don't need things perfect
That's my secret

 Him I drain of terrifying waters
This one I feed
This one's thirst I quench

And you child put on a chain
a necklace or a crown
of blossom coins

Now bright and handsome
don't you feel like dancing
let me seed your breathing

OCCASIONS
Five-Day Lesson Plan

Day 1   Many times, writing a poem is a clearly social act. List occasions that poems may address. Have students go to the library, find as many poems as they can about occasions (e.g., death, birth, saying good-bye, etc.) and copy their favorite poem into their poetry notebook. Then have them write a response piece focusing on what makes the poem effective.

Day 2   Students share their favorite poem by reading it aloud. Assess each student's reading in terms of articulation, audibility, and pace.

Day 3   Have students choose an occasion that has meaning to their own life and write a poem that speaks to that occasion. Students must consider the audience for the poem (Is it for a sister, a friend, a parent? It may be for someone who is no longer living.)

Have students start another poem based on the premise that every poem offers the opportunity to celebrate the occasion of being alive. Put all the students' names in a container and have each student draw a name. Now, have each student compose a poem that celebrates that person.

Day 4   Students work on their drafts for the two poems.

Day 5   Students finalize their two poems.

Beyond the Week

Write a poem that addresses a school occasion. (E.g., a student might write a poem entitled, "On Taking My SAT's" or "On Driving My Mother's Car to School for the First Time")

OCCASIONS
Bibliography

Poems

"In Memory of the Unknown Poet, Robert Boardman Vaughn" by Donald Justice from *The Sunset Maker*, Alfred A. Knopf, 1987; "Thelonious" by Reuben Jackson from *Fingering the Keys*, Gut Punch Press, 1991; "Alfred Corning Clark [1916–1961]" by Robert Lowell from *Selected Poems*, Farrar Straus Giroux, 1977; "Poem in October" by Dylan Thomas from *The Collected Poems 1934–1952*, New Directions, 1956; "Rosa Revisited" by Kate Rushin from *The Black Back-Ups*, Firebrand Books, 1993; "Phoebe, Phoebe, Phoebe" by Irene McKinney from *Six O'Clock Mine Report*, University of Pittsburgh Press, 1989; "Late Autumn, Late in the Century" by Jeffrey Skinner from *The Company of Heaven*, University of Pittsburgh Press, 1992; "Voice from the Crack Between Gutter and Curb" by Peter Wood from *Horsetongue*, Demarais Studio Press, 1996.

19

Variations (Found Poem, Prose Poem, Shaped Poem)

Summary

The line is the basic unit of the poem but there are types of poems that redefine the line. In the prose poem, the line is that of the prose sentence; the poem looks like a prose paragraph (or number of paragraphs) in which each line runs all the way to the right margin. As it considers itself a poem while renouncing the poetic line, the prose poem is an intentional contradiction. In the found poem, the line is present in regular poetic fashion but the "poem" is a prose text that has been set into lines. It is a case of poetry kidnapping prose for its own ends. In the shaped poem, the line shapes a silhouette on the page—a pattern, a figure, a geometric or organic form. The shaped poem draws with words.

Traditionally a poem has been defined as a verbal composition written in lines. This distinguishes poetry from prose whose unit of composition is the sentence rather than the line. Modern times, however, have not been great respecters of traditions, and in nineteenth-century France various poets began writing paragraph-like blocks that looked like prose but which were, according to the poets, prose poems. What the poets were seeking was not complicated: On one hand, they wanted to demystify lyric poetry. By taking away the line, they forced the rhythmic stride of poetry into the functional gait of prose. In addition, poetry's aura of inspiration ("This is not a piece

315

of journalism or a report or a business letter. This is a poem.") did not look quite so highfalutin within the prosaic confines of the paragraph. On the other hand, poets were able to make prose seem much more self-conscious by labeling a paragraph or two or three a poem. Clearly no genre was immutable. Poetry, which prided itself on its distinctiveness, took a tumble of sorts.

The chief advantage of the prose poem is its ambivalence, the way it partakes of and yet opposes two forms. As it exists in opposition to poetry, it is defined negatively and hence seems more certain about what it isn't, than what it is. This negativity, however, hasn't stopped various poets writing in English (Gertrude Stein, William Carlos Williams, and Robert Bly among many) from constructing prose poems that mirror each artist's particular concerns. Perhaps the constant thread among different poets working in different cultures is that the prose poem is subversive. It questions the notion of what a poem is. **(1)**

The prose poem nowadays is not a curiosity but a respectable form (or anti-form, depending on how you look at it) with a very creditable lineage in a number of languages. It continues to offer a unique approach: self-aware of its hybrid status and indifferent to poetry's line-making traditions. Here is a contemporary example of the prose poem entitled "Langdon, North Dakota" and written by the American poet, Campbell McGrath:

Just across the Red River of the North we pulled over at dusk to watch a farm auction near Langdon, North Dakota. Pickup trucks were parked for a quarter mile in either direction. Wind shook the waist-high grass and weeds, lifting conic sections of dust swirling into the white, slanting, late-summer sunlight. As we came into the yard crowded with farmers and farmers' wives and children the family guns were on the block: shotguns, deer rifles, down to a bolt-action .22, "just right for a youngster." By the barn, Charlie deciphered a family history in farm equipment: '41 tractor, '51 truck and spreader, '72 tractor, '78 combine—good times and fallow, all going. The auctioneer was a friend from the next county, and the women laughed softly at his jokes, self-consciously, caught somewhere between a wake and a square dance, while the farmers smiled then gazed off into the trees as if listening to the wind. It was a wind that pulled the auctioneer's words from his mouth and left him working his jaws broadly and soundlessly, a grey-haired man in a cowboy hat waving his arms while the buzz of grasshoppers from the endless fields and the noise of thrashing leaves roared and roared. It was a dry, hard wind that blew until it was the sound of the citizens of Langdon singing hymns in the one-story Lutheran church at the edge of town, as their forebears had offered up prayers of thanks a hundred years earlier at the first sight of the borderless grasslands, moving west in the curl of the great human wave of migration, Swedes and Norwegians off the boats from Oslo or Narvik or Trondheim, sent out by train to the home of relatives in Chicago—an uncle whose pickling plant already bore the promise of great wealth—and on north and west, some falling out among the prosperous lakes of Wisconsin, the meadows and pinewoods of Minnesota, the white birch forests like home and the green hills like heaven, through the last of the moraine and glacial defiles, across the lithe Mississippi and into the edge of the vast prairie, the Great Plains of North America still raw with Sioux and locust plagues, the last massive buffalo hunts flashing in the hills of Montana no more than a generation gone, the Arctic wind massing a thousand miles to the north and barrelling down the continent, along the width and breadth of grass, the Dakotas, Nebraska, sod and wild flax in the spring, limitless land, a place to plant and sow that neither Indians nor winters fierce as Stockholm's nor the virulent range wars could take away from the Vorlegs and Johannsens and Lindstroms, a tide of settlers moving out across the heartland, naming lakes for Icelandic heroes, founding towns like Fertile and Walhalla, islands in the great grass delta. It was the sweet wind of Capitalism in the inland Sargasso.

The auction began at noon, was almost over when we arrived. Gone already were the canoe, wading pool, camper, motorcycles, lawn furniture, toys, old clothes, the house, the land itself. Through the window I could see a stag's head over the mantel. Charlie's boots were thick with dust. As we left they were auctioning off an artificial Christmas tree, a last-ditch offering from Sears or Woolworth's. "A real handy article, folks, only gotta wait four months to get your money's worth—do I hear a dollar, do I hear four bits?"

It was nearing the day the smiling auctioneer spoke of, that promised Christmas, a season of hope and redemption. I have carried the draggled plastic tree across the continent and back in my heart. I have felt the silvered needles sting, heard them rustle in the glow of blinking Christmas lights like wheatfields in the first wind of autumn. It is a wind which carries the seeds of life and the dust of extinction. I have dreamt of tinsel and glass balls, of a living room in the heart of the Great Plains. It is a winnowing wind. It is a bitter wind.

By the standards of either poetry or prose, McGrath's prose poem is a compelling piece of writing and in its mingling of metaphor and detail it seems very much a poem. One senses that the poet could have cast the piece into long, Whitman-like lines and let the repetitions do their incantatory work. He chose not to, however, and the interesting question is, "What does he gain by writing the poem this way?" No doubt each reader will have her or his answers to this question (including some that may feel McGrath would have done better to put the poem into lines). For our part, we feel that McGrath gains from the prosaic look of "Langdon." His prose poem describes an auction at which a whole way of life is being sold off. Is this event the stuff of lineated poetry? As McGrath sees it, the answer is "no." The prose poem refuses the consolation of being poetry; this refusal mirrors the fact that there is no consolation for the people who once owned the farm. That farm, as those people lived on it, is done for, and in its stoic, unlineated way the poem is a gesture of solidarity. For its part, the prose poem seeks to record what happens with a minimum of poetic interference. Everything is allowed into McGrath's prose poem: Its embrace is total and it makes no distinctions. The "wind" gathers a lot of history while the various realities of the situation ("do I hear a dollar, do I hear four bits?") impose themselves forthrightly. There is no consolation: "It is a bitter wind." The prose poem, in McGrath's hands, refuses to turn its face from the reality it confronts. (2)

The prose poem at once devalues its poemness—"No lines here"—and values it—"Still a poem of sorts." It testifies to the degree that a poem is a state of mind: Poemhood has become over the course of the twentieth century a slippery entity to define, but however one sees it, a poem retains a degree of almost numinous feeling. To say the word "poem," is to say a word with connotations of vision and insight and feeling that do not go away. The so-called "found" poem pushes poemhood to its limit by conferring poem status on material lifted directly from the world of prose. In a found poem the author recasts the prose into lines and stanzas and—*voila!*—declares it a poem. The author has written nothing new but rather has imagined what was prose as a poem. This sleight of hand takes audacity and sensitivity. Indeed, although the contents of any newspaper article or bureaucratic memorandum can be rearranged so as to look on the page like a poem, the reader may ask what has been gained by this act beyond a degree of self-consciousness. What is the point?

There are a couple of worthwhile points, one of which is unrepentant fun. One thing the found poem can be is a prank that poetry plays on the heedless world of prose. By situating some unsuspecting piece of prose within the norms of poetic form, a scrutiny of the words is provoked that otherwise would not be forthcoming. Among other things, this can highlight the sheer goofiness of some writing. Annie Dillard has such a found poem in her collection of found poems. The book is entitled *Mornings Like This* and the poem is entitled "Junior High School English." Here is the first section of the poem (the words are taken from *Junior High School English, For the Eighth Grade*, 1926):

A CHALLENGE TO YOUR SPIRIT

Girls and boys of America, you
Are the hope of the world!
You can't evade it, young America.

And are you going to go on dancing
And spinning on your ear?
What are you thinking about, sitting

There staring into the dark?
Haven't you been lying around long
Enough? Shouldn't you go to work?

Find as interesting a subject as possible.
Write as vivid a sketch as you can
Of a person who attracts you or an animal.

The present day is entitled to its jokes about the past, particularly if they make the present day think a bit uneasily about what strictures its own junior high school English textbooks are dispensing. As Dillard casts the sentences of the authors into poetic form, she is having a deserved joke at their expense and also one at poetry's expense. The last way Briggs, McKinney and Skeffington would want to think about their words is that they formed a sort of poem. "Perish the thought!"—as those authors might have exclaimed. The rhythmic breadth of free verse allows Dillard to turn the prose into lines and stanzas that are quite uniform. The wonderfully wacky "or an animal" that squats at the end of the poem gains some of its wackiness from being situated as part of a final line of a final stanza. Its anti-climactic, afterthought quality jounces against the reader's expectation that some conclusion is going to be reached. Dillard's sensitivity to poetic form has fun with her authors' bumptious prose. The poem creates a frame for the uplift that once distinguished textbooks. (3)

Sarah Gorham's found poem "Dear Growing Teen: a Found Poem" is culled from the pages of magazines that advise teenage girls. The uplift Gorham zeroes in on is much hipper but the peppy tone is recognizable:

> Mom walks into your room and trips.
> It's probably because
> > a) she's clumsy
> > b) she's blind
> > c) there's stuff all over the floor
>
> What your room reveals about you!
> Brooke Shields, Drew Barrymore,
> Fiona Apple, Gwynneth Paltrow.
> Hippie chic tie-dye, creative crochet
> simply sleek, or glittery glam.
>
> A little extra coverage can be kinda sexy.
> What's a girl to do with all those glands?
> Tie them, tassel them, add
> a hair extender. In short, take defensive action.

Imagine! Pressing your lips together
in an almost perfect way. Fakin' it
so they'll never guess
how many dreams you have per night,

what band broke your heart when they broke up,
what singer's voice goes straight to your soul,
how the actor is handling all this.
You can still sizzle
even if you don't
bare all.

The wonderful salad Gorham makes from the breathless pronouncements of *Teen* and *YM* gives a strong sense of how screwy all this advice is in the first place. By running various sentences together,
Gorham highlights the absurdity of the language and the vulnerability of the readers of that language. By using poetic form, Gorham is
able to call attention to words so that they are defenseless: They
can't hide in the thicket of a prose paragraph. In the poet's hands,
prose repetitions become anaphora and the punchy rhythms of magazine writing become staccato lines that leave the reader feeling
breathless. The syntactic mix of exclamations, complete sentences,
fragments, imperatives, and even a question never lets the reader
settle down. The final sentence is a *coup de grace* as the words are
granted three full lines: Anything less would be a disservice to the
passion the words proclaim. Gorham did not write the words but she
certainly assembled the poem. (4)

To cast prose into a form of some sort is an exercise in thinking
about form. Why couplets or tristichs or quatrains or individual
lines or lines of the same length or different lengths or lines that all
begin at the margin or some of which begin at the margin? The issues
are almost endless as the poet reinvents prose as poetry. How best to
do it? Here is a found poem taken (word for word) from a piece about
slugs (the garden variety) by Herman G. Wheeler that first appeared
in *The Journal of College Science Teaching*. We've titled it "The Questions of Slugs":

I had expected to be asked
My first questions by some of nature's
Larger forest animals or plants,
So I was a little nervous
About giving control over
My learning process to slugs.
But I listened closely to their questions.
Each slug seemed to ask:
"I am here on the barely moist
Jogging path for what purpose?
Why am I not farther out,
On the soggy forest floor?"

We wanted to create a form that called attention to itself and hence chose to lineate according to natural syntactic units. Similarly, we wanted a block-like form that would make the experience all-of-a-piece. And we wanted capital letters at the beginning of each line to indicate that this was self-consciously a poem. But someone else could put Weller's paragraph into some other form and come up with a perfectly reasonable explanation for those decisions. The found poem entertains the arbitrary quality of form that art seeks to banish. *Paradise Lost* has to be in blank verse and William Carlos Williams's brief, imagistic poems have to have an informal look to their lineation, but a found poem opens up a whole range of equally plausible options. The sort of fiddling around that the found poem invites is obliquely imaginative. As Dillard notes, "This is editing at its extreme: writing without composing." How the found poem is read depends on how it appears as a poem. Form, as it creates a plausible context, lets the reader see the words in a new light. (5)

By putting a group of words in a formal setting, the found poem reframes a piece of language. How much material the author wants to consider depends on the author's intentions. Sarah Gorham quarried a number of teenage magazines for her found poem. All manner of texts can be examined (documents, testimonies, diaries) and from a mass of words an essence may be distilled. Such found poems have an order that is the work of the poet but no words that are in the source have been changed. Nancy Richardson's poem "An Everyday Thing" is constructed from the notes of lawyers representing the families of students who were killed and injured at Kent State. (Richardson's sister was one of the trial researchers.) Here is the poem:

> one round was fired on the hill.
> what did they say?
> you can see smoke in the pictures.
> good hair, the jury likes him.
> find the impeaching part.
> cause she's so pretty.
> watch out for hearsay and conclusions.
> did you see anyone carry any bodies?
> he put the blame on me for his fuck-up.
> you have any phenobarbital?
> he gave the order to kneel and take aim.
> if he hadn't heard the order to fire.
> he's getting scattered, tell him to sit down.
> can you help me cash my paycheck?
> one person in troop G emptied their whole clip.
> he's been ineffective lately.
> the net gain is clearly worth the cost.
> he had his hand on his holster.
> Bill was not dead there.
> I yawn to mask my true sentiments.
> when you play in the mud you get dirty.
> say thanks to Charlie.
> isn't death an everyday thing for everyone?
> this guy is a professional witness.
> he said if they rush us shoot them.
> how come you're saving all the notes?

The end-stopped form the author uses is, at once, self-aware and uncommon. Over and over again the reader has to slightly pause and pick up the poem again. Each line is a world unto itself. The text is focused but, nonetheless, has a random feeling since so many diverse remarks appear. The order in which the notes are presented is intuitive yet logical as the poem leads to its final, self-reflexive question. The poet is literally sifting through history; she turns the jumble of actuality into art. (6)

Richardson's poem opens up an enormous door. As the found poem respects the authenticity of its source(s), it is journalistic; but as it orders and forms the words, it is imaginative. Our age has seen a blurring of the line between reality and fiction, but poetry has, in fact, always been comfortable with that blurring. The truths poetry offers are of a poetic sort; they don't pretend to be reportorial or legal or documentary or scientific truths. Poetic statements are just that: they occur in a poem. Their validity is aesthetic and emotional. How much we believe in that validity is up to each one of us. Those who indict poetry for being impractical (a common enough complaint) might ponder two notions: Since facts exist in a social context they have an emotional tenor and any attempt to banish or expunge feeling from a social context carries a price, since suppressed feeling comes out sooner or later. Whether a feeling results in a poem depends on a thousand circumstances; what the found poem illustrates is how transforming the tenor of poetry is, how the framing of words in the structures of poems changes the import of those words—even as they remain the words they always were.

The prose poem and the found poem are hybrids as they traffic with the world of prose. The shaped poem, on the other hand, is a hyper-poem. It is so much a poem that its form on the page has a pictorial dimension that is an embodiment of the poem's topic. The overall words of the poem create a shape and that shape is the silhouette of a form, be it a column, a pair of spectacles, a bus, or a swarm of gnats. The shaped poem (also known as the pattern poem) draws with words.

The shaped poem is a novelty but that does not mean it is a triviality. George Herbert, for one, used the shaped poem to great and serious effect in the seventeenth century. In one poem Herbert represented on the page a pair of wings and in another he represented an altar. Here is "The Altar":

A broken A L T A R, Lord, thy servant rears,

Made of a heart, and cemented with tears:

   Whose parts are as thy hand did frame;

   No workman's tool hath touched the same.

       A H E A R T alone

       Is such a stone,

       As nothing but

       Thy pow'r doth cut.

       Wherefore each part

       Of my hard heart

       Meets in this frame,

       To praise thy Name:

   That, if I chance to hold my peace

   These stones to praise thee may not cease.

O let thy blessed S A C R I F I C E be mine,

And sanctify this A L T A R to be thine.

Herbert is a poignant poet who frequently addresses the disparity between the debility of his spiritual efforts and, what was for him, the
consummate strength to be found in Christianity. He was a man who
genuinely felt the pangs of his shortcomings; yet he respected the lessons humility taught him. An altar is a made thing and Herbert
adroitly contrasts the sense of the altar as a whole, constructed entity
with the human reality of a heart that only God could construct. The
unyielding form of the poem contrasts with the "broken" aspect of the
poet's heart. At the same time, the shape of the altar on the page
graphically testifies to the firmness of faith and praise. The shape is a
witness to the resolution of a spiritual dilemma.

    The trick of shaped poetry is to make the words speak to the shapes
they construct. In his remarkable series of shaped poems entitled "Vision and Prayer" Dylan Thomas represents a spiritual experience in
the forms of a diamond and a geometric hourglass. The shapes provide
a tautness that dramatizes the poet's experience as the lines expand
and contract. Here is the final poem in the series of twelve poems:

I turn the corner of prayer and burn
In a blessing of the sudden
Sun. In the name of the damned
I would turn back and run
To the hidden land
But the loud sun
Christens down
The   sky.
I
Am found.
O   let   him
Scald me and drown
Me in his world's wound.
His lightning answers my
Cry. My voice burns in his hand.
Now I am lost in the blinding
One. The sun roars at the prayer's end.

Though the poem as a whole, as it uses a simple vocabulary to such powerful effect, is a *tour de force*, the placement of the "I" all by its single self qualifies to our minds as a stroke of genius. The physicality of poetry could not be more emphatic as the feeling of intense pressure almost literally shouts from the page. Rhyme, syntax, and word choice work within the confines of the shape; if the shape was not present their collective energy would be diminished. The shape is an actualization of an inner moment, the invisible made truly visible. (7)

The poems of Herbert and Thomas emphasize expressive energy. The shaped poem can, however, be drolly mimetic as it imitates one shape or another. In his book of shaped poems entitled *Types of Shape*, John Hollander proffers a remarkable array of shapes ranging from the utterly physical—a key or an arrow—to the unphysical—an idea, an ego. To everything there is a shape and anyone interested in how utterly inventive a poet can be is advised to consult Hollander's book. In his introduction to that book Hollander notes that the shaped poem that fascinated him as a child was the tale told by the mouse in

Alice's Adventures in Wonderland, a poem that appears on the page in the form of a mouse's tail (a visual pun) and indeed is not only shaped but also makes use of type size so that the final words of the poem—the little end of a mouse's tail—are teeny-tiny.

Shaped poems gravitate to either geometric forms—cross, triangle, diamond—or imitations of made things—cars, escalators, buildings. Some shaped poems, however, create organic shapes on the page. Jeffrey Harrison's "Swifts at Evening" is such a poem:

> The whoosh of rush hour traffic washes through my head
> as I cross the bridge through the treetops into my neighborhood
> and what's left of my thoughts is sucked up suddenly
> by a huge whirlwind of birds, thousands of chimney swifts
> wheeling crazily overhead against a sky just beginning
> to deepen into evening—turning round and round
> in their erratic spiral ragged at the edges
> where more chittering birds join in the circling
> flock from every direction, having spent all
> day on the wing scattered for miles across
> September skies and now pulled into the
> great vortex that funnels into the air-
> shaft of the library, the whole day
> going like water down a drain with
> the sucking sound of traffic and
> the birds swirling like specks
> of living sediment drawn from
> the world into the whirlpool
> into the word-pool flapping
> like bats at the last
> moment diving and
> turning into
> words.

Thanks to Harrison's deft shaping we experience the physical form that the birds make as they are "pulled into the / great vortex that funnels into the air- / shaft of the library ... " The poem's final word acknowledges the written quality of the experience as it affirms the power of language. Words (and the vortex they form on the page) enable us to witness something remarkable and compelling. To form all the words against the left margin would be to take the empathetic, whirling joy out of the poem. The shape is a phenomenon just as a poem is a phenomenon, something that happens in time, in some form, and is, in its particularity, unique. (8)

VARIATIONS
In the Classroom

1. Read some prose poems in English by different poets. Given that all the poems are in the same form, write a response piece detailing the differences you note among them concerning elements such as tone and occasion.

2. Write a prose poem of your own. After you have written the poem, write a brief piece about why the subject of the poem seemed appropriate for the prose poem form.

3. Take a passage from any of your textbooks and lineate it so that it becomes a found poem. By making the passage into a poem, what qualities of the prose become more noticeable? Write a brief piece explaining why you lineated it the way you did.

4. Choose a section from a magazine column that gives advice and turn it into a found poem. You can construct your poem from one, uninterrupted passage or you can string passages together to form your own poem.

5. Read a found poem constructed by another student. Write a response piece as to the formal decisions the student has made about elements such as line and stanza.

6. Read a primary source document of American history—a diary, a polemic, a first-hand account of an event, a testimony. Construct a found poem from your source. Limit yourself to no more than two pages in length.

7. Read the entirety of "Vision and Prayer" by Dylan Thomas. Choose one poem and write a response piece about the art of the shaped poem. Consider the effect on the words that the shape exerts and whether the poem would be the same if the shape were removed.

8. Think about which sort of shaped poem—geometric, mimetic, organic—appeals to you and write your own.

VARIATIONS
Five-Day Lesson Plan

Day 1   Have students create a shaped poem based on examples provided by the teacher. (See chapter bibliography.)

Day 2   Once the poem has been revised to the satisfaction of the student and the teacher, it is time to collaborate with the art department to silk screen poetry tee shirts.

Days 3 Through 5

Work on and finish poetry tee shirt collaboration.

Beyond the Week

Stage a poetry/art event in which students display their tee shirts and read their poems.

VARIATIONS
Bibliography

Poems

"Langdon, North Dakota" by Campbell McGrath from *Capitalism*, Wesleyan University Press, 1990; "Junior High School English" by Annie Dillard from *Mornings Like This*, HarperCollins, 1996; "Vision and Prayer" by Dylan Thomas from *The Collected Poems 1934–1952*, New Directions, 1956; "Swifts at Evening" by Jeffrey Harrison from *Signs of Arrival*, Copper Beech Press, 1996.

Types of Shape by John Hollander, Yale University Press, 1991.

For various sorts of prose poems in various contexts see *This Body is Made of Camphor and Gopherwood* by Robert Bly, Harper & Row, 1977; *The Morning Glory* by Robert Bly, Harper & Row, 1975; *Kora in Hell* by William Carlos Williams, reprinted in *Imaginations*, New Directions, 1970; *Tender Buttons* by Gertrude Stein, reprinted in *Selected Writings of Gertrude Stein*, Random House, 1946. Also, *Models of the Universe: An Anthology of the Prose Poem*, edited by Stuart Friebert and David Young, Oberlin College Press, 1995.

Prose

On the prose poem see *A Tradition of Subversion: The Prose Poem in English from Wilde to Ashbery* by Marguerite S. Murphy, University of Massachusetts Press, 1992, and *A Poverty of Objects: The Prose Poem and the Politics of Genre* by Jonathan Monroe, Cornell University Press, 1987.

20

Coaching the "Moves": On Teaching Poetry in the Classroom

One way to look upon the preceding chapters is as a playbook, a collection of strategies, for the teaching of poetry. The question for the classroom teacher is how to best use it. As a teacher you want your students to be able to master the strategies. How well the students learn them depends upon how well "the moves" are taught. The teacher is a facilitator who affords the students an opportunity to attempt, practice, and familiarize themselves with the art of poetry.

A good coach teaches all the moves consistently over a period of time. Teaching poetry is a yearlong endeavor. During that time, the teacher imparts the basic aspects of poetry and builds upon them. Accordingly, we have structured this book so that one rudiment of the art of poetry builds upon another. We suggest that the teacher approximate our sequence of chapters. Of course, this depends upon what the teacher wishes to emphasize. What is crucial is that the moves be taught so that the students have a complete perspective on poetry. Failure to do this is likely to lead to dogmatic assertions that cripple the teaching of poetry such as, "If it doesn't rhyme, it isn't a poem."

A playbook is only as good as how the coach teaches it. A good coach (and of course a coach is a teacher) knows that the playbook in and of itself is not a guarantee of success. Rather, it is how the player utilizes the information that matters most. "Utilize" implies the ability to use what one has been taught for one's own ends. The joy of basketball lies in playing it; the joy of poetry lies in actively reading and writing it.

Teaching poetry means having a set of objective methods that, over time, will broaden the students' subjective experience of poetry. Subjectivity, after all, is the quintessence of poetry, and it need not be downplayed in the classroom. The teacher's job is to enable students to articulate how poems work. This is invaluable knowledge because it makes students place subjective experience in an objective context; for example, "I like it because the poet uses line breaks to convey a feeling of uncertainty." Choosing, liking, feeling are subjective notions, but the art of poetry is rooted in objective actualities—sounds, words, accents.

TEACHING POETRY

What does it mean to teach poetry? First of all, it means being comfortable with poetry. Poetry is a cultural activity and teaching it is a cultural act. A teacher who is comfortable with poetry recognizes its cultural import and is accordingly engaged with the traditions of poetry and with the contemporary practice of poetry. Often, teachers exhibit a degree of aloofness when poetry is taught. This is understandable.

Teachers are in a double bind: On one hand, they are expected to have objective answers about a subjective art; on the other hand, they are confronted with the discrepancy between their knowledge of poetry and their students' lack of knowledge about it. Cultivating an attitude of separateness may seem a way out. Nancy Atwell has remarked upon this: "My students never found poetry anywhere. Real poetry was for me, for the teacher's sublime mind." Through experience, she came to realize that such a stance inhibited her teaching and her attempts at connecting with her students. This is hardly atypical. Being a proprietor of poetry is not the same thing as being a facilitator of it.

The facilitator is comfortable with the knowledge base of the art of poetry and with the cultural implications of poetry. Poetry is an environment; it is not something that is simply trotted out for 2 weeks in

May. To dwell in an environment one needs to know its landscape (knowledge base) and experience the satisfaction of living in that landscape (culture). Poetry, after all, is about feelings. The teacher who recognizes this, recognizes the validity of the emotional life—both the teacher's and the students'. This recognition allows the facilitator to acknowledge individuality. No two people like the same poets to the same degree. They don't have to.

What we call the poetry-based classroom allows for emotional input without compromising the teacher's authority. No one 'owns' poetry. What the teacher offers is familiarity with the knowledge base and a willingness to investigate the uses of poetry. We are the first to say that this is easier said than done.

The real-world classroom is formidable. Consider the following three scenarios from our experience:

Scenario No. 1: Senior English class. Discussion of Emily Dickinson's "After great pain ... ," A student, Sarah, mentions that, *"This poem is all about nervousness and how you feel when you are nervous."* The teacher replies, *"Well, maybe but it's really about much more than that, really, isn't it, when you think about it? Now let's look at the first few lines and you can see what I mean."*

Scenario No. 2: A student asks the teacher "What's a 'quartz contentment' or 'dimities of blue'? These words just don't make any sense. Seems kind of stupid to me. How's this stuff going to get me a job?" The teacher responds with, "Don't worry about it. Just get the overall idea of what Dickinson is trying to say so you can write your essay next week. We don't have time to look at every figure of speech."

Scenario No. 3: A teacher has just asked her class to look at a section of Whitman's "Song of Myself." To help them along she reads the piece aloud, with heart and clarity. After she finishes, during the moment when she is silently admiring the section, a student raises his hand and says, "What good is this stuff? Is it on the SAT? Do we have to know this? You've got your own agenda here, Ms. C., don't you ... you like Whitman that's why we have to read it, huh?"

The teacher, and the coach, inevitably deals with these situations. Why do we need to do this? What good will this do us? All we want to do is play the game. All we want to do is get good grades. For the teacher of poetry a large issue always looms: how to allow students to learn that poetry is an art and that as an art it can have intrinsic value for them, that it is a personal, meaningful way to understand their own emotions and thoughts about the world around them.

STRATEGIES

We emphasize a methodological approach that allows the teacher to present poetry so the student can use it to learn about the art of language. Our approach allows the teacher to examine poetry in terms of artistic practice. The various teaching methods are ways for students to *explore* poetry. They are sequenced approximately according to cognitive difficulty.

The first step in presenting poetry is to read it aloud. The teacher reads the poem and the students write it down, preferably in a notebook that they maintain over the course of the year for all poetry-related work. We see the poetry notebook as the focal point for all activities: writing poems down that have been read aloud, writing response pieces, drafting poems, writing down poems from other sources, compiling vocabulary lists based on poems, and keeping a journal of ideas, images, and questions. The poetry notebook is an expanded portfolio and can be assessed according to a rubric that takes into account all the dimensions of the notebook.

Listening to a poem being read and writing it down accomplishes a number of goals. As a "focused listening" exercise it reinforces the oral nature of poetry and how it has been passed on. Students do not know what the next word or line will be. Thus, they experience the narrative aspect of poetry in its most rudimentary and captivating form.

To listen to a poem and write it down is to experience the poem word by word. To our minds this process is the truest way to sensitize students to language because every word is crucial and multi-dimensional as it engages aspects of sound, rhythm, syntax, etymology, tone, and the sheer meaning (or meanings) of the word. Poetry is accordingly an important entryway into literacy. If literacy represents informed reading, then poetry is a crucible of literacy because it asks for complete attention to words as words.

After students have written a poem down in their notebooks, they are faced with the task of identification. What are the essential artistic elements of the poem? Do metaphors dominate the poem? How is enjambment used in the poem? What is the nature of the poem's rhythm?

Identification of artistic elements naturally leads to higher-order thinking. Students can compare and contrast artistic elements in other poems; they can evaluate the merits of particular poems based on evidence gleaned from them; and they can defend judgments about taste as to why they like one poem more than another. Such critical thinking skills produce confident readers.

When students analyze poems, they demonstrate how they understand a poem's external qualities; when students write imitations, they have the opportunity to internalize a poet's art. For example, by asking students to imitate Whitman's long lines, they will have to consider what goes into a long line—details, place names, strings of verbs. In part, writers learn to write by imitating masters of the art. Imitation leads to assimilation, as aspects of the art become part of the students' poetry repertoire.

That repertoire extends beyond the classroom. Once the students have demonstrated a knowledge base, they can pursue poems outside of the classroom. Finding examples that use various aspects of the art means that students must apply their personal understanding to poetry in general. Applying this understanding to a new poem requires inductive thinking. Such thinking demands that the student be able to locate a particular aspect of poetry in a new context. This calls for the confidence that accompanies close reading, that is to say, the commitment to paying careful attention to every aspect of the poem.

If students read poems, they are bound to want to write poems. To write one's own poems is to practice the art of poetry according to one's own inspiration. To do this is to consider the whole range of moves available to a poet. After the first draft has been written, the writer and someone else (teacher or peer) can consider how the moves work. This conferencing initiates the process of revision that leads to a completed poem.

As readers and writers, students can begin to see themselves as part of the community of writers. This community extends in many directions; it is multicultural in nature and includes many traditions. To investigate different traditions is to learn to appreciate different experiences. Democracy depends on our ability to empathize with a broad range of experiences. Every poem has a past; it comes from somewhere. By exploring different heritages, students come to appreciate how poets continually respect and reinvent the past.

Also, the classroom itself represents an immediate community of writers. It is the place where writers work cooperatively, as they share notions about language, art, and creativity. It is the place where students can talk poetry, as they observe and comment upon the various drafts of poems, where they can evaluate one another's work, and where they can encourage each other through intelligent critical discussion.

The more students work with poetry, the more imagination will become tangible for them. Imagination is intuitive but it is also concerned with strategizing. A good example of imaginative strategizing is the "what if ... " approach. This can be used when examining any poem, as the writer asks, "What if x becomes y?" "What if 'small' becomes 'little?'" "What if 'blue' becomes 'azure'?" Since every word choice is a multi-faceted decision, small questions can lead to big issues.

The classroom experience with poetry begins when a teacher reads a poem aloud. It can meaningfully conclude with students reading poems aloud. Oral interpretation shows how much a student has explored the art of the poem. Aspects such as rhythm, intonation, and pronunciation figure crucially in the convincing reading of a poem.

If reading a poem aloud demonstrates insight about it, memorizing a poem confirms how poems have lived for millennia. Memorization should not be a rote action; it is a way of making the poem part of the person.

THE POETRY-BASED CLASSROOM

The classroom in which these methods are used is what we call the "poetry-based classroom." In such a classroom, poetry is esteemed as the primary lens through which the student engages language. The "poetry-based classroom" is a language arts classroom in the true sense of that term—the art of language. Thus, the English classroom is not organized around grammar drills or literary history, per se.

Rather, it is built around the responsible use of language—be it aesthetic or practical. This is not to say that the English classroom abandons its typical concerns such as grammar and literature. It is to say that the "poetry-based classroom" uses poetry each day as a way of scrutinizing language usage. Such scrutiny is what we call "site based" in the sense that poems provide an experiential context for learning.

The "poetry-based classroom" advocates an integrated approach to language study. For instance, when grammar is taught, specific aspects can be examined through the lens of specific poems. Thus, usage can be examined in an actual and carefully constructed setting rather than as an isolated example in a textbook. This type of praxis shows the student that grammar is an active component of language use and not a topic taught for its own sake. Such an approach harkens to John Dewey's concept of experiential learning, a concept that values students' lived experience.

Language is rooted in feeling, and the "poetry-based classroom" values emotional growth. Poems raise all sorts of emotional issues. This is a benefit to students and teachers alike as it provides a forum to discuss and analyze how responsible language conveys feeling. Since each student is a user of language, this forum has personal implications for each student's responsible use of language. Thus, literature is not placed on a pedestal but is viewed as part of the continuum of language use.

MANAGING THE POETRY-BASED CLASSROOM

How does the teacher manage a "poetry-based classroom"? Primarily, the teacher is a facilitator. The teacher coaches the student in the responsibilities and pleasures of language. The teacher as coach does not diminish the stature of the teacher; it enhances it. What the teacher offers is not ultimate control—"I know what the poem means and you don't."—but experience in guiding students through the arts of language—"I've been here, experienced this, and here are some things to consider." In the "poetry-based classroom," the teacher demonstrates rather than explicates. The facilitator is not the guardian of meanings, but a guide to the art of poetry.

Accordingly, teaching poetry focuses not only on the *feeling* for process—how poems are made—but on the *process* of feeling—how readers respond. As the British educator, David Holbrook, observes, "Poetry is not 'writing about,' but exploring experience metaphorically." Metaphor typifies the inner/outer dynamic of the poetry experience. The facilitator recognizes this. On one hand, the teacher recognizes the validity of emotional responses to poetry and does not seek to short-circuit them. On the other hand, the teacher recognizes that responses that do not have demonstrable points to make are doomed to the futility of "I don't know why I like it, but I do." It is incumbent upon the teacher to demonstrate "the moves" so that the student can articulate responses.

A lot is going on in the "poetry-based classroom." Since the teacher uses poetry as the basis from which all other classroom work emanates (which is not to say, of course, that prose should be forgotten), poetry will be used in the classroom on a daily basis. This doesn't mean that every class period is taken up completely by poetry. It can mean 5 minutes, and it can mean 3 consecutive weeks of full periods. The activities are flexible: Students will be listening to poems, copying them in notebooks, reading poetry books, sharing drafts of poems, using dictionaries, conferencing with peers, reading poems aloud, posing questions about poems, and analyzing aspects of the art of poetry.

As someone who actively esteems language, the teacher in the "poetry-based classroom" is a model to students. The teacher brings poems to the classroom and makes them part of the environment. Poems are on the walls; poetry books are on the shelves. The teacher makes known to students the contemporary world of poetry, be it readings, journals, workshops, or Internet sites. The teacher helps to bring poets into the classroom. In terms of professional development, the teacher will stay abreast of pedagogical strategies, work with other teachers, and participate in conferences and workshops. All in all, the teacher will make students aware of poetry's active place in society.

The teacher is a planner who creates short-term and long-term designs for the use of poetry over the entire school year. Using poetry as a lens, the teacher can continually refine aspects of the art and of language. In this way, teachers can create curricula by sequencing activities. This can be accomplished over the high school years as a whole. From the student's point of view, long-term planning offers the opportunity to progress from novice to aficionado.

Everyone in a school community, teachers, students, parents, administrators, and the community at large, is concerned with outcomes. In the "poetry-based classroom," outcomes are measured in typical ways. A quiz on lineation would present students with new poems concerning which students would have to discuss how the lineation works in the poems. Students would be graded on how well they identified and articulated aspects of lineation. In similar fashion, student writing is graded according to clarity, vividness, coherence, and grammar, to name a few criteria. Poetry isn't fuzzy. To read and write poetry is to be conversant with an art.

FINAL THOUGHTS

Teaching the art of poetry in the classroom is a sort of rhetoric. The teacher provides models for students to examine, analyze, imitate, and emulate. Rhetoric is not some foggy, ancient, dead term. Rather, it presents a structured means to understand poetry as a living art. Rhetoric prizes practice, and the "poetry-based classroom" is the place for students to practice the art of language.

Poetry is an incalculable cultural treasure. Although poetry has an increasingly higher profile in society at large, its presence in secondary schools has diminished. Indeed, at the beginning of the twentieth century, poetry comprised a full 50% of the reading material in standard school texts; today it is less than 3%. Every adult in America was in high school. What did they learn about poetry? To fear and avoid it or to engage and enjoy it? The choice is each teacher's to make.

Epilogue:
Getting Started

As poets, teachers, and writers about poetry and teaching, we are often asked by teachers what they can do on a daily basis to get poetry into their classrooms. The segregation of poetry into occasional units frustrates them, but they have to contend with the tentacles of curriculum, standardized testing, and time constraints. What to do?

Our very simple answer is to read poems aloud to students and have them write the poems down in a notebook. This is hardly an earth-shaking proposal, but years of teaching have convinced us of its efficacy. There is, to our minds, no more concise way to process language. Literacy and poetry are literally and figuratively on the same page. Listening to a poem and writing it down allows students to focus on language word by word, comma by comma, sentence by sentence. In our speeded-up world, this is no little thing.

We read the poem line by line and indicate punctuation and capitalization as we proceed. Students who are not sure about spellings must check them later in a dictionary. Yes, it takes time to read poems aloud and write them down. It is, however, time very well spent in that students must pay careful attention to what is being said. Part of their grade lies in the accuracy of their writing the poem down. If they are

343

inattentive, their grade reflects it. The poet took pains to get it just so: you can take pains too.

We begin the semester with quite short poems—couplets and haiku that are complete poems. The brevity of the poems is inviting and makes students aware of how much a poet can do in a few lines. Quantity is not necessarily quality—always a good lesson for prospective writers. We build from there. Since there is a galaxy of poems in the English language from all eras that are no longer than thirty lines, material is not a problem. We need never repeat a poem.

And why not, we are often asked, give them photocopies and save valuable time for discussion? The fact is that writing a poem down *is* a valuable use of time in and of itself because it forces the student to listen to each word. It asks students to consider language on the most basic level—one word after another. Doing this work with a poem allows the student to construct a *context*, to discover a connection to the words and poem on his or her own *from within.* Thus, when students begin to ask questions about the poem as they hear and write it, they are *predicting.* In doing so, they inevitably will encounter ambiguities as they construct interpretations. This is as it should be, for the students are, in effect, making a move toward comprehension. Such questioning generates a dynamic between the teacher and the students, one that allows the students to *recognize* the sense of the poem. This important work, this learning about the relationships between words and poems, ups the ante since such primary literacy tasks naturally widen a student's vocabulary. There is no substitute for listening and writing down what one hears. It harkens to the very origins of poetry as an oral art and it stimulates enormous interest in the sheer narrative of the poem: What will the next line be? Photocopies of poems are expedients we resort to in the case of longer poems, but even there we insist that our students write down a passage of the poem.

Interestingly enough, we have found that after the initial grousing ("Don't they let you use the photocopier?"), students enjoy the listening and writing. Students enjoy this work because it is an innately "organizing" experience. As Frank Smith, in *Reading Without Nonsense,* would say, it is not nonsense; it is work that leads to purposeful reading. The poem becomes their own in the sense that they wrote it down, and the listening and writing is a sort of sanctuary, a quiet place we all go to and respect. From the teacher's point of view, it is an ideal way to begin a class period. The class knows what is coming in terms of structure, but the content is always new and it keeps them engaged and alert. The class also knows it has to be silent for the poem to be heard. Noise and attention to language do not go together.

The talkative fun begins once the poem has been written down. Discussion can be postponed until another day (the poem is there in the notebook to be consulted) or can begin immediately, depending on curricular concerns. In this activity, students are doing "real" reading. They are naturally creating a *context* for what they are hearing and writing. This work assists the student in thwarting the overload of information which Smith and others call "tunnel vision," the limited ability of anxious readers to process what they see. In fact, this exercise pointedly helps students avoid what Smith sees as the major pitfalls. They do not grapple with something that makes no sense; they do not need relevant knowledge; they do not become reluctant to use non-visual knowledge; they do not have to worry about their reading habits. Instead, they are free to dig below the surface structure of the poem and explore its deep structure (again, to use Smith's terms). Thus, the poem on the page is a gateway to language study—be it vocabulary, grammar, punctuation, capitalization, or issues about writing such as coherence, purpose, economy of language, word choice, or aspects of poetry *per se* such as metaphor, rhythm, sound, image, or literary history. We state an objective and all we ask is that our discussion stay with the poem. Students must continually focus on what is there in front of them. Writing proceeds from discussion but sometimes we reverse the order and have students immediately write a response piece or begin a draft of a poem.

Inevitably what we find is that students become very close and challenging readers and questioners. Why is there a comma at the end of line twelve? Why so many metaphors at the poem's beginning? Why is this in first person? Why is the poem in quatrains? Once the students see the poem as the stuff of living art, the questions are endless. By asking these questions, students are making explicit their theories about the direct experience that they had while listening to, writing down, and reading the poem. The questions they ask about this experience reflect how they make sense out of what they are reading.

Again, in terms of literacy, they are attempting to predict. They may not be good at it initially, but over time they become quite adept. The more questions they ask, the more knowledge they gain. They lose that "residual uncertainty" to which Smith and others refer.

And the data as to the efficacy of this approach? Well, students like it and learn to think about language very concretely. They learn all the terms about poetry in a context so they can use the terms. They learn to make judgments based on actual artistic issues rather than whim. They learn to write their own poems based on models that make sense to them. Not the least of virtues, they lose their fear of poetry. We believe that a curriculum that puts poetry at its center would boost test scores. After all, working with poetry builds a basic foundation of literacy with the art of language (the poem) as the prime exemplar. Such work allows the teacher and student to move beyond the pitfalls of differentiated reading instruction and into the realm of the good practice of reading instruction on the secondary level. As Dornan, Rosen, and Wilson, the authors of *Multiple Voices; Multiple Texts* note, both the teacher and the students become aware of their own reading process when engaging the poem. The poem listened to and written down becomes a "friendly text." We think it would have to boost test scores because students would be at close quarters with language day in, and day out. What better way to become skilled than immersion in the art of language? The poem can then become a reliable and valid source to assess student language skills both informally and formally depending on the instructional needs of the student.

The genius of poetry is that style is meaning in poetry. If you can talk about what the poet is doing in terms of rhythm and word choice and form and metaphor, you are going to be talking about meanings. What we have found over the years is that the ability to talk about poetry is not only a powerful builder of self-esteem but of language skills. Students can see themselves as active readers and writers of poems because they experience again and again, the poem blooming word by word in their notebooks through their own hands.

Many people in the field talk about reinventing English in order to deal with recent notions of literacy, of instructional models, of teaching and learning (just to name a few concepts). By reading poetry to students and having them write it down on a consistent basis, an English teacher truly can begin to remake the teaching of language and literature in the classroom. Teachers can begin to connect reading and writing so that it makes instructional sense. They can enable students to connect their life experiences to the varied experiences of our contemporary poets in an exploratory manner. Also, they can change the relationship between themselves and their students in exciting, genuine ways. To do these things is to reinvent English.

To use poetry in this way is to stress to students the idea that aesthetic experience is based upon their ordinary, everyday life but in a heightened way through the art of language. This is basic John Dewey. Also, in regards to teaching English, it is pure Louise Rosenblatt, who observes in *The Reader, The Text, The Poem* that the efferent day-to-day life is recognized through "a certain shift of interest, attention or awareness ... to the immediately qualitative aspects." To us, such experience in the English classroom is essential because it epitomizes the imaginative quality of everyday life. Students need to have this quality nurtured over time. To reinvent the classroom, to allow the students to listen to and write down poetry, is to allow the "shift" that Rosenblatt describes to occur. To use poetry in this manner is the first step in helping all students acquire real skills in the art of language. There is nothing like it.

Acknowledgments

Chapter One: Rhythm

Page 2, N. Scott Momaday. Excerpt from "New World" by N. Scott Momaday from *The Gourd Dancer*, Harper and Row, 1976. Copyright N. Scott Momaday. Reprinted by permission of the author.

Page 5, Robert Frost. Excerpt from "Birches" by Robert Frost from *The Poetry of Robert Frost* edited by Edward Connery Lathem. Henry Holt and Company, Inc., Publisher, New York, 1969. Reprinted by permission of Henry Holt and Company, Inc. and by permission of the Estate of Robert Frost, the editor Edward Connery Lathem, and Jonathan Cape, Ltd.

Page 6, Hart Crane. Excerpt from "For the Marriage of Faustus and Helen, II," from *Complete Poems of Hart Crane* by Marc Simon, editor. Copyright 1933, 1958, 1966 by Liveright Publishing Corp. Copyright 1986 by Marc Simon. Reprinted by permission of Liveright Publishing Corp.

Page 10, William Carlos Williams. Excerpt from "Love Song" from *Collected Poems: 1909 – 1939, Volume I*, by William Carlos Williams, copyright 1938 by New Directions Publishing Corp., reprinted by permission of New Directions Publishing Corp. and Carcanet Press, Ltd.

Page 11, Denise Levertov. Excerpt from "Overland to the Islands" from *Collected Earlier Poems 1940 – 1960* by Denise Levertov, copyright 1958, 1979 by Denise Levertov, reprinted by permission of New Direction Publishing Corp. and by permission of Bloodaxe Books Ltd.

Page 12, Wesley McNair. Excerpt from "Seeing Mercer, Maine" from *The Town of No & My Brother Running* by Wesley McNair. Reprinted by permission of David R. Godine, Publisher, Inc. Copyright 1997 by Wesley McNair.

Page 13, Jeanne Marie Beaumont. Excerpt from "Childhood of the Invisible Woman" from *Placebo Effects* by Jeanne Marie Beaumont. Copyright 1997 by Jeanne Marie Beaumont. Reprinted by permission of W.W. Norton & Co., Inc.

Page 13, Yusef Komunyakaa. Excerpt from "Somewhere Near Phu Bai" from *Neon Vernacular: New and Selected Poems* by Yusef Komunyakaa, Wesleyan University Press, copyright 1993 by Yusef Komunyakaa. Reprinted by permission of the author.

Page 13, Martín Espada. Excerpt from "Who Burns for the Perfection of Paper" from *City of Coughing and Dead Radiators* by Martín Espada. Copyright 1993 by Martín Espada. Reprinted by permission of W.W. Norton & Co., Inc.

Page 14, James Schuyler. Excerpt from "A Few Days" from *Collected Poems* by James Schuyler. Copyright 1993 by the Estate of James Schyuler. Reprinted by permission of Farrar, Straus & Giroux, Inc. and by permission of Carcanet Press, Ltd.

Page 15, Robert Lowell. Excerpt from "Middle Age" from *For the Union Dead* by Robert Lowell. Copyright 1959 by Robert Lowell. Copyright renewed 1987 by Harriet Lowell, Caroline Lowell, and Sheridan Lowell. Reprinted by permission Farrar, Straus & Giroux, Inc. and by permission of Faber & Faber, Ltd.

Page 16, Dana Gioia. Excerpt from "Bix Beiderbecke (1903 – 1931)." Copyright 1986, Dana Gioia from *Daily Horoscope* (Graywolf Press), reprinted by permission of the author.

Page 16, T. S. Eliot. Excerpt from "Burnt Norton," copyright 1943 by T. S. Eliot and renewed 1971 by Esme Valerie Eliot, reprinted by permission of Harcourt Brace & Company and by permission of Faber & Faber, Ltd.

Chapter Two: Sound

Page 25, Charles Wright. Excerpt from "Meditation on Song and Structure" from *Black Zodiac* by Charles Wright. Copyright 1997 by Charles Wright. Reprinted by permission of Farrar, Straus & Giroux, Inc.

Page 27, W. H. Auden. Excerpt from "On This Island." Copyright © 1937 and renewed 1965 by W. H. Auden. Reprinted by permission of Random House Inc. and by permission of Faber & Faber, Ltd.

Page 27, Louise Bogan. Excerpt from "Putting to Sea" from *The Blue Estuaries: Poems, 1923 – 1968* by Louise Bogan. Copyright renewed © 1996 by Ruth Limmer. Reprinted by permission of Farrar, Straus and Giroux, Inc.

Page 27, W. H. Auden. Excerpt from "Domesday Song" from *W. H. Auden: Collected Poems* by W. H. Auden, edited Edward Mendelson, copyright 1945 by W. H. Auden, reprinted by permission of Random House, Inc. and by permission of Faber & Faber, Ltd.

Page 28, Richard Wilbur. Excerpt from "Junk," copyright 1961 and renewed 1989 by Richard Wilbur, reprinted by permission of Harcourt, Brace & Company and by permission of Faber & Faber, Ltd.

Page 32, Thomas Hardy. Excerpt from "The Best She Could" by Thomas Hardy. Reprinted with the permission of Simon & Schuster from *The Complete Poems of Thomas Hardy*, edited by James Gibson. Copyright 1978 by Macmillan London Ltd.

Page 33, Wilfred Owen. Excerpt from "A Terre" by Wilfred Owen from *The Collected Poems of Wilfred Owen*. Copyright 1963 by Chatto & Windus, Ltd. Reprinted by permission of New Directions Publishing Corp. and by permission of Chatto & Windus, Ltd.

Page 34, Wilfred Owen. Excerpt from "Exposure" by Wilfred Owen from *The Collected Poems of Wilfred Owen*. Copyright 1963 by Chatto & Windus, Ltd. Reprinted by permission of New Directions Publishing Corp. and by permission of Chatto & Windus, Ltd.

Page 34, Stanley Kunitz. Excerpt from "River Road," copyright 1966 by Stanley Kunitz, from *Passing Through: The Later Poems New and Selected* by Stanley Kunitz. Reprinted by permission of W.W. Norton & Company, Inc.

Page 35, Robert Francis. "Overhearing Two on a Cold Sunday Morning" by Robert Francis. Reprinted from *Robert Francis: Collected Poems, 1936 – 1976*. (Amherst: University of Massachusetts Press, 1976). Copyright 1956, 1976 by the University of Massachusetts Press.

Chapter Three: Line

Page 43, Thomas Hardy. Excerpt from "During Wind and Rain" by Thomas Hardy. Reprinted with the permission of Simon & Schuster from *The Complete Poems of Thomas Hardy*, edited by James Gibson. Copyright 1978 by Macmillan London Ltd.

Page 44, Norman Williams. Excerpt from "Skonoke's Barber Chair" by Norman Williams from *The Unlovely Child*, Alfred A. Knopf, copyright 1984 by Norman Williams. Reprinted by permission of the author.

Page 45, Norman Williams. "Plovers" by Norman Williams. Reprinted by permission of the author.

Page 46, John Betjeman. Excerpt from "The Arrest of Oscar Wilde" by John Betjeman from *Collected Poems*, John Murray (Publishers) Ltd. Reprinted by permission of John Murray (Publishers) Ltd.

Page 48, Jane Kenyon. Excerpt from "The Three Susans" copyright 1996 by the Estate of Jane Kenyon. Reprinted from *Otherwise: New and Selected Poems* by Jane Kenyon with the permission of Graywolf Press, St. Paul, Minnesota.

Page 49, Shaun T. Griffin. "A Metered Vision" from *Snowmelt* by Shaun T. Griffin, Rainshadow Editions, The Black Rock Press, University of Nevada, Reno, copyright 1994. Used with permission of the author.

Page 50, Donald Hall. Excerpt from "For an Exchange of Rings" from *The Happy Man* by Donald Hall. Copyright 1981, 1982, 1983, 1984, 1985, 1986 by Donald Hall. Reprinted by permission of Random House, Inc. and Gerard McCauley Agency, Inc.

Page 51, Robert Creeley. Excerpt from "The Cracks" by Robert Creeley from *Collected Poems of Robert Creeley, 1945 – 1975*, copyright 1983 The Regents of the University of California. Reprinted by permission of the publisher.

Page 51, Gerald Barrax. Excerpt from "Slow Drivers" reprinted by permission of Louisiana State University Press from *From a Person Sitting in Darkness: New and Selected Poems*, by Gerald Barrax. Copyright 1984 by Gerald Barrax.

Page 52, Li-Young Lee. Excerpt from "Braiding," copyright 1986 by Li-Young Lee. Reprinted from *Rose* with the permission of BOA Editions, Ltd., 260 East Avenue, Rochester, NY 14604.

Page 53, Thomas McGrath. Excerpt from "Praises" from *Selected Poems: 1938 – 1988* by Thomas McGrath. Reprinted by permission of Copper Canyon Press, P. O. Box 271, Port Townsend, WA 98368.

Page 53, Jim Harrison. Excerpt from "A Domestic Poem for Portia," copyright Jim Harrison. Used with permission of the author.

Page 54, Marianne Moore. Excerpt from "Critics and Connoisseurs" by Marianne Moore. Reprinted with the permission of Simon & Schuster from *The Collected Poems of Marianne Moore*. Copyright 1935 by Marianne Moore; copyright renewed 1963 by Marianne Moore and T.S. Eliot and by permission of Faber & Faber, Ltd.

Page 55, Hayden Carruth. Excerpt from "Loneliness: An Outburst of Hexasyllables" from *Collected Shorter Poems 1946 – 1991*, © 1992 by Hayden Carruth. Reprinted by permission of Copper Canyon Press, P. O. Box 271, Port Townsend, WA 98368.

Page 56, A. David Cappella. "Two Haiku" by A. David Cappella. Reprinted by permission of the author.

Page 58, Randall Jarrell. Excerpt from "Lady Bates" from *The Complete Poems* by Randall Jarrell. Copyright © 1969 and copyright renewed © 1997 by Mary von S. Jarrell. Reprinted by permission of Farrar, Straus & Giroux, Inc. and by permission of Faber & Faber, Ltd.

Chapter Four: Syntax

Page 66, Eleanor Wilner. "Of a Sun She Can Remember" from *Reversing the Spell: New and Selected Poems* © 1998 by Eleanor Wilner. Reprinted by permission of Copper Canyon Press, P. O. Box 271, Port Townsend, WA 98368.

Page 68, David Ignatow. "Self-Employed" from *David Ignatow: Poems 1934 – 1969* © 1970 by David Ignatow, Wesleyan University Press by permission of University Press of New England.

Page 69, Alberto Ríos. "What a Boy Can Do," from *Teodoro Luna's Two Kisses* by Alberto Ríos. Copyright © 1990 by Alberto Ríos. Reprinted by permission of W.W. Norton & Company, Inc.

Page 70, Ted Kooser. "Notes on the Death of Nels Paulssen, Farmer, at the Ripe Old Age of 93" from *Sure Signs: New and Selected Poems* by Ted Kooser, University of Pittsburgh Press, 1980. Reprinted by permission of the author.

Page 72, Mark Strand. Excerpt from "The Room" from *Selected Poems* by Mark Strand. Copyright © 1979, 1980 by Mark Strand. Reprinted by permission of Alfred A. Knopf Inc.

Page 73, David Henderson, "Lee Morgan" from *The Low East* by David Henderson. Copyright © 1980 by David Henderson. Used by permission of North Atlantic Books, Berkeley, California, USA.

Page 74, Leo Connellan. "Boxing" by Leo Connellan, copyright by Leo Connellan. Reprinted from *Short Poems, City Poems: 1944– 1998* by Leo Connellan, Hanover Press, with the permission of the author.

Page 75, Gary Snyder. Excerpt from "Hay for the Horses" by Gary Snyder. Reprinted with permission of the author. Originally published in *Riprap*, the Origin Press, 1959.

Chapter Five: Grammar, Punctuation, and Capitalization

Page 82, George Oppen. "Street" by George Oppen, from *Collected Poems*. Copyright © 1975 by George Oppen. Reprinted by permission of New Directions Publishing Corp.

Page 84, Yusef Komunyakaa. Excerpt from "Soliloquy: Man Talking to a Mirror" from *Neon Vernacular: New and Selected Poems* by Yusef Komunyakaa, Wesleyan University Press, copyright 1993 by Yusek Komunyakaa. Reprinted by permission of the author.

Page 84, Maxine Kumin. "Continuum: a Love Poem," copyright © 1982 by Maxine Kumin, from *Selected Poems 1960 – 1990* by Maxine Kumin. Reprinted by permission of W. W. Norton & Company, Inc.

Page 86, Rita Dove. "Sunday Greens" from *Thomas and Beulah*, Carnegie – Mellon University Press, © 1986 by Rita Dove. Reprinted by permission of the author.

Page 87, E. E. Cummings. Excerpt from "nobody loses all the time," copyright 1926, 1954, © 1991 by the Trustees for the E. E. Cummings Trust. Copyright © 1985 by George James Firmage, from *Complete Poems: 1904 – 1962* by E. E. Cummings, edited by George J. Firmage. Reprinted by permission of Liveright Publishing Corporation.

Chapter Six: Word Choice

Page 98, Laure-Anne Bosselaar. "English Flavors," copyright © 1997 by Laure-Anne Bosselaar. Reprinted from *The Hour Between Dog and Wolf* with the permission of BOA Editions, Ltd., 260 East Avenue, Rochester, NY 14604.

Page 99, Howard Nemerov. Excerpt from "The View from an Attic Window" by Howard Nemerov. Reprinted by permission of Margaret Nemerov.

Page 99, Mona Van Duyn. Excerpt from "The Miser" by Mona Van Duyn, from *To See, To Take*, Atheneum, 1970. Reprinted by permission of the author.

Page 100, Haki Madhubuti. Excerpt from "Gwendolyn Brooks" by Haki Madhubuti from *Don't Cry, SCREAM* by Haki R. Madhubuti. Copyright 1969 by Haki R. Madhubuti, reprinted by permission of Third World Press, Inc., Chicago, Illinois.

Page 100, John Haines. Excerpt from "Watching the Fire" from *Collected Poems, The Owl in the Mask of the Dreamer*, Graywolf Press, St. Paul, Minnesota, 1993. Reprinted with permission of the author.

Page 101, W. D. Snodgrass. Excerpt from "Winter Bouquet" from *Heart's Needle* by W. D. Snodgrass. Copyright © 1959 by William Snodgrass. Reprinted by permission of Alfred A. Knopf Inc.

Page 101, Emily Dickinson. "# 1144." Reprinted by permission of the publishers and the Trustees of Amherst College from *The Poems of Emily Dickinson*, Thomas H. Johnson, ed., Cambridge, Mass.: The Belknap Press of Harvard University Press, Copyright © 1951, 1955, 1979, 1983 by the President and Fellows of Harvard College.

Page 102, Robert Frost. Excerpt from "The Pasture" by Robert Frost from *The Poetry of Robert Frost* edited by Edward Connery Lathem. Henry Holt and Company, Inc., Publisher, New York, 1969. Reprinted by permission of Henry Holt and Company, Inc. and by permission of the Estate of Robert Frost, the editor, Edward Connery Lathem, and Jonathan Cape. Ltd.

Page 102, Frank O'Hara. Excerpt from "The Spirit Ink" from *Collected Poems* by Frank O'Hara, copyright © 1971 by Maureen Granville-Smith, administratrix of the Estate of Frank O'Hara, reprinted by permission of Alfred A. Knopf Inc.

Page 102, Robert Lowell. Excerpt from "For the Union Dead" from *For the Union Dead* by Robert Lowell. Copyright 1959 by Robert Lowell. Copyright renewed 1987 by Harriet Lowell, Caroline Lowell, and Sheridan Lowell. Reprinted by permission Farrar, Straus & Giroux, Inc. and by permission of Faber & Faber, Ltd.

Chapter Seven: Details

Page 111, Ellen Bryant Voigt. Excerpt from "The Last Class" by Ellen Bryant Voigt from *The Lotus Flower*, W. W. Norton and Company, Inc., 1987. Reprinted by permission of the publisher.

Page 112, Gjertrud Schnackenberg. "Thanksgiving Day Downstairs" by Gjertrud Schnackenberg from *Portraits and Elegies*, David R. Godine, copyright © 1982 by Gjertrud Schnackenberg. Reprinted by permission of the author.

Page 113, Greg Pape. "A Job on the Night Shift" from *Black Branches*, by Greg Pape, © 1984. Reprinted by permission of the University of Pittsburgh Press.

Page 116, C. K. Williams. Excerpt from "The Regulars" by C. K. Williams from *Selected Poems* by C.K. Williams. Copyright © 1994 by C.K. Williams. Reprinted by permission of Farrar, Straus & Giroux, Inc. and by permission of Bloodaxe Books Ltd.

Page 117, Toi Derricotte. "St. Peter Claver" by Toi Derricotte from *Captivity*, © 1989 by Toi Derricotte. Reprinted by permission of the University of Pittsburgh Press.

Page 118, Debra R. Nowak. "Bliss" by Debra R. Nowak. Reprinted by permission of the author.

Page 120, Belle Waring. Excerpt from "Ending Green" by Belle Waring from *Dark Blonde*, copyright 1997 by Belle Waring, is reprinted by permission of the author and of Sarabande Books.

Page 120, Richard Wilbur. Excerpt from "Love Calls Us to the Things of This World" by Richard Wilbur, copyright © 1956 and renewed 1984 by Richard Wilbur. Reprinted by permission of Harcourt, Brace & Company and by permission of Faber & Faber, Ltd.

Page 121, Galway Kinnell. "Break of Day" from *Three Books* by Galway Kinnell. Copyright © 1993 by Galway Kinnell. Reprinted by permission of Houghton Mifflin Company. All rights reserved.

Chapter Eight: Metaphor

Page 131, Emily Dickinson. Excerpt from "# 986." Reprinted by permission of the publishers and the Trustees of Amherst College from *The Poems of Emily Dickinson*, Thomas H. Johnson, ed., Cambridge, Mass.: The Belknap Press of Harvard University Press, Copyright © 1951, 1955, 1979, 1983 by the President and Fellows of Harvard College.

Page 131, Emily Dickinson. Excerpt from "# 925." Reprinted by permission of the publishers and the Trustees of Amherst College from *The Poems of Emily Dickinson*, Thomas H. Johnson, ed., Cambridge, Mass.: The Belknap Press of Harvard University Press, Copyright © 1951, 1955, 1979, 1983 by the President and Fellows of Harvard College.

Page 131, Emily Dickinson. Excerpt from "# 831." Reprinted by permission of the publishers and the Trustees of Amherst College from *The Poems of Emily Dickinson*, Thomas H. Johnson, ed., Cambridge, Mass.: The Belknap Press of Harvard University Press, Copyright © 1951, 1955, 1979, 1983 by the President and Fellows of Harvard College.

Page 131, Emily Dickinson. Excerpt from "# 784." Reprinted by permission of the publishers and the Trustees of Amherst College from *The Poems of Emily Dickinson*, Thomas H. Johnson, ed., Cambridge, Mass.: The Belknap Press of Harvard University Press, Copyright © 1951, 1955, 1979, 1983 by the President and Fellows of Harvard College.

Page 131, Emily Dickinson. Excerpt from "# 744." Reprinted by permission of the publishers and the Trustees of Amherst College from *The Poems of Emily Dickinson*, Thomas H. Johnson, ed., Cambridge, Mass.: The Belknap Press of Harvard University Press, Copyright © 1951, 1955, 1979, 1983 by the President and Fellows of Harvard College.

Page 131, Emily Dickinson. Excerpt from "# 712." Reprinted by permission of the publishers and the Trustees of Amherst College from *The Poems of Emily Dickinson*, Thomas H. Johnson, ed., Cambridge, Mass.: The Belknap Press of Harvard University Press, Copyright © 1951, 1955, 1979, 1983 by the President and Fellows of Harvard College.

Page 132, Emily Dickinson. "# 875." Reprinted by permission of the publishers and the Trustees of Amherst College from *The Poems of Emily Dickinson*, Thomas H. Johnson, ed., Cambridge, Mass.: The Belknap Press of Harvard University Press, Copyright © 1951, 1955, 1979, 1983 by the President and Fellows of Harvard College.

Page 132, Emily Dickinson. "# 889." Reprinted by permission of the publishers and the Trustees of Amherst College from *The Poems of Emily Dickinson*, Thomas H. Johnson, ed., Cambridge, Mass.: The Belknap Press of Harvard University Press, Copyright © 1951, 1955, 1979, 1983 by the President and Fellows of Harvard College.

Page 134, Emily Dickinson. Excerpt from " #288." Reprinted by permission of the publishers and the Trustees of Amherst College from *The Poems of Emily Dickinson*, Thomas H. Johnson, ed., Cambridge, Mass.: The Belknap Press of Harvard University Press, Copyright © 1951, 1955, 1979, 1983 by the President and Fellows of Harvard College.

Page 134, Anne Sexton. Excerpt from "Iron Hans" by Anne Sexton from *Transformations*. Copyright © 1971 by Anne Sexton. Reprinted by permission of Houghton Mifflin Company. All rights reserved. Reprinted by permission of Sterling Lord Literistic, Inc. copyright 1971 by Anne Sexton.

Page 134, Anne Sexton. Excerpt from "Cinderella" by Anne Sexton from *Transformations*. Copyright © 1971 by Anne Sexton. Reprinted by permission of Houghton Mifflin Company. All rights reserved. Reprinted by permission of Sterling Lord Literistic, Inc. copyright 1971 by Anne Sexton.

Page 135, Anne Sexton. Excerpt from "One Eye, Two Eyes, Three Eyes" by Anne Sexton from *Transformations*. Copyright © 1971 by Anne Sexton. Reprinted by permission of Houghton Mifflin Company. All rights reserved. Reprinted by permission of Sterling Lord Literistic, Inc. copyright 1971 by Anne Sexton.

Page 135, Etheridge Knight. "Hard Rock Returns to Prison from the Hospital for the Criminal Insane" from *The Essential Etheridge Knight*, by Etheridge Knight, © 1986. Reprinted by the permission of the University of Pittsburgh Press.

Page 137, Tadeusz Borowski. "Night Over Birkenau" by Tadeusz Borowski, translated by Tadeusz Pioro with Larry Rafferty and Meryl Natchez from *Selected Poems* by Tadeusz Borowski, hit & run press, copyright 1990. Reprinted by permission of Larry Rafferty.

Chapter Nine: Image

Page 146, Ezra Pound. Excerpt from "In a Station of the Metro" by Ezra Pound from *Personae*, copyright © 1926 by Ezra Pound. Reprinted by permission of New Directions Publishing Corp. From *Collected Shorter Poems* by Ezra Pound, Faber & Faber Ltd. Reprinted by permission of Faber & Faber, Ltd.

Page 147, T. S. Eliot. Excerpt from "Preludes" by T. S. Eliiot. Reprinted by permission of Faber & Faber, Ltd.

Page 148, Robert Lowell. Excerpt from "Skunk Hour" by Robert Lowell from *Life Studies*. Copyright 1959 by Robert Lowell. Copyright renewed 1987 by Harriet Lowell, Caroline Lowell, and Sheridan Lowell. Reprinted by permission Farrar, Straus & Giroux, Inc. and by permission Faber & Faber, Ltd.

Page 149, Ezra Pound. Excerpt from "Taking Leave of a Friend" by Ezra Pound from *Personae*, copyright © 1926 by Ezra Pound. Reprinted by permission of New Directions Publishing Corp. From *Collected Shorter Poems* by Ezra Pound, Faber & Faber Ltd. Reprinted by permission of Faber & Faber, Ltd.

Page 150, Robert Bly. Excerpt from "Snowfall in the Afternoon," reprinted from *Silence in the Snowy Fields* by Robert Bly, Wesleyan University Press, Middletown, Conn. © 1962 by permission of the author.

Page 151, James Wright. "Rain" from *Above the River: The Complete Poems* by James Wright, © 1990 by Anne Wright, Wesleyan University Press, by permission of University Press of New England.

Page 152, Billie Bolton. "To the Crossing" by Billie Bolton. Reprinted by permission of the author.

Chapter Ten: Architecture

Page 158, Emerson Gilmore. "I am Fifteen" by Emerson Gilmore. Used with permission of the author.

Page 160, William Carlos Williams. Excerpt from "At the Ball Game" from *Collected Poems: 1909 – 1939, Volume I*, by William Carlos Williams, copyright 1938 by New Directions Publishing Corp., reprinted by permission of New Directions Publishing Corp. and by permission of Carcanet Press, Ltd.

Page 161, Donald Justice. Excerpt from "Psalm and Lament" from *New and Selected Poems* by Donald Justice. Copyright © 1995 by Donald Justice. Reprinted by permission of Alfred A. Knopf Inc.

Page 162, Mark Doty. Excerpt from "Almost Blue" from *My Alexandria: Poems*. Copyright 1993 by Mark Doty. Used with the permission of the poet and the University of Illinois Press.

Page 163, Wallace Stevens. Excerpt from "Notes Toward a Supreme Fiction" from *Collected Poems* by Wallace Stevens, copyright 1942 by Wallace Stevens, reprinted by permission of Alfred A. Knopf Inc. and permission of Faber & Faber, Ltd.

Page 164, William Carlos Williams. Excerpt from "The Pink Locust" by William Carlos Williams from *Collected Poems: 1939 – 1962, Volume II*. Copyright © 1962 by New Directions Publishing Corp. Reprinted by permission of New Directions Publishing Corp. and by permission of Carcanet Press, Ltd.

Page 165, Sue Payne. "Mother May I" by Sue Payne. Reprinted by permission of the author.

Page 167, Al Young. Excerpt from "Lester Leaps In" by Al Young from *Heaven: Collected Poems 1956 – 1990*, Creative Arts Book, 1992.

Page 168, X. J. Kennedy. Excerpt from "B Negative" from *Nude Descending a Staircase*, by X. J. Kennedy, Carnegie – Mellon University Press. Copyright © 1995 by X. J. Kennedy. Reprinted by permission of the author.

Page 168, Richard Wilbur. Excerpt from "The Walgh-Vogel," copyright 1947 and renewed 1975 by Richard Wilbur, reprinted by permission of Harcourt, Brace & Company and by permission of Faber & Faber, Ltd.

Page 168, Kenneth Rexroth. Excerpt from "Stone and Flower" by Kenneth Rexroth, from *Collected Shorter Poems*. Copyright © 1944, 1963 by Kenneth Rexroth. Reprinted by permission of New Directions Publishing Corp.

Page 169, Robert Hayden. " 'Lear is Gay' ", copyright © 1970 by Robert Hayden, from *Collected Poems of Robert Hayden* by Frederick Glaysher, editor. Reprinted by permission of Liveright Publishing Corp.

Page 171, Timothy B. McCall. "Beatle Boots (Milwaukee, Wisconsin, 1964)" Reprinted by permission of the author.

Page 172, Rosa Maria Arenas. "What I Can't Tell You" reprinted by permission of the author. First published in *River Styx*.

Page 174, Elisabeth Bishop. "Jerónimo's House" from *The Complete Poems 1927 – 1979* by Elizabeth Bishop. Copyright © 1979, 1983 by Alice Helen Methfessel. Reprinted by permission of Farrar, Straus and Giroux, Inc.

Page 175, Robert Duncan. Excerpt from "A Set of Romantic Hymns" by Robert Duncan, from *Roots and Branches*. Copyright © 1964 by Robert Duncan. Reprinted by permission of New Directions Publishing Corp.

Chapter Eleven: Form

Page 188, Marilyn Hacker. Excerpt from XIV of "Separations." Reprinted by permission of Frances Collin Literary Agent. Copyright © 1994 by Marilyn Hacker. Copyright © 1976 by Marilyn Hacker, from *Selected Poems: 1965 – 1990*. Reprinted by permission of the author and W. W. Norton and Company, Inc.

Page 190, Baron Wormser. "A Later Death" by Baron Wormser, from *The White Words* by Baron Wormser, Houghton Mifflin Company, 1983. Reprinted by permission of the author.

Page 191, Christopher Jane Corkery. "The Song" by Christopher Jane Corkery from *Blessing*. Copyright © 1985 by Princeton University Press. Reprinted by permission of Princeton University Press.

Chapter Twelve: Tone and Lyric

Page 201, Hayden Carruth. Selections from *The Sleeping Beauty*, # 17 and # 23 from *Collected Longer Poems* © 1994 by Hayden Carruth. Reprinted by permission of Copper Canyon Press, P. O. Box 271, Port Townsend, WA 98368.

Page 208, Sylvia Plath. Excerpt from "Daddy" by Sylvia Path from *The Collected Poems* by Sylvia Plath. Poems copyright © 1960, 1965, 1971, 1981 by the Estate of Sylvia Plath. Reprinted by permission of HarperCollins Publishers and by permission of Faber & Faber, Ltd.

Page 209, Sylvia Plath. Excerpt from "The Applicant" by Sylvia Plath from *The Collected Poems* by Sylvia Plath. Poems copyright © 1960, 1965, 1971, 1981 by the Estate of Sylvia Plath. Reprinted by permission of HarperCollins Publishers and by permission of Faber & Faber, Ltd.

Page 209, Sylvia Plath. Excerpt from "Lady Lazarus" by Sylvia Plath from *The Collected Poems* by Sylvia Plath. Poems copyright © 1960, 1965, 1971, 1981 by the Estate of Sylvia Plath. Reprinted by permission of HarperCollins Publishers and by permission of Faber & Faber, Ltd.

Page 209, Sylvia Plath. Excerpt from "Sheep in Fog" by Sylvia Plath from *The Collected Poems* by Sylvia Plath. Poems copyright © 1960, 1965, 1971, 1981 by the Estate of Sylvia Plath. Reprinted by permission of HarperCollins Publishers and by permission of Faber & Faber, Ltd.

Chapter Thirteen: Repetition

Page 218, Langston Hughes. Excerpt from "Interne at Provident" from *Collected Poems* by Langston Hughes, copyright © 1994 by the Estate of Langston Hughes, reprinted by permission of Alfred A. Knopf Inc. and by permission of Harold Ober Associates Incorporated.

Page 219, Cornelius Eady. "The Dance" by Cornelius Eady. Reprinted from Cornelius Eady: *Victims of the Latest Dance Craze* by permission of Carnegie-Mellon University Press © 1997 by Cornelius Eady.

Page 221, Jim Harrison. "Lullaby for a Daughter" copyright Jim Harrison. Used with the permission of the author.

Page 224, T. S. Eliot. Excerpt from "Ash Wednesday" copyright 1936 by Harcourt Brace & Company, copyright © 1964, 1963 by T. S. Eliot, reprinted by permission of the publisher and by permission of Faber & Faber, Ltd.

Page 224, T. S. Eliot. Excerpt from "The Love Song of J. Alfred Prufrock" reprinted by permission of Faber & Faber, Ltd.

Page 225, Theodore Roethke. "The Cycle"," copyright 1941 by *The Virginia Quarterly Review*, The University of Virginia, from *The Collected Poems of Theodore Roethke* by Theodore Roethke. Used by permission of Doubleday, a division of Random House, Inc. and by permission of Faber & Faber, Ltd.

Chapter Fourteen: Endings

Page 234, Molly Peacock. "Petting and Being a Pet" by Molly Peacock from *Raw Heaven*, Random House, 1984. Copyright Molly Peacock. Reprinted with permission of the author.

Page 235, Bin Ramke. "Why I am Afraid to Have Children" by Bin Ramke from *White Monkeys*, University of Georgia Press, 1981. Reprinted by permission of the author.

Page 236, Debora Greger. "The Light Passages" from *Movable Islands* is reprinted by permission of the author. Copyright 1980 by Debora Greger.

Page 238, Naomi Shihab Nye. "The Use of Fiction" by Naomi Shihab Nye from *Words Under the Words: Selected Poems* by Naomi Shihab Nye, Far Corner Books, 1995. Reprinted by permission of the author.

Page 239, Robert Morgan. "Passenger Pigeons" from *At the Edge of Orchard Country* © 1987 by Robert Morgan, Wesleyan University Press by permission of University Press of New England.

Page 240, James Richardson. "The Lake" by James Richardson, from *Reservations*, Princeton University Press, 1977. Reprinted by permission of Princeton University Press.

Chapter Fifteen: Narrative

Page 250, Joe-Anne McLaughlin. "Complicated" from *The Banshee Diaries* by Joe-Anne McLaughlin. Text copyright © Joe-Anne McLaughlin 1998. Copyright © Exile Editions Limited 1998. Reprinted by permission of the author and Exile Editions Limited.

Page 251, Louis Simpson. "To the Western World" from *At the End of the Open Road* © 1963 by Louis Simpson, Wesleyan University Press by permission of University Press of New England.

Page 252, Richmond Lattimore. "The Crabs" from *Poems from Three Decades* by Richmond Lattimore, Charles Scribner's Sons, 1972. Reprinted by permission of The Bryn Mawr Trust Company, Paul C. Benedict, Trustee of Richmond A. Lattimore, Residency Trust.

Page 253, Christianne Balk. "Dusk Choir," copyright 1995 by Christianne Balk, from *Desiring Flight*, published by Purdue University Press. Reprinted by permission of the author.

Page 255, David Keller. "The Man Who Knew the Words to *Louie, Louie*" by David Keller. First appeared in *The Ohio Review*. Reprinted by permission of the author.

Page 257, Chitra Banerjee Divakaruni. "Cutting the Sun" by Chitra Banerjee Divakaruni. From *Leaving Yuba City* by Chitra Banerjee Divakaruni. Copyright © 1997 by Chitra Banerjee Divakaruni. Used by permission of Doubleday, a division of Random House, Inc. and by permission of Sandra Dijkstra Literary Agency.

Chapter Sixteen: The Didactic Poem (How Poems Instruct)

Page 264, Tom Lowenstein. "How the Raven Became Black" translated by Tukummig and Tom Lowenstein from *Ancient Land, Sacred Whale: The Inuiut Hunt and Its Rituals* by Tom Lowenstein. Copyright © 1993 by Tom Lowenstein. Reprinted by permission of Farrar, Straus and Giroux Inc.

Page 265, Hesiod. Excerpt from *Works and Days*, by Hesiod, translated by Stanley Lombardo, by permission of Hackett Publishing Company. Copyright © 1993 by Hackett Publishing Company Inc. All rights reserved.

Page 266, Smith Palmer Bovie. Excerpt from *Virgil's Georgics* translated by Smith Palmer Bovie, copyright 1956. Reprinted by permission of the University of Chicago Press.

Page 267, Ovid. Excerpt from *Ovid: The Art of Love and Other Poems*, translated by J. H. Mozley, William Heinemann, 1929.

Page 268, Wendell Berry. Excerpt from "Manifesto: the Mad Farmer Liberation Front" from *Collected Poems 1957 – 1982* by Wendell Berry, North Point Press, 1985. Originally published in *The Country of Marriage*, Harcourt Brace Jovanovich, 1973. Reprinted by permission of Counterpoint Press.

Page 269, Denise Levertov. "Didactic Poem" from *Poems 1960 – 1967* by Denise Levertov, copyright 1966 by Denise Levertov, reprinted by permission New Directions Publishing Corp. and Jonathan Cape, Ltd.

Page 270, Thomas Lux. Excerpt from "River Blindness (Onchocerciosis)" from *Split Horizon* by Thomas Lux, Houghton Mifflin Company, 1994 reprinted by permission of the author.

Page 271, Gary Snyder. Excerpt from "How to Make Stew in the Pinacate Desert" by Gary Snyder, from *The Back Country*. Copyright © 1968 by Gary Snyder. Reprinted by permission of New Directions Publishing Corp.

Page 271, Nancy Willard. Excerpt from "How to Stuff a Pepper" by Nancy Willard from *Carpenter of the Sun* by Nancy Willard. Copyright © 1974 by Nancy Willard. Reprinted by permission Liveright Publishing Corp.

Page 272, Philip Booth. Excerpt from "How to See Deer" from *Lifelines, Selected Poems 1950 – 1999*, by Philip Booth, Viking Penguin, 1999.

Page 272, May Swenson. Excerpt from "How to be Old" by May Swenson. Used with the permission of the Literary Estate of May Swenson.

Chapter Seventeen: Place and Politics

Page 280, Gary Snyder. "Thin Ice" by Gary Snyder. Reprinted with permission of the author. Originally published in *Riprap*, the Origin Press, 1959.

Page 281, Faye Kicknosway. "Linoleum," from *Who Shall Know Them?* By Faye Kicknosway. Copyright © 1978, 1980, 1981, 1983, 1985 by Faye Kicknosway. Used by permission of Viking Penguin, a division of Penguin Putnam Inc.

Page 283, Linda Hogan. "Map" from *The Book of Medicines* by Linda Hogan, Coffee House Press, 1993. Reprinted by permission of the publisher.

Page 285, Howard Levy. "Jackson, MS, 1966" by Howard Levy. Reprinted by permission of the author.

Page 287, Joe Bolton. "Speaking of the South: 1961" by Joe Bolton from *Days of Summer Gone*, published by The Galileo Press, 1990. Used with the permission of the Galileo Press.

Page 288, Tim Dlugos. Excerpt from "East Longmeadow" by Tim Dlugos from *Powerless: Selected Poems 1973-1990* by Tim Dlugos (High Risk Books, 1996). Copyright © 1996 Estate of Tim Dlugos. Reprinted by permission of the Estate of Tim Dlugos.

Page 289, W. S. Merwin. "Lackawanna" from *Selected Poems* by W. S. Merwin, Atheneum, 1988. Reprinted by permission of the author.

Page 291, Jane Gentry. "Exercise in the Cemetery" reprinted by permission of Louisiana State University Press from *A Garden in Kentucky: Poems*, by Jane Gentry. Copyright © 1995 by Jane Gentry.

Chapter Eighteen: Occasions (The Social Contexts of Poems)

Page 297, Donald Justice. "In Memory of the Unknown Poet, Robert Boardman Vaughn." From *New and Selected Poems* by Donald Justice. Copyright © 1995 by Donald Justice. Reprinted by permission of Alfred A. Knopf Inc.

Page 299, Reuben Jackson. "Thelonious" copyright © 1991 by Reuben Jackson from *Fingering the Keys*, Gut Punch Press, by permission of the author.

Page 300, Robert Lowell. "Alfred Corning Clark" from *For the Union* by Robert Lowell. Copyright 1959 by Robert Lowell. Copyright renewed 1987 by Harriet Lowell, Caroline Lowell, and Sheridan Lowell. Reprinted by permission of Farrar, Straus & Giroux, Inc. and by permission of Faber & Faber, Ltd.

Page 302, Dylan Thomas. Excerpt from "Poem in October" by Dylan Thomas from *The Poems of Dylan Thomas*, copyright 1945 by The Trustees for the Copyrights of Dylan Thomas, first published in *Poetry*. Reprinted by permission of New Directions Publishing Corp. and J. M. Dent.

Page 305, Kate Rushin. "Rosa Revisited" from *The Black Back-Ups* by Kate Rushin, copyright 1993 by Kate Rushin, by permission of Firebrand Books, Ithaca, New York.

Page 307, Irene McKinney. "Phoebe, Phoebe, Phoebe" from *Six O'clock Mine Report* by Irene McKinney, © 1989. Reprinted by permission of the University of Pittsburgh Press.

Page 308, Jeffrey Skinner. "Late Afternoon, Late in the Century" by Jeffrey Skinner from *The Company of Heaven*, University of Pittsburgh Press, © 1992 Jeffrey Skinner. Reprinted by permission of the author.

Page 312, Peter Wood. "Voice from the Crack Between Gutter and Curb" by Peter Wood from *Horsetongue*, Demarais Studio Press, 1996. Reprinted by permission of the author.

Chapter Nineteen: Variations
(Found Poem, Prose Poem, Shaped Poem)

Page 316, Campbell McGrath. "Langdon, North Dakota" from *Capitalism* © 1990 by Campbell McGrath, Wesleyan University Press by permission of University Press of New England.

Page 319, Annie Dillard. Excerpt from "Junior High School English" from *Mornings Like This: Found Poems* by Annie Dillard copyright © 1995 by Annie Dillard, reprinted by permission of HarperCollins Publishers, Inc. and by permission of Russell & Volkening as agents for the author. Copyright © 1995 by Annie Dillard.

Page 320, Sarah Gorham. "Dear Growing Teen" by Sarah Gorham used with the permission of the author.

Page 323, Nancy B. Richardson. "An Everyday Thing" by Nancy B. Richardson. Reprinted by permission of the author.

Page 326, Dylan Thomas. Excerpt from "I Turn the Corner of Prayer and Burn" by Dylan Thomas from *The Poems of Dylan Thomas*. Copyright © 1939 by New Directions Publishing Corp. Reprinted by permission of New Directions Publishing Corp. and J. M. Dent.

Page 327, Jeffrey Harrison. "Swifts at Evening" by Jeffrey Harrison from *Signs of Arrival*, © 1996 by Jeffrey Harrison. Used by permission of Copper Beech Press.

Author Index

Subject Index

About the Authors

Baron Wormser is an educator and retired librarian who has worked in public schools and universities in Maine for over 25 years. He also teaches at the Robert Frost Place in Franconia, New Hampshire, and is the author of five books of poetry including *Mulroney and Others* and *When*, both published by Sarabande Books. He has been the recipient of fellowships from the National Endowment for the Arts and the John Simon Guggenheim Memorial Foundation.

David Cappella is a poet and teacher, currently serving as Acting Director of the Teacher Education Program at Wabash College. A former secondary school teacher, he holds a doctorate from Boston University in Curriculum and Instruction with a specialty in English Education. His educational research focuses on how poetry is taught in the classroom.

PN
1101
.W67

2000

Wormser, Baron.
Teaching the art of
poetry

Date Due

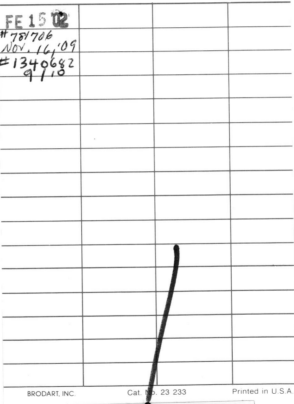

FE 15 02
#781706
Nov. 16, '09
#1340682
9/10